Elizabeth Bishop's Poetics of Intimacy, a biographical and critical study of one of the great poets of this century, offers a fresh look at Bishop's published and unpublished writing over the course of her career. Informed by pragmatic, postmodern, and feminist theories, Victoria Harrison's study also makes extensive use of Bishop's archives, many pieces of which have never been discussed, to reveal the process of the poet's writing. Harrison explores Bishop's childhood memoirs, journals, letters, Brazilian travel prose, unfinished poems, and draft material, researching dates of undated material and reproducing Bishop's revisions, cancellations, and idiosyncratic spellings. Attentiveness to the detail of this archival writing gives Harrison a broad foundation for arguing that Bishop treats some of our largest concerns – family relationships, sexuality, war, and cultural differences – within poetry and prose that are intimate but not self-revelatory and daily but never ordinary. Elizabeth Bishop charges the moments of her writing with the desires, fears, and passions of her life.

CAMBRIDGE STUDIES IN AMERICAN LITERATURE AND CULTURE

Elizabeth Bishop's Poetics of Intimacy

CAMBRIDGE STUDIES IN AMERICAN LITERATURE AND CULTURE

Editor

Books in the series

Continued on pages following the Index

Elizabeth Bishop's Poetics of Intimacy

VICTORIA HARRISON
University of California, Santa Barbara

CAMBRIDGE
UNIVERSITY PRESS

Published by the Press Syndicate of the University of Cambridge
The Pitt Building, Trumpington Street, Cambridge CB2 1RP
40 West 20th Street, New York, NY 10011-4211, USA
10 Stamford Road, Oakleigh, Victoria 3166, Australia

First published 1993

Printed in the United States of America

Library of Congress Cataloging-in-Publication Data
Harrison, Victoria.
Elizabeth Bishop's poetics of intimacy / Victoria Harrison.
p. cm. – (Cambridge studies in American literature and
culture)
Includes bibliographical references (p.   ) and index.
ISBN 0-521-43203-0 (hardback)
1. Bishop, Elizabeth, 1911–1979 – Criticism and interpretation.
2. Intimacy (Psychology) in literature. I. Title. II. Series.
PS3503.I785Z69   1993
811'.52 – dc20   92-18960
                                                      CIP

A catalog record for this book is available from the British Library.

ISBN 0-521-43203-0 hardback

In memory of
Dr. Dora Moszkowski,
1901–1991

Contents

Acknowledgments

My first and profoundest debt is to the late David Kalstone, who introduced me to Elizabeth Bishop's poetry and taught me, through his own exquisite example, to study her "inner landscapes." I can only hope to offer my students what Alicia Ostriker gave me as thesis adviser: demanding, thorough, trusting, and generous, she was and continues to be my finest audience and guide. At a crucial stage in the manuscript's life Giles Gunn saw through to the core of my underarticulated argument and helped me toward my thinking. In addition, George Kearns, Helen Tartar, Lynn Keller, and Stephen Yenser have read the manuscript in its entirety over the years, objecting, querying, cajoling, and offering me insights with which I could discover its next stage. Other colleagues, friends, and family members have given the gift of their expertise and their questions, have puzzled with me over lines and critiqued chapters, have moved my writing to a new place; I thank them for their generosity: Dora Moszkowski, Ada Harrison, Elsee Layton, Ilse Barker, Carol Braun Pasternack, Alan Liu, Porter Abbott, Eloise Hay, Mary Wood, and Lloyd Schwartz. Throughout an encouraging friend, co-detective, and scrupulous editor, Alice Methfessel has been for me much more than Elizabeth Bishop's executor. Bishop's archives have challenged me as a scholar, but not without the invaluable assistance of Vassar College Library's curators, Lisa Browar and Nancy MacKechnie, or the warm home of Marianne Begemann and Steven Kenney. Eric Sundquist, series editor, Julie Greenblatt, humanities editor, and Mary Racine, production editor, for Cambridge have made the publishing process quite joyful. Madelyn Detloff and Amy Rabbino have eased the work of permissions and indexing with their enthusiastic assistance. Throughout, Peter Ullmann has welcomed this book into the circle of our daily intimacy.

I gratefully acknowledge the permission that has been granted by the following libraries to examine, and by the following executors and cor-

respondents to examine and quote, the manuscript material in this book:
Vassar College Library, Poughkeepsie, N.Y.; Princeton University Library, Princeton, N.J.; Houghton Library, Harvard University, Cambridge, Mass.; Rosenbach Museum and Library, Philadelphia, Pa.; Henry
W. and Albert A. Berg Collection, New York Public Library; Olin
Library, Washington University, St. Louis, Mo.; Harry Ranson Humanities Research Center, University of Texas at Austin; Alice Methfessel, literary executor of the estate of Elizabeth Bishop; Frank Bidart, literary executor of the estate of Robert Lowell; Marianne Craig
Moore, literary executor of the estate of Marianne Moore; Rozanne
Knudson, literary executor of the estate of May Swensen; Houghton
Mifflin Company; James Merrill; Anne Stevenson. All manuscript material throughout the book, including notebooks, unpublished writing,
and drafts toward published writing, not otherwise noted, are in the
Elizabeth Bishop Collection at the Vassar College Library.

In addition I acknowledge permission to cite the following:

Excerpts from *The Collected Prose,* by Elizabeth Bishop. Copyright ©
1984 by Alice Methfessel. Reprinted by permission of Farrar, Straus and
Giroux, Inc.

Excerpts from *The Complete Poems, 1927–1979,* by Elizabeth Bishop.
Copyright © 1979, 1983 by Alice Helen Methfessel. Reprinted by permission of Farrar, Straus and Giroux, Inc.

Excerpts from *The Diary of "Helena Morley,"* translated and edited by
Elizabeth Bishop. Copyright © 1957 by Elizabeth Bishop. Reprinted by
permission of Farrar, Straus and Giroux, Inc.

Excerpts from the introduction to *The Ballad of the Burglar of Babylon,*
by Elizabeth Bishop. Copyright © 1964, 1968 by Elizabeth Bishop.
Reprinted by permission of Farrar, Straus and Giroux, Inc.

Excerpts from *The Complete Poems,* by Marianne Moore. Copyright
© 1969, 1972 by Marianne Moore. Reprinted by permission of Macmillan
Publishing Company.

Excerpt from *Notebook,* by Robert Lowell. Copyright © 1967, 1971
by Robert Lowell. Reprinted by permission of Farrar, Straus and Giroux.

Portions of Chapter 6 were published under the title "The Dailiness
of Her Center: Elizabeth Bishop's Late Poetry," *Twentieth Century Literature* 37.3 (1991): 253–72, and are reprinted by permission of Hofstra
University.

Note on the Text

Because my discussion often depends on a precise reproduction of Elizabeth Bishop's texts, I have developed a system of parentheses, brackets, and braces for distinguishing my marks from hers. Parentheses within a quotation are Bishop's own. Empty brackets [ ] immediately following a word and letters within brackets signify my revision of the form of the word, to serve the syntactic clarity of my own sentence. I bracket my own ellipses to distinguish them from Bishop's. For consistency's sake, I use these same markers in quoting all other writers as well. Empty braces { } mark a word in Bishop's manuscript that I have been unable to decipher, and a question mark within braces signifies transcriptions about which I have doubt.

I have tried to reproduce exactly the texts of all letters and manuscript material, without normalizing spelling or punctuation. Typographical errors in Bishop's manuscripts or letters, therefore, are hers. In the case of letters through much of the book, I use Bishop's last version: where she crossed out words, I transcribe the corrected version, as I do with Bishop's correspondents. Beginning in Chapter 4, however, where I make extensive use of Bishop's unfinished poems and prose excerpts, unless I note that I am transcribing only her revised version, I reproduce her texts, including all errors and corrections, as precisely as possible.

Introduction

Elizabeth Bishop's poetic diet was typical for the poets of her generation: her grandfather's recitations of Burns, supplemented by her own reading in the family library of the romantics and the Victorians, were followed by the thrill of the modernists, when in 1923 she received a gift of the Harriet Monroe anthology, *The New Poetry*.[1] At Vassar from 1930 through 1934, she learned her moderns and, in proper Eliotian/New Critical fashion, read and loved Donne, Herbert, and Hopkins. And, like many of her contemporaries, she inherited the legacy of the modern poets, as her own poetry was departing from it. When she defined her position it was to ally herself with the "late-late Post World War I generation," because "I went to Europe earlier than most of my 'contemporary' poets – and I am a few years older than some of them" (letter to Stevenson, 20 Mar. 1963, WU). She wrestled in the mid-1930s with questions raised by modern poets and philosophers about the materiality of poetic language. Yet her poetry is generationally apart from the moderns' stylistic experimentation, tonal impersonality, and ideological effort to "make it new." But it is also unlike the poetry of her contemporaries. She never wrote poetic applications of New Critical methodologies, as did the Fugitives; neither did she feel anxiety over the moderns' influence, nor the weight of American history, as did the early Lowell, who was an intimate friend of hers. Her poetry underwent no major transformations in the 1950s, as Lowell's did, when he met the Beat poets, as Berryman's did, when he attempted the intimate tones of a dialogue with Anne Bradstreet,[2] and as several women poets' did – Levertov, Plath, Rich – when they discovered within the emerging poetic modes ways to write as women. Indeed, Bishop's poetic language is colloquial, her settings local, her address direct and personal, like those of many of her contemporaries.[3] Yet her residency in Brazil in the 1950s and 1960s removed her from the rising schools of postmodern poetry – San Francisco's Beat poetry, Black Mountain poetry, and that of the New York school.

Situating Elizabeth Bishop within her poetic field, as most critics who try to do so attest, runs one up against the idiosyncrasy Robert Lowell articulated upon reading "From Trollope's Journal":

> I think you never do a poem without your own intuition. You are the only poet now who calls her own tune – rather different from even Pound or Miss Moore who built original styles then continue them – but yours, especially the last dozen or so, are all unpredictably different. (Letter to Bishop, 12 July 1960, VC)

Her poems are "different," Lowell asserts, each from the other and all from the poetry around her. Indeed, "From Trollope's Journal" was oddly matched with the other poems in the issue of *Partisan Review* in which it appeared – Jarrell's "Hope," about his wife and mother, Rich's "A Marriage in the 'Sixties," and several confessional Sexton poems, including one called "The Abortion."[4] Bishop's persona poem, twenty-eight lines that were, in the draft she sent Lowell, divided, as if to spotlight its tight, double sonnet form, is all the odder in this company. Its political intent – she wrote Lowell it was about Eisenhower (18 Nov. 1965, HL) – seems all the more disguised, surrounded here by her contemporaries' openness. Most recently David Kalstone faced Bishop's odd fit in his posthumously published *Becoming a Poet,* which began, as his editor notes, as a book about the relations of post–World War II poets with their predecessors. Gradually, Kalstone admitted in his drafted introduction, Elizabeth Bishop's "intense difference as a poet[ ] eventually took over my book. We write and rewrite literary history. It becomes increasingly clear, the more we know about Elizabeth Bishop, that she makes us describe poetry in a different light" (ix).

Attempting to define this difference, the Irish poet Eavan Boland calls Bishop "the one un-Romantic American poet of her generation" (75). In other words, Boland observes:

> She never suggests that her fishhouses and hymn-loving seals, her Nova Scotia kitchens and Tantramar marshes depend on her. She never intimates to us, as Yeats might in "The Wild Swans at Coole" or Byron in "Childe Harold," that these objects will vanish without her intervention. Her earth is not represented as a dramatized fragment of her consciousness. Instead, she celebrates the separateness, the awesome detachment of the exterior universe. (77)

Bishop rejects the powerful romantic consciousness as a poetic center; she refuses to "exercise the privileges and powers of th[is] Romantic mechanism" (Boland 77). Explaining this mechanism by contrasting it with that of pragmatism, Richard Rorty distinguishes the two movements by the degrees to which they depart from a monologic discourse of truth: while romanticism, particularly in the hands of Hegel, situates truth not in science but in the different and potentially new discourses of literature, pragmatism, or Boland's "un-Romanticism," abandons all claims to truth.[5] A pragmatic world, in which the relations between things are necessarily as real as the things themselves, is left with inter-acting subjects discovering the use or pleasure of any reality, without a higher authority – poet, God, language, science – encompassing and controlling the process. Recognizing her intimacy with – and not her centrality amid – an interesting world, Bishop listens to the unlikely connections and mutual discoveries of the subjects of her writing, as she recognizes her subjects' unfolding.

Articulating her unromanticism in her own terms in her 1934 note-book, Bishop distinguished between the materiality and the spirituality of poetry:

> It's a question of using the poet's proper materials, with which he is equipped by nature, i.e., immediate, intense physical reactions, a sense of metaphor and decoration in everything – to express something not of them – something I suppose, spiritual. But it proceeds from the material, the material eaten out with acid, pulled down from under-neath, made to perform and always kept in order, in its place.[6] Some-times it cannot be made to indicate its spiritual goal clearly (Some of Hopkins', say, where the point seems to be missing) but even then the spiritual must be felt. [. . .] The other way – of using the supposedly "spiritual" – the beautiful, the nostalgic, the ideal and poetic, to produce the material – is the way of the Romantic, I think – and a great perversity. This may be capable of being treated by a mere studying of simile and metaphor – This is why genuine religious poetry seems to be about as far as poetry can go – and as good as it can be – (Notebook, late July 1934)

Bishop unwittingly invokes something like Remy de Gourmont's belief that "all abstract words are the figuration of a material act."[7] Like him, she insists on the primacy of the poem's own materiality. That this material force is, for her, "eaten out with acid," discolored, raw, and charged with a potency of its own defines well the distinction Boland and Rorty articulate differently between the romantic's faith in essence and Bishop's postromantic, pragmatic slippage, whereby she engages the poet's ordering mechanisms but celebrates most highly what is "not of them," or the element of spiritual surprise that makes the trust in those external forces worthwhile.

This fascination with the mind's processes has invited comparison between her poetry and that of her stylistic mentors, Hopkins and Her-bert,[8] and in his book on Bishop, Thomas Travisano draws the connec-

tion between Bishop's efforts to capture the process of a poet's knowing
and that of the baroques. He cites her college essay on Hopkins, in which
she quotes Morris Croll's "The Baroque Style in Prose": the baroque
writers' "purpose," Croll states and Bishop quotes, "was to portray, not
a thought, but the mind thinking [. . .,] the moment in which the truth
is still *imagined*" (Travisano 11–12). Therein, Travisano argues, the baroques "attended to the twists and turns of perception" (11), achieving
surprise, the poetic quality Bishop most admired.

Although Bishop never articulated her interests as such, it is a short
step from Travisano's description of what most fascinated Bishop in the
baroque to the terms of an American pragmatism that informed American
thinking around Bishop in the late modern period. Though she did no
systematic reading of pragmatism, she and Marianne Moore read the
"Christian pragmatism"[9] of Reinhold Niebuhr in 1938; John Dewey and
she were acquaintances in Key West in the 1940s and perhaps shared
conversation about his work; and in response to a query about whether
she had seen Leon Edel's biography of Henry James, she responded with
pride that the Jameses were hardly new to her: she had read them thoroughly twenty years before, and now, because "Lota has a lot of Wm.
James [, . . .] I've even been trying to cope with pragmatism again recently" (letter to Barkers, 23 Mar. 1956, PU). I do not intend, however,
to draw the direct links between poet and philosophers as much as to
suggest a tradition that embraces them each – a "vocabulary of practise
rather than of theory, of action rather than contemplation, in which one
can say something useful about truth" (Rorty 162).

Postromanticist, empiricist, and pragmatist, James and Dewey articulated for the modern American period a vision that had its roots in
Emersonian thinking and found its way into the poetic practice of such
twentieth-century poets as Frost, Stevens, and, I will argue, Elizabeth
Bishop. Tracing this tradition in *The Renewal of Literature*, Richard Poirier
sets forth some of the terms that link these writers:

> Consider: the emphasis on action, on transitions as a valuable form of
> action, both in Emerson and in James; the need stressed by both of
> them for movement *away* from substantives or "resting-places" or set-
> tled texts; Frost's definition of a poem as only "a momentary stay against
> confusion," and the virtue attached by Stevens to becoming "an ig-
> norant man again." (16)

William James asserts that vital to any event are the "prepositions,
copulas, and conjunctions" that link the parts, often coincidentally (216).
In fact, he argues, "we ought to say a feeling of *and*, a feeling of *if*, a
feeling of *but*, and a feeling of *by*, quite as readily as we say a feeling of
blue, or a feeling of *cold*" (38). Bishop recognized precisely these feelings

in "Over 2,000 Illustrations and a Complete Concordance," a poem
whose tourist, back home with the comprehensible, orderly renditions
of the world in her engraved Bible, is nonetheless overwhelmed by the
proliferation of sensation and emotion experienced in a different world.
The closing stanza of the poem begins with the fragment: "Everything
only connected by 'and' and 'and,' " as if to suggest that no more definitive connections between the emotions or between the experienced and
the observed worlds would suffice. Or rather, as James asserted, these
transitive states – these "*tendencies* of the nascent images [. . .] among
the *objects* of the stream" (45), this "*psychic overtone, suffusion,*" and these
"fringes of relation" (48, 54, his emphases) – participate fully in the
making of those worlds: "A man walks suddenly into my field of view,
and forthwith becomes part of it. [. . .] I may entirely overlook and fail
to notice even so important an object as a man, until the inward event
of altering my attention makes me suddenly see him with the other
objects there" (159–60). James's very prose method, which layers ar-
guments with anecdotes so that each shades the others, reinforces his
premise, allowing his readers to experience the tendencies of his often
oddly juxtaposed examples as we are discovering the line of thought
they share. With such a pragmatic impulse at play, Bishop's poems enact
relationships by means of often surprising conjunctions and transitions.
Bringing together land and sea in "The Map," an almanac, a teakettle,
and an effusion of tears in "Sestina," or the Vietnam War and her nighttime desk in "12 O'Clock News," she explores the relationships born
of often surprising meetings. Bishop was fascinated by the coincidental,
musing in her 1935 journal about the mysterious life of the things stuck
together in a mail-order catalogue and fantasizing an attic room where
the smells, colors, and textures of her life's things would decay together
to produce oddly new combinations.

John Dewey was likewise interested in the impact such things have
on the one experiencing them, or rather on the interrelations of thought
and thing:

> The odor knows the rose; the rose is known by the odor; and the import of
> each term is constituted by the relationship in which it stands to the other.
> [. . .] The smell which knows is no more merely mental than is the
> rose known. [. . .] It denotes only the fact that the smell, a real and
> nonpsychical object, now exercises an intellectual *function*. This new
> property involves, as James has pointed out, an *additive* relation – a new
> property possessed by a non-mental object, when that object, occurring
> in a new context, assumes a further office and use. (*Darwin* 88, 104,
> his emphases)[10]

Or, as he would argue some fifteen years later, "The qualities never were
'in' the organism; they always were qualities of interactions in which

both extra-organic things and organisms partake" (*Experience* 212). Whereas in James's sentence the individual's thought or imagination inevitably has a grammatical primacy over the thing and its fringes or overtones, Dewey is careful to consider both the grammar and the psychology of the relationship between the seemingly animate and the seemingly inanimate. Especially interested in revising the tendency of empiricism toward dualisms of mind and body, as a means toward a more culturally situated, process-oriented, and consequence-minded philosophy of education, Dewey focuses on what he calls our "undergoing" in *Democracy and Education,* or the significant "flux" produced "when the change made by action is reflected back into a change made in us" (163).

Dewey's carefully articulated effort to give integrity to both changes – in this case they balance each other as equally passive subjects – nicely situates my interest in this book in the images, actions, tones, prosodic structures, and language of Bishop's writing that foregrounds what I will call its "subject–subject relationships." It matters absolutely that these subjects have, as Boland understood, an interactive separateness with and from their author and one another. Reading Bishop's poetry through American pragmatism offers insight into how her poems structurally and thematically enact these relations between. And it gives us a way of reading Bishop's localism – her attention to the ordinary, daily emotions and conversations among subjects. Richard Rorty is particularly interested in this local aspect of pragmatism:

> It is the doctrine that there are no constraints on inquiry save conversational ones – no wholesale constraints derived from the nature of the objects, or of the mind, or of language, but only those retail constraints provided by the remarks of our fellow-inquirers. [...]
> Our identification with our community – our society, our political tradition, our intellectual heritage – is heightened when we see this community as *ours* rather than *nature's, shaped* rather than *found,* one among many which men have made. In the end, the pragmatists tell us, what matters is our loyalty to other human beings clinging together against the dark, not our hope of getting things right. (165–6)

Recognizing what pragmatism gives up – "there is no method for knowing *when* one has reached the truth, or when one is closer to it than before" (165–6) – Rorty finds some measure of compensation in its offer of local, human communities. But despite his own postmodern situation, Rorty articulates a notion of community that is seemingly gender-, class-, and race-neutral, inevitably rendering hegemonic that which he claims to be *"ours."* Thus, Rorty's examination of pragmatism leaves unquestioned its often implicit humanism. Vital as are the transitive parts of James's stream of thought, James's confluence of tones, shades, and values never quite loses its central subject or fully embraces multiplicity; nor does Rorty's. James's fringes are, finally, a "halo or penumbra that surrounds and escorts" the subject (46); Rorty's "shaped" community is "one among many which [undifferentiated] men have made." While Dewey gets as close as empirical pragmatism will to a recognition of the mutuality and multiplicity of subject–subject relationships, his vision as well does not go as far as I need toward a reading of the particularly gendered or the particular sexually and racially oriented subjects of Bishop's poetry.

Grounded by the kind of antiessentialism toward which pragmatism reached, postmodern feminism and cultural anthropology are in turn opening out the field of discourse precisely at this juncture, where they can question the politics of a James-like confluence by deconstructing our assumptions about subjectivity and considering means toward redefinition and revision. Three theorists – Teresa de Lauretis, Clifford Geertz, and Gayatri Spivak – offer three quite different readings of subjectivity, readings implicitly in conversation with one another and each vitally extending the pragmatic frame.

Feminist film theorist Teresa de Lauretis is interested first in the inherent gendering of all subjectivity and further in the politics of that gendering process. Embracing Foucault's methods of theorizing sexuality to unravel the ways we have essentialized and then exploited our gender system, she counters, in *Technologies of Gender,* that the "relations of subjectivity to sociality" are

> constituted in gender, to be sure, though not by sexual difference alone, but rather across languages and cultural representations; a subject engendered in the experiencing of race and class, as well as sexual, relations; a subject, therefore, not unified but rather multiple, and not so much divided as contradicted. (2)

Complicating what we mean when we speak of gender, this feminist theory offers a model not of a head with its halo of significances but of multiple and unequally powerful heads, some receding as others come forward, some wholly shadowed by others more imposing, but each nonetheless constituting a share of the gendered subject. De Lauretis reads the contradiction as follows:

> It is a movement between the (represented) discursive space of the positions made available by hegemonic discourses and the space-off, the elsewhere, of those discourses: those other spaces both discursive and social that exist, since feminist practices have (re)constructed them, in the margins [. . .] of hegemonic discourses and in the interstices of institutions, in counter-practices and new forms of community. [. . .] The movement between them, therefore, is [. . .] the tension of contradiction, multiplicity, and heteronomy. (26)

Whereas both Rorty and de Lauretis are concerned with understanding the forces that make possible a community, de Lauretis begins where Rorty leaves off. She assumes that only when we recognize the contradictory layers across which we are each constituted by such technologies as gender can we assess the ways in which we might in turn "shape" culture or participate as subjects in the community – "in the micropolitical practices of daily life and daily resistances" (25).

Cultural anthropologist Clifford Geertz approaches our shaping of culture not from the perspective of a micropolitics of dispersed authority but from the particular authoritative position of the ethnographer. Fully the pragmatist who recognizes the daily, transitive progress of culture and trusts that the suffusions and fringes will shift every meaning, Geertz at the same time responds, in *Works and Lives* and elsewhere, to the inadequacy of humanist notions of truth, insisting that we acknowledge the "highly situated nature of ethnographic description – this ethnographer, in this time, in this place, with these informants, these commitments, and these experiences, a representative of a particular culture, a member of a certain class" (5). Geertz is more optimistic than are many of his colleagues that if the ethnographer recognizes and makes textually available his position "here," he will discover a means of access to what is "there":[11]

> One of the major assumptions upon which anthropological writing rested until only yesterday, that its subjects and its audience were not only separable but morally disconnected, that the first were to be described but not addressed, the second informed but not implicated, has fairly well dissolved. (132)

Gayatri Spivak, who comes to cultural criticism from the fields of deconstruction, feminism, and Marxism, reads differently what Geertz calls "this inter-confusion of object and audience" (133). Whereas he discusses the problem of who indeed one writes for, "Africanists or Africans," for instance, Spivak sees the inter-confusion as far more basic:

> I am progressively inclined [. . .] to read the retrieval of subaltern consciousness as the charting of what in post-structuralist language would be called the subaltern subject-effect. A subject-effect can be briefly plotted as follows: that which seems to operate as a subject may be part of an immense discontinuous network ("text" in the general sense) of strands that may be termed politics, ideology, economics, history, sexuality, language, and so on. [. . .] Different knottings and configurations of these strands, determined by heterogeneous determinations which are themselves dependent upon myriad circumstances, produce the effect of an operating subject. Yet the continuist and homogenist deliberative consciousness symptomatically requires a continuous and homogeneous cause for this effect and thus posits a sov-

ereign and determining subject. This latter is, then, the effect of an
effect, and its positing a metalepsis, or the substitution of an effect for
a cause. (*Worlds* 204)

As if reexamining de Lauretis's discursive spaces to find no "space-off"
but only subject effects in the subaltern's discursive position, Spivak
would reject Geertz's optimism as well. Geertz's suggested project of
making ethnographic discourse " 'heteroglossial,' so that Emawayish can
speak within it alongside the anthropologist in some direct, equal, and
independent way" (145), is, in Spivak's terms, flawed from the start: the
voice of Michel Leiris's Ethiopian woman, Emawayish (Geertz 129), is
already interwoven with the strands of a range of determining textualities,
so that listening to it is listening to those other texts.

Like Rorty, Geertz closes his text on a note of optimism, that ethnography can enable conversation across societal lines. But Geertz moves
beyond Rorty's universalized community to reassert antiessentialism in
the terms of a contemporary pragmatism: concerning himself with "eth-
nicity, religion, class, gender, language, race," he asserts that

> the next necessary thing [. . .] is to enlarge the possibility of intelligible
> discourse between people quite different from one another in interest,
> outlook, wealth, and power, and yet contained in a world where, tum-
> bled as they are into endless connection, it is increasingly difficult to
> get out of each other's way. (147)

Where Spivak might agree with the desirability of such a conversation,
she would insist on its impossibility: because her voice is occupied by
the network of subject effects that speak on her behalf, "the subaltern
cannot speak."[12]

Though this discussion seems to have moved far from the philosophy
of pragmatism, Elizabeth Bishop's poetry has required that I look not
only at her American interest in what, in James's words, "link[s] the
parts, often coincidentally," but also at what pragmatism only begins to
open up – the multiplicity and power dynamics inherent both within
subjectivity itself and in the relations between subjects. While I regard
Bishop as a pragmatist whom Richard Poirier could have included hand-
ily in his reading of the tradition, she was at the same time challenging
the authority of the subject, in ways Frost and Stevens were not and in
terms to which pragmatism can only point me. Here, then, I will turn
for assistance to postmodern theory. Bishop poses these latter questions
not, of course, with the political or intellectual commitment of these
theorists, but with a similar intuitive response to centers, wholes, subjects, and objects.

Vital to my reading of Bishop's response is her construction of subjectivities that are at their core relational.[13] These subject–subject relations

need not be and are often not between people, nor are they necessarily between clearly demarcated entities at all. In her first major published poem, "The Map," the relationship is between interwoven bodies of land and water. The relationships need not be contained within the borders of the poem; Bishop sometimes expects her reader to feel the responsibilities of the poem's "you." Sometimes they are between figures unconscious of their connection, as in "The Moose" or "In the Waiting Room," until the poem's process records and adjusts their awarenesses. Often, Bishop reveals relationship through variations in metrical form, which might itself support or contradict the poem's articulated emotion. Perhaps most significantly, Bishop discovers over the course of a career an ability to give her poetic objects agency – that sense of "awesome detachment" – which in turn gives them a vital role in the poem's working emotion. "Sestina's" almanac and teakettle provide a domestic ground that can accommodate the child's inscrutable tears; the child depends on these stable, ordinary objects, which assume the power of subjects and can thus bear some of the weight of this roomful of heightened emotions.

Animating her poetic objects, her tonal and grammatical shifts, and her poetic structures with the force and engagement of intimate emotions, Bishop challenges assumed hierarchies between and definitional distinctions of subjects and their others, rendering these fully if not painfully revisable. Essential to such revisions is a recognition of subjectivity as not only multiplicitous to its core but also, from its origins, relational. Whether her poem's subject is a man-moth, a weed, a Brazilian murderer, or a Nova Scotian grandparent, her figure's "multiple and contradicted" "tendencies" (de Lauretis; James) are determined by its changing interactions with its equally multiple and contradicted other. Writing a poetry that enacts same-sex love, for instance, Bishop disorders and variously reconfigures the subjectivity of poetic sexuality. When she explored ethnic subjectivity, as I will argue in Chapters 3 and 5 particularly, she was aware of and attempted to achieve what she called in a drafted introduction to her never-completed book of prose essays on Brazil "a double point of view." Occasionally, her intimacy with Brazilian friends did offer her Brazilian writing a perspective "~~more-three-dimensional~~[ ]" than either a foreigner's or Brazilian's alone: the collaborative nature of her authorial position makes possible her most profound inquiries into cultural difference. Her poetry repeatedly engages the questions of her subjects' continuity and discontinuity, both at home among the objects of a grandmother's kitchen or beside a lover in bed, and abroad, amid foreign countries, whose cultural and political practices both challenge and confirm her own. Bishop "call[s her] own tune," I argue in this book, because her poetry's concerns are very simple and quite unique:

she enacts subject–subject relations in their dailiness. Whether she writes about people riding a bus together, one woman shampooing another's hair, or land and water finding each other, her poetry inevitably listens to the voices of layered and changeable subjectivities, so as to explore their daily and profound connections.

In discussing her work, Bishop's early critics formed themselves into two rough camps. There were those who admired the morality of Bishop's emotion and those who, after Marianne Moore, appreciated the disguise of that emotion and the technical accuracy of her art. Moore introduced Bishop's work in *Trial Balances* as follows:

> The specific is judiciously interspersed with generality, and the permitted clue to idiosyncrasy has a becoming evasiveness. We are willing to be apprised of a secret – indeed glad to be – but technique must be cold, sober, conscious of self-justifying ability. Some feminine poets of the present day seem to have grown horns and to like to be frightful and dainty by turns; but distorted propriety suggests effeteness. One would rather disguise than travesty emotion; give away a nice thing than sell it; dismember a garment of rich aesthetic construction than degrade it to the utilitarian offices of the boneyard. One notices the deferences and vigilances in Miss Bishop's writing, and the debt to Donne and to Gerard Hopkins. We look at imitation askance; but like the shell which the hermit-crab selects for itself, it has value – the avowed humility, and the protection. Miss Bishop's ungrudged self-expenditure should also be noticed – automatic, apparently, as part of the nature. Too much cannot be said for this phase of self-respect. (82–3)[14]

If self-expenditure was not quite self-revelation, if one's aesthetics were "accurate and modest," a feature for which Moore praised Bishop in her 1946 review of *North & South* (*CPr* 406), and if, finally, one's poetry was neither utilitarian nor distorted by emotion, especially female emotion, then one began to meet Moore's high moral standards for poetry. With Moore's (and Moore's mother's) mentorship and editorial assistance over the years, Bishop did.

Louise Bogan, who was similarly pleased that Bishop had sloughed what she considered to be the invasive sentimentalism of the Teasdale–Wylie type of female poetry, praised Bishop's poems for their objectivity:

> They strike no attitudes and have not an ounce of superfluous emotional weight, and they combine an unforced ironic humor with a naturalist's accuracy of observation, for Miss Bishop, although she frequently writes fantasy, is firmly in touch with the real world and takes a Thoreaulike interest in whatever catches her attention. (Schwartz and Estess 182)

The opening of James Southworth's 1959 essay epitomizes this sort of criticism: "The poetry of Elizabeth Bishop, except for some ten poems [which he did acknowledge are, by contrast, "passionately subjective"], is as objective as poetry can well be." He further defined Bishop's objectivity in terms similar to Bogan's: "She is not interested in the abstract truth at the end of the road, but in the concrete truths that lie along the way." To illustrate the type of truths he meant, he invoked captured moments in painting, "a bowl of peaches by Cézanne, a wheat field by Van Gogh, a lady playing the lute by Ter Borch" (213–14).

While he accepted the clichés about what is good in women's poetry, addressing Bishop's "restraint, calm, and proportion" in his 1946 review, Randall Jarrell was most interested in the "emotional weight" that Bogan was glad to see constrained. Bishop's art, he showed, serves a postwar morality:

> Her work is unusually personal and honest in its wit, perception, and sensitivity – and in its restrictions too; all her poems have written underneath, *I have seen it.* She is morally so attractive, in poems like "The Fish" or "Roosters," because she understands so well that the wickedness and confusion of the age can explain and extenuate other people's wickedness and confusion, but not, for you, your own; that morality, for the individual, is usually a small, personal, statistical, but heartbreaking or heartwarming affair of omissions and commissions the greatest of which will seem infinitesimal, ludicrously beneath notice, to those who govern, rationalize, and deplore; [. . .] that beneath our lives "there is inescapable hope, the pivot," so that in the revolution of things even the heartsick Peter can someday find "his dreadful rooster come to mean forgiveness"; that when you see the snapped lines trailing, "a five-haired beard of wisdom," from the great fish's aching jaw, it is then that victory fills "the little rented boat," that the oil on the bilgewater by the rusty engine is "rainbow, rainbow, rainbow!" – that you let the fish go. (Schwartz and Estess 181)

Jarrell's review, pressured by his own postwar sensitivities, is stunning in its distinction between self-consciousness and consciousness of the other outside. Although his closing lines seem to leave Bishop behind in their excitement of layered quotation and projection of a "you" beyond her, Jarrell nonetheless argues with passion that one can derive a moral vision from Bishop's poetic moments.

Interested likewise in this vision in his 1947 review, "Thomas, Bishop, and Williams," Robert Lowell discussed not its isolatable moments but the emotional oppositions inherent in her poems' process.[15] Seeing restless motion and equally unsettling closure as paradoxical counterpoints in Bishop's art, he traced the course between. She appreciated the insight:

his "is the only review that goes at things in what *I* think is the right way" (letter to Lowell, 14 Aug. 1947, HL):

> There are two opposing factors. The first is something in motion, weary but persisting, almost always failing and on the point of disintegrating, and yet, for the most part, stoically maintained. This is morality, memory, the weed that grows to divide, and the dawn that advances, illuminates and calls to work. [...] The second factor is a terminus: rest, sleep, fulfillment or death. This is the imaginary iceberg, the moon which the Man-moth thinks is a small clean hole through which he must thrust his head. [...]
> The motion-process is usually accepted as necessary and, therefore, good; yet it is dreary and exhausting. But the formula is mysterious and gently varies with its objects. The terminus is sometimes pathetically or humorously desired as a letting-go or annihilation; sometimes it is fulfillment and the complete harmonious exercise of one's faculties. (Schwartz and Estess 186–7)

Lowell's review confronted unsettling turns in Bishop's poetry decades before postmodern theory opened up the disruptive as a fruitful angle of literary inquiry. But he did so by labeling the opposing factors "a single symbolic pattern" that encompasses "at least nine-tenths" of the poems in *North & South,* thus making academic the potentially disturbing movement, now safe within a New Critical establishment.

In the first full-length book on Bishop, Anne Stevenson engaged in an early form of interdisciplinarity, applying the varied theories of Hofmannsthal (58), Wittgenstein (114–16), David Bohm's modern physics, and Roberto Bonola's non-Euclidean geometry (118) to Bishop's work. Moving in quite the opposite direction, in keeping with the psychological forms of inquiry of the mid-1970s, Jerome Mazzaro offered the first turn inward toward an Elizabeth Bishop who makes her personal conflicts available to her poetic perception. Near the end of his essay, Mazzaro defined Bishop's difference from Roethke's, Lowell's, Jarrell's, and Berryman's ego promotion – their "rarity" – and their imposition of will on their surroundings:

> One has the sense particularly in these late poems that she has lived the life she imagined – with all its necessary disappointments – and, despite the narrow range of choice and the pain of disappointment, she is willing to see her past as the only kind of life she could have lived. (195)

Using as much as he knew of her life as guide, he teased out what he called the "Imagist attachment of emotion to objects" (167), in his readings of dozens of her poems and prose pieces. Although he was sometimes wrong, particularly when he allowed stereotypes of femaleness to determine his response, his essay is important for its boldness. David Kalstone's penetrating analyses in his posthumously published *Becoming a Poet* and in several earlier essays increasingly turned toward what he called in 1977 her "inner landscapes." "These poems," he wrote about her first two books of poetry,

> both describe and set themselves at the limits of description. Bishop lets us know that every detail is a boundary, not a Blakean microcosm. Because of the limits they suggest, details vibrate with a meaning beyond mere physical presence. Landscapes meant to sound detached are really inner landscapes. They show an effort at reconstituting the world as if it were in danger of being continually lost. (*Temperaments* 22)

Kalstone is particularly interested here in the point of juncture between Bishop's emotions and memory and her world. In the later book, where he explores the meeting of these personal queries and her intimate relationships with Moore and Lowell, Kalstone makes the moment of her poems immediate to us, as he is offering personal, poetic, and historical contexts for them. Kalstone was perhaps Bishop's most kindred spirit as a critic. When he quotes from her letters and notebooks his insights match hers, their two voices yielding up her life and poetry as if in intimate conversation.

Feminist critics have approached Bishop less with such unconditional affection than with a challenge: she is a woman poet, now how? In 1983 Adrienne Rich discussed Bishop's lesbianism as the means to her insight about and sympathy with the position of the outsider ("Outsider" 17). Rich's article is self-reflexive; it is as much about her ability now to revise her 1971 dismissal of Bishop as it is about Bishop's poetics.[16] The explorations of academic feminists in the 1980s have taken at least two directions. Searching for a female line that includes Bishop, Joanne Feit Diehl and co-writers Lynn Keller and Cristanne Miller discuss Dickinson as a precursor to Bishop. While Feit Diehl explores the ways that Bishop, like Dickinson, gains authority by becoming a "transsexual self-as-poet," subverting her female or lesbian voice so that it speaks palimpsestically within male or genderless personas (135), Keller and Miller use feminist studies of language and gender to argue a tradition wherein both writers use clichéd feminine speech patterns and various forms of indirection to empower their images and language. "Bishop creates a breezy chatter within which weighty emotions become bearable and radical suggestions possible" (542–3). In combination, the two essays are valuable in their exploration of how Bishop wrote as and seemed not to write as a woman. Three essays that came out within months of each other plumb Moore and Bishop's correspondence in analyzing this important modernist literary relationship;[17] in her 1990 book, Jeredith Merrin studies the relationship through an analysis of their literary influences, or the "maternity

and paternity," as she puts it, of influence itself. Such critics as Susan
Lurie and Lois Cucullu read Bishop through the insights of feminist
psychoanalytic and materialist theories in order at once to claim and
problematize Bishop's feminism. Lois Cucullu, for instance, argues that
Bishop's "eye/I" is politically radical; her poems "become a method of
interrogating language as a coding system, the ideology (political, racial,
sexual) inscribed within its discourses, and the subject positions it delimits
for women" (264).

While such theories are essential to our understanding both of the work
of Bishop's poetic images and of her situation within a feminist literary
canon, still, there is a large gap. In the absence of both published letters
and a biography of Bishop,[18] and in the virtual silence from her of any
discussion of poetics, the literary or theoretical prescriptions of much
current study of Bishop have the effect of distancing us from her writing.
Four full-length studies of Bishop have recently been published, Thomas
Travisano's and Robert Dale Parker's (1988), Bonnie Costello's (1991),
and Lorrie Goldensohn's (1992). Travisano's is especially helpful to me
for its explorations into Bishop's contemporizing of baroque process,
and Goldensohn's recovery in Brazil of Bishop's 1940s and 1950s notebooks has been invaluable for my reading of this period of Bishop's
work. Costello's book is, like her writing on Bishop for more than a
decade, beautiful and evocative; indeed, all four books provide important
readings of Bishop's poems. But still much of the essential work among
the yellowed fragments, the pen scratches, and the miserable typing of
Bishop's archival material, at the Vassar College Library and elsewhere,
is yet to be done. David Kalstone's *Becoming a Poet* goes farther in this
direction than any previous study; having nearly completed my book
before his was published, I have been pleased to discover how closely
my readings complement and extend the study of Bishop's wide range
of texts that Kalstone began. We must go like Bishop's sandpiper, "preoccupied, looking"[19] at irrelevant but curiously colored sand, if we are to
approach her submerged voices. Letters, notebooks, drafts toward published writing, unpublished poems and prose, fragments, and the mis-
cellaneous texts in a writer's life help to answer many of our stumbling
questions, as they complicate, disorganize, and force us to discard our
more comfortable theoretical assumptions. One important lesson of postmodern theory is that these disorganizations are necessarily the point.
Understanding the sexuality and politics, the forms of intimacy and
confrontations with the world in Elizabeth Bishop's writing requires a
careful inquiry into territory of which she was aware and which she
inhabited unwittingly. This book participates in that inquiry.

I begin with some of the important details of Bishop's life, to set a
context for my discussion of her work.[20] Then, in an introduction to her

career as poet, I study Bishop as a "literary critic," who had definite, albeit often idiosyncratic, opinions about poetry and about her fellow poets. Reading letters, occasional published and unpublished reviews, and marginal jottings in the books she read, I discuss the importance to her of the accurate but nonetheless surprising details that lead a poem to move one emotionally. This consistently local – and in a Rortian sense thoroughly pragmatic – turn of her comments serves her urge toward connection: whether she was reading an author she liked, responding to a friend's poetry, or preparing a review of one of her contemporaries, she gravitated toward the personal, daily details of the writing as a means to relationship with the writer and struggled, in some sketchy but fascinating discussions, with writing that refused her this dailiness.

In the five chapters that follow, I approach Bishop's writing roughly chronologically, dividing, in the case of her early poetry and her Brazil writing, the more directly personal work from that more public in nature, so as to isolate the different yet overlapping patterns. Feminist, lesbian, and object-relations theories hover behind the close readings of the second chapter, which more directly engage letters and notebook entries in their effort to unpack the multilayered subjectivities of this poetry. In these 1930s and 1940s poems, Bishop explores mother–daughter and love relationships by enacting their emotional states – dependency and assertions of independence, aggression, playfulness, competitiveness, alienation, loss, and desire. Concerned with the emotions bred by difference and the insights of what she called an "inverted" vision, her poems record the multiple and contradicted positions of her subjects' intimacies.

In the third chapter I explore Bishop's poetic engagement with 1930s Left politics and 1940s antiwar sentiment and black–white race relations in Key West in order to watch her particularly pragmatic process, whereby historical crises and cultural memories meet individuals in their daily lives. Several of Bishop's finest poems of these years are located at these brief but insightful moments of juncture, where her subjects' inner and outer wars are fought on a single turf. Hers is an effort toward inclusivity: righteous remove, even in the face of terrible world events, has no voice in this poetry; there is no unimplicated position. Rather, Bishop reveals the flexibility of historical fact, as viewed from the ordinary individual's perspective. By setting history into such a daily frame she avoids ideological stances but nonetheless explores and challenges cultural norms and values.

The fourth and fifth chapters study the writing of Bishop's Brazil years, the 1950s and 1960s, the fourth examining her Nova Scotia memoirs in prose and poetry. Through an analysis of manuscript material that dates back to the 1930s, I trace the development of her most important memoir, "In the Village," and then discuss her published and unpublished representations of her family and childhood. Trust in the stability, even the agency, of objects – her intense focus on "something <u>real</u> coming along like a piece of wood bobbing on the waves," as she put it in her notebook in 1950 – provided access to inscrutable emotions and to the elusive moments at which related but alienated subjects conjoin, an especially important task for the child, Elizabeth, in this writing, desperately in need of a family feeling. While in the second chapter I discuss the multiple and contradicted nature of subjectivity primarily in terms of the people involved, here I am interested as well in the roles played by objects, sounds, and gestures in the making and remaking of subjectivity. Dispersing the emotion among the poem or story's members, be they animate or inanimate, Bishop offers us a relational subjectivity at once flexible and connective: the subject–subject relationships in this family writing are made up not of discrete individuals but of interacting memories, objects around the familiar rooms, sounds and their resonances, repeated gestures, and individuals who are themselves composites of one another.

While the family poems often confront the layers of subjectivity at a level of poetic symbol, Bishop was at the same time increasingly alert in Brazil to the cultural difference that distances speaking subject from spoken other. Throughout the 1950s and 1960s, she wrote about individual Brazilians, immersing herself for three years, for instance, in the tones of rural Brazil as she translated *The Diary of "Helena Morley."* Guided again by pragmatism's suggestiveness and by the more specific discussions of Clifford Geertz and Gayatri Spivak regarding the roles of the ethnographer and the subaltern subject effect, I explore in the fifth chapter Bishop's increasing awareness of and poetic engagement with the economic, racial, and gendered structures of power in Brazil. Articulating subject–subject relationship in Brazil required acknowledging her position as writer and co-creator of her other, as she does most poignantly in "Brazil, January 1, 1502," where she explores the power politics of knowing, having, and controlling the unknown. In her translations, particularly, Bishop locates the points of conversation between an outsider's insight and a Brazilian familiarity. Translating, or creating a "new" poem founded in an interaction between two writers' perspectives and voices, Bishop extended her own range of political and cultural concerns by working with poems more confessional or more political than her own writing.

Bishop's late poetry, I argue in the sixth chapter, is a locus for her life's convergences and closure. When she returned to Boston in the early 1970s and began writing retrospective verse, she turned most consistently to the moments yielded up by memory, where she could render culture and politics in terms of daily relationships of power, alienation, curiosity, identification, and love. Choosing to read culture by thus decentering it, this poetry poses the sorts of questions Gayatri Spivak asks in "French Feminism in an International Frame" – Who am I? Who is she? How do we name each other? (*Worlds* 150) – by listening to ordinary, traditionally marginalized individuals as they constitute culture daily.

Throughout this book my interest in Bishop's work is more practical than theoretical, more focused than comparative: the depth of her simplicity seems to demand such an approach. While certain theoretical approaches in feminist, anthropological, and cultural studies have given me insights about how to proceed, I endeavor, finally, to write pragmatically myself, developing my terms for reading relationships in Bishop's poetry by listening to the turns of her writing itself. This writing, like any author's, is, of course, never a self-completing cycle; it is inevitably immersed in economic, racial, and gendered structures, of which it is only occasionally and partially aware. But in order to explore the process by which Bishop's poetry enacts ordinary, uneventful, subject–subject relationships, I must give closest attention to the turns, breaks, juxtapositions, and odd moments of Bishop's published and unpublished writing over a career.

1

Articulating a Personal Poetics

G.S.: Did it seem important to notice what women poets were doing?
E.B.: No, I never made any distinction; I never make any distinction.
However, one thing I should make clear. When I was in college and
started publishing, even then, and in the following few years, there
were women's anthologies, and all-women issues of magazines, but I
always refused to be in them. I didn't think about it very seriously, but
I felt it was a lot of nonsense, separating the sexes. I suppose this feeling
came from feminist principles, perhaps stronger than I was aware of.[1]

Interview with George Starbuck 322

What Bishop does not say in this 1977 interview is that she had, with a
few important exceptions, dissociated herself from women's writing,
both as an influence and as a movement contemporary with her own
poetry. On the one hand, she subscribed to a feminism that maintained,
as Louise Bogan put it in a 1963 review of women's poetry: "To separate
the work of women writers from the work of men is, naturally, a highly
unfeminist action."[2] Although academic and cultural feminism was in
1977 actively asserting and exploring gender difference, Bishop believed
that gender marking (as well as racial marking) contributed to inequality.
On the other hand, her refusal to take a stand as a woman writer was
consistent with her general privacy regarding most things personal, including, especially, her sexual identity and, until some interviews in the
1960s and 1970s, her political views. In the midst of highly politicized
times – among her leftist friends in the 1930s, her rightist friends in Brazil
in the 1950s and 1960s, her openly lesbian and homosexual friends
throughout her life – Bishop maintained a principle of privacy in her
work that would necessarily find problematic the ideology of a single-
sex anthology. Her most powerful poetry, she wrote Anne Stevenson,
was that in which she was unconscious of the politics ([Mar. 1964], 15

19

Aug. 1965, WU). Although her own writing reveals an engagement with issues of class hierarchy, war politics, and gender and race relations in the United States and then in Brazil, she asserted that she "was always opposed to political thinking as such for writers. . . . Politically, I considered myself a socialist [in the 1930s], but I disliked 'social conscious' writing.")[3] Likewise, she told Wesley Wehr, after living on the West Coast during the rise of Beat poetry, "I *hate* confessional poetry, and so many people are writing it these days. Besides, they seldom have anything interesting to 'confess' anyway" (327).

She did not like open display in life any more than she did in writing. Overt homosexuality in San Francisco in the late 1960s, for instance, bothered her enough that she did not finish a prose piece, entitled "The Fairy Toll-taker," whose description of San Francisco's fog-colored lights is disturbed by the title figure, a diminutive, doll-like San Francisco Bay Bridge toll taker. Though she had lived as a lesbian for the past several decades, this man's display of his sexual identity – "An obvious homosexual. Perhaps he picks up men on his odd job?" – wrenched her out of her fantasy of color and light; this question stopped her half-page description short, and she could not or would not go on. We may attribute Bishop's effort to submerge her politics, her sexuality, and, in the early writing especially, her personal "I" to the more conservative tenets of New Criticism or to her own shyness and sense of privacy. Yet her writing is nonetheless a record of how the world impinged daily on her life: war, issues of class and race, feminism, and lesbianism enter her writing not as confessional and not within larger political frames, but as everyday relationships among ordinary subjects.

In this chapter I approach these relationships from two unrelated directions. Beginning with a condensed biography I foreground important intimacies of Bishop's life, so that these will resonate in or provide a backdrop for my discussion of her poetry's enacted relationships between, for instance, friends, lovers, a mother and a daughter. I am particularly interested in the terms in which Bishop encoded and revealed her life, and these will be relevant throughout to my readings of individual works. In this chapter I also approach Bishop's assessments of writers and literary movements, which offer insight into not only where she placed herself but also how she found within the rather formal genre of literary analysis the details, once again, of homey relationships between herself and her subject. In her assessments of other writers, Bishop looks first to the surprising, often seemingly insignificant details of their writing, reserving her most acerbic criticism for writing whose emotions are imposed from above rather than grounded in the necessity of the objects themselves. In her literary criticism as elsewhere, Bishop's localism prevails: she searches among everyday details for the material that might offer bonding between her and her subjects or between her poetic subjects themselves.

If we gather together the details of Bishop's life, as she recorded them in letters, contracts and documents, published and unpublished autobiographical poems, sketches, and stories, and as they have been preserved by others in oral and written histories,[4] we can offer a setting in which to explore her enactment of subject–subject relationships. Elizabeth Bishop was born on 8 February 1911. Her father, William T. Bishop, president of his father's contracting firm, the J. W. Bishop Company of Worcester, Massachusetts, died of Bright's disease in October 1911, leaving his wife and infant daughter in financial ease and emotional disarray. Gertrude Bulmer Bishop was ten years her husband's junior; she was twenty-nine when her husband died, after three years of marriage. At that time she had her first of a series of breakdowns. Though she continued to care for her child with the help of her family for a few years, by 1915 she was hospitalized at the McLean sanatorium outside Boston and Elizabeth was living at her grandparents' in Great Village, Nova Scotia. She records her mother's traumatic homecoming in "In the Village," as well as her permanent leave taking, to a state-run mental institution in Dartmouth, Nova Scotia, where she died in May 1934.[5] In one of Bishop's rare letters about her mother, she wrote Robert Lowell, on his admission to McLean Hospital, about her mother's stay there and about a picture she had of her mother on the lawn, healthy looking and well dressed (11 Dec. 1957, HL).

In moving, unpublished poems and briefly in her 1952 *Poetry* review,[6] Bishop recorded some memories of events with her mother in Boston and Salem in 1914. But her written memories of childhood center mostly on the brief period in the home of her grandparents, William and Elizabeth Hutchinson Bulmer, or Boomer (both spellings were used). Still at home were her mother's younger sisters, Grace and Mary; Bishop's Uncle Arthur had moved out but also lived in the village. For these few years Great Village was home, and Bishop was surrounded by an extended family who loved her and about whom she wrote poems and stories, many of which she never published.

It was only in the early 1950s, when she was living in Brazil, that she felt ready to publish her writing explicitly about her Nova Scotia childhood. Rio de Janeiro was a stop on a freighter trip Bishop was taking around South America (letter to Lowell, 26 Nov. 1951, HL); it became a permanent stay, as a result of a debilitating allergic reaction to the fruit of the cashew (letter to Baumann, 8 Jan. 1952, VC) and the care and love of Lota de Macedo Soares, a Brazilian friend she had met in New York in 1942. Macedo Soares invited her to live with her in the home she was having built, "Samambaia," in the mountains above Petrópolis, and the Brazilian setting re-created "home" for Bishop for the first time in more than thirty-five years. In a letter to Ilse and Kit Barker, Bishop remarked on the ready connection between her two family worlds: "It is funny to come to Brazil to experience total recall about Nova Scotia – geography must be more mysterious than we realize, even" (12 Oct. 1952, PU). Elaborating on this connection in a 1964 letter to Anne Stevenson, Bishop wrote about the early period's vital return:

> The village [Great Village] was 50 years or so backwards – We made yeast from the hopvine on the barn; had no plumbing, oil lamps etc. My grandmother was a famous butter-maker. Everything is quite changed now, of course. But when I came to live first in Samambaia and we had oil lamps for two or three years, etc. a lot came back to me. I helped design our sitting-room stove, for example (needed up there "winters") and without ever having done such things before I found myself baking bread, making marmalade, etc. – When the need arises apparently the old Nova Scotian domestic arts come back to me! ([Mar.] 1964, WU)

Although she drafted memoirs about her childhood and her family as far back as 1934, publishing such stories as "Gwendolyn" and "In the Village" in 1953 seemed to depend on the mysteriousness of a geography that had so returned her home.

Her early letters from Brazil were the most consistently positive of her life. She wrote Lowell, for instance, that

> here I am extremely happy, for the first time in my life. I live in a spectacularly beautiful place; we have beteen us about 3,000 books now; I know, through Lota, most of the Brazilian "intellectuals" already and I find the people frank, – startlingly so, until you get used to Portugese vocabularies – extremely affectionate – an atmosphere that I just lap up – no I guess I mean loll in – after that dismal year in Washington and that dismaler winter at Yaddo when I thought my days were numbered and there was nothing to be done about it. – I arrived to visit Lota just at the point where she really wanted someone to stay with her in the new house she was building. [. . .] She wanted me to stay; she offered to build me a studio – picture enclosed – I certainly didn't really want to wander around the world in a drunken daze for the rest of my life – so it's all fine & dandy. (28 July 1953, HL)

Macedo Soares descended from old aristocratic Brazilian families on both sides, and so knew many of the major Brazilian architects, artists, writers, and political leaders. Both Bishop and Macedo Soares were interested in every aspect of art and architecture; they oversaw and took part in the designing and building of their home, making the decisions, especially, about terraces, interiors, and Bishop's studio, which was a short walk from the house, overlooking a cliff and waterfall. While they entertained occasionally, they were more often simply surrounded by "grandchildren," the constantly multiplying family of an adopted, married son of Macedo Soares, and by the servants' children.

The years between Nova Scotia and Brazil, Bishop's childhood and her formative years as a writer, were fragmented ones. In 1917 she was moved against her child's will to her paternal grandparents in Worcester, where she lived for less than a year. "The Country Mouse"[7] tells the story of life with her grandparents, reimagining through a child's eyes her fearful anticipation of it on the train ride from her home in Great Village to Worcester and her sad identification with the dog Beppo, who "immediately adopted me, perhaps as being on the same terms in the house as himself" (21). When her reaction to life in her grandparents' formal home, incapacitating asthma and eczema, became too obvious to ignore, her mother's older sister, Aunt Maud, took her into her Revere apartment, north of Boston, and slowly nursed her back to health. From the age of twelve on, Bishop spent summers either in Great Village or at the Nautical Camp for Girls on Cape Cod; she went away for high school to the Walnut Hill School in Natick, Massachusetts. When she was admitted to Vassar College in 1930, she permanently left "home, wherever that may be," as she put it in her poem "Questions of Travel."

In the mid-1930s, Bishop traveled restlessly in Europe. In the late 1930s and early 1940s, she moved back and forth between Key West and New York, where her address was more often than not a hotel, until the early 1940s, when she rented a forty-dollar apartment in Greenwich Village. There were trips to Canada, Haiti, Mexico. She traveled, seemingly, whenever she was dissatisfied with her present state. She had very occasional and short-lived jobs outside her writing – a few months just after college at the U.S.A. School of Writing, about which she wrote her humorous story by that title,[8] and five days (until her eczema returned) in 1943 cleaning and adjusting binoculars at a navy optical shop in Key West, a job that Marianne Moore encouraged her to take, so "that you can then have a refuge – profitable or not, for the blanker and more inside side of the umbrella" (letter to Bishop, 8 Oct. 1943, VC).

When Bishop and Moore met in the spring of 1934, within months of both Bishop's college graduation and the death of her mother, a living absence to her since she was five, Moore readily took on the role of mother/mentor. She looked after Bishop's health and negotiated for Bishop the world of publishing, which she herself had known closely for more than a decade because of her own writing and her editorship at *The Dial*. She served as literary mediator for Bishop during the 1930s, introducing her and her work to publishers and encouraging both her fine eye for detail and her verbal generosity, what Moore called in *Trial Balances* "that phase of self-respect" (23).

Their admiration and their usually playful competition were mutual. Bishop respected Moore's judgment, as she was rebelling against it, always explaining politely just why she could not make the revision Moore had suggested. They were closest and most in contest in the 1930s and 1940s, when they exchanged visits or long letters, in which their disputes about principles of poetry emerge in their squabbles over details in Bishop's poems and their love emanates out of their detailed descriptions of, say, a swan's nesting habits (Bishop to Moore, 11 June 1935, V:04:30, RM) or the antics of Bishop's cat Minnow (Moore to Bishop, 11 Jan. 1937, VC). By the late 1940s their friendship and competitiveness became more simply pleasurable: Bishop's poem "Invitation to Miss Marianne Moore" and prose tribute "As We Like It," which were included in the Spring 1948 *Quarterly Review of Literature* Marianne Moore issue, convey this great affection in their anecdotes and their tone, as does Bishop's posthumously published memoir, "Efforts of Affection."[9] As if teasingly to outdo Moore in her own method of layered quotation, in her opening of "As We Like It" Bishop drops line after line of stunning moments in Moore's poetry to demonstrate that "As far as I know, Miss Marianne Moore is The World's Greatest Living Observer" (129).

Her other important literary friendship was with Robert Lowell, whom she met through Randall Jarrell in 1947. As David Kalstone shows in "Prodigal Years" and again in *Becoming a Poet,* Bishop's relationship with Lowell was charmed by the moment of their meeting. They were both riding the success of their first books of poetry; they felt fresh on the scene, together, and they liked each other (and each other's writing) immediately. When Moore turned down a job as Library of Congress poetry consultant for the year 1950–1, because she was working on her La Fontaine translations, Lowell, who had been consultant in 1947–8, secured the position for her. The following winter, on his convincing, she spent at Yaddo. As Ian Hamilton argues in his biography of Lowell and as the correspondence of Bishop and Lowell concurs, their friendship was complicated by Lowell's seemingly unreciprocated romantic love for Bishop, by Bishop's moves first to Florida and then to Brazil, and by Lowell's repeated manic-depressive breakdowns, to which Bishop could only respond, by letter, with cautious reaffirmations of her affection and respect. Nonetheless, throughout their lives they visited each other whenever possible and wrote with animation and love about each other's writing, about politics, books, writers, and the literary New York that Bishop made repeated efforts to escape.

Though the 1940s and early 1950s were difficult years for Bishop, during which she reacted to feelings of personal and professional insecurity with bouts of drinking,[10] asthma, and depression, she was at the same time becoming prominent in midcentury American poetry. Her 1945 Houghton Mifflin Poetry Award for a first book, *North & South*,[11] was followed in 1947 by a Guggenheim Fellowship, a 1950 American Academy of Arts and Letters Award, a 1951 Lucy M. Donnelly Fellowship from Bryn Mawr College, a 1952 Shelley Memorial Award, and a 1956 Pulitzer Prize for poetry. The list continues; Bishop received awards and fellowships throughout her career, and, especially in the early years, Moore and Lowell were instrumental in many of these, nominating her at every turn.

Bishop's friendships with Moore and Lowell, and her acquaintanceships with other major poets and writers of their rather undefined circle, Edmund Wilson, Elizabeth Hardwick, Randall Jarrell, and, later, James Merrill and Frank Bidart, are well known. So are her claims in several interviews that her poetic influences were George Herbert, Gerard Manley Hopkins, Wallace Stevens, and, of course, Marianne Moore.[12] But it is less well known that, particularly in the 1930s and well into the 1940s, when she was establishing herself as a poet, she consistently turned to women for love, financial and emotional support, and professional advice. Marianne Moore was her professional mainstay. Her traveling companions in the 1930s and most of her friends in New York were her Vassar friends and intimates who had stayed in the area. In Key West she lived with Louise Crane until, with Crane's financial help, she bought a house there. During much of the war, she rented out the house and lived with Marjorie Stevens. Most of her Key West friends were women, including Pauline Pfeifer Hemingway, Ernest Hemingway's second wife. Meeting Jarrell and then Lowell, serving as consultant at the Library of Congress, and living at Yaddo, she began to meet and become close friends with many more writers and artists. She visited Ezra Pound at St. Elizabeth's; her letters to Lowell in 1950 and 1951 are filled with stories about the writers she was meeting. When she moved to Brazil, however, she immersed herself in a life of domesticity – cooking, baking, grandmothering – that was mostly a setting of women and children and a chosen far cry from the New York poet's world. As she wrote in a letter to Ilse Barker, "It ["go-getting"] is one reason why I am content to leave New York for good. I think – everybody is so intent on using everybody else that there is no room or time for friendship any more" (8 Oct. 1953, PU).

Though there has been important discussion of Moore and Bishop's mutual impact on each other's lives and writing, Bishop's connection to other women writers is only now beginning to be explored.[13] Bishop wanted not to appear the "woman writer," especially in the 1950s, when American women writers were beginning to discover their common voice, so she encouraged her critics to look the other way: hers was not a woman's but a genderless artist's vision. Despite her dissociation from the genre of women's writing, her connections with individual women writers were deep. Her relationship with the poet May Swenson has been wholly undiscussed; their thirty-year correspondence began in the early 1950s, when Swenson was in New York typing Bishop's short stories for a book Bishop wanted to offer Houghton Mifflin.[14] Bishop played the role of mentor in this relationship, as she did in her intimate friendship with Ilse Barker, German-born writer and translator, recorded in a similarly rich correspondence. She met Ilse and her husband Kit, a British painter, at Yaddo, and they wrote their lives consistently for close to thirty years.

In the 1950s in Brazil, Bishop had the time to develop these correspondence friendships and the freedom in her letters to test literary judgments and generalizations, exploring her politics and her feminism. For almost a decade, she had what she called later, when she felt she was losing it, "the necessary elimination, sequestration, concentration" (letter to Barkers, 14 Oct. 1963, PU). By the early 1960s, however, Brazil was becoming less paradisaical for Bishop and Macedo Soares, as Brazilian politics became unstable and intrusive in their lives. In 1960, when Carlos Lacerda was elected governor, Macedo Soares's friendship with him led to her appointment as coordinator of architects and landscape designers in the planning and building of a six-kilometer park in Rio de Janeiro. Though Macedo Soares enjoyed the position, her work was exhausting, and their life became irreversibly politicized by her closeness with Lacerda, a radical rightist. So that Macedo Soares could be near her work, she and Bishop moved to an apartment in Rio, returning to their quiet Samambaia life only one or two weekends a month. As governor of the state of Guanabara, Lacerda perpetuated his battle with the former dictator-president Getúlio Vargas by setting himself in defiant opposition to Vargas's protégé, President João Goulart. In October 1963, when Goulart's men purportedly attempted an assassination of Lacerda, he used Macedo Soares's Petrópolis home as a hideout.[15] Bishop could not help but be embroiled in Brazilian politics.

She continued to write consistently through the first half of the 1960s, poetry and prose about Brazil, translations of the work of several Brazilian authors, and long, detailed letters of personal and professional retrospect to Anne Stevenson, who was writing the first book on Bishop. Cautious at first, Bishop became forthcoming and introspective in these letters, once she realized how much she cared that Stevenson render her version of her life. At the same time, however, Bishop was becoming restless in what she referred to as her "exile" in a 1963 letter to Ilse Barker, feeling her own precariousness as she helplessly watched Macedo Soares grow disillusioned and suffocated by her work with the government and emotionally ill as a result. She did find ways to escape the political and the personal stress: she and Macedo Soares went to Europe in 1964 and 1966. Bishop took several trips alone, for work and rest, to Ouro Prêto, an area she was mesmerized by, "18th century pure and simple" (letter to Barkers, 17 Jan. 1965, PU). In August 1965 she bought an eighteenth-century house there as a renovation project and spent two and a half months living next door at a friend's, writing and overseeing the work. In Ouro Prêto, at least, she could joke about the distractions of her daily life in Rio:

> I rarely seem to finish even a thought, or a good long look through binoculars, without something interrupting: the maid's problems, or the telephone ringing, or a political upheaval, or a dressmaker's appointment, or someone coming to dinner and I have to make the soup – since our maid isn't a very good cook. (Letter to Stevenson, 15 Aug. [1965], WU)

After much deliberation, she accepted her first teaching job, a semester at the University of Washington, Seattle, in 1966. But the times away served, finally, as added aggravation. Under the strain of her own troubles and her sense of betrayal in Bishop's escapes to new places, friendships, and intimacies, Macedo Soares's physical and emotional illnesses worsened, and her doctor recommended that she and Bishop remain apart for several months. In August 1967 Bishop went to New York to try to work on a book of prose pieces about Brazil, for which she had received a Rockefeller research fellowship in 1966. (She repeatedly mentioned the volume of prose in letters from 1956 on, though she never completed it.) Macedo Soares came to visit her in September; the evening she arrived she took an overdose of Valium and never regained consciousness.

Bishop spent most of the next several years trying to hold her life together. She moved to San Francisco with an intimate friend from Seattle and her two-year-old child.[16] There, with her friend acting as secretary, she continued research on her prose book and began assembling *An Anthology of Twentieth-Century Brazilian Poetry* with Emanuel Brasil. Late in 1969 she and her friend returned to Ouro Prêto, where they faced a flood of corruption, both from lawyers handling Macedo Soares's still unsettled will and from the contractors and workmen she had hired for her house. Bishop reported in letters her loneliness and alienation: Brazilians she had thought were her friends had abandoned her and were now either blaming her for Macedo Soares's death or simply avoiding her. Strained by the barrage of anxieties, her friend suffered a nervous breakdown and returned home with her child. Bishop responded by immersing herself in work. Alone in her home in Ouro Prêto, writing became possible and pleasurable for the first time in years; she wrote several poems and continued work on the *Anthology*.

As her life gradually reached emotional calm in the early 1970s, Bishop became more active than she ever had been, professionally. She began teaching at Harvard in the fall of 1970, temporarily replacing Lowell, who was himself on leave because of a breakdown. From then until her death in 1979, she taught at least one semester a year, often two, at Harvard, University of Washington, New York University, and Massachusetts Institute of Technology and gave several readings a year beginning in the mid-1970s. Various ailments slowed her down, but still she traveled a great deal in this country and abroad in the last nine years of her life, with her friend Alice Methfessel, whom she had met her first year at Harvard, when living at Kirkland House where Methfessel worked. She bought a house at Lewis Wharf on the Boston Harbor, writing about its stability with a mixture of desire and irony: "I've already had the walls all arranged to suit me and orderd a Franklin stove, etc. so I guess I'm settled for the rest of my life now" (letter to Barkers, 30 July 1973, PU). Of course, she was no more settled here than anywhere, nor would she have wanted to be, but she now had a stable place from which to roam, actually or imaginatively. Bishop's poem "Sonnet," which was published in the *New Yorker* twenty-three days after her death,[17] enacts this doubled position. In "Sonnet," which I will discuss in the last chapter, disjointed images are "Caught" in the opening sestet; others are "Freed" in the closing octave, which ends in flight, "wherever/ it feels like, gay!" Confining the enigmatic release within an extremely loose sonnet form, she has it both ways: the "walls [are] all arranged," and the images escape definition. They have coexisted here across the semicolons and periods of their juxtaposition, and they have left their relationships underarticulated and altogether un-"settled," seemingly fluxional with every reading, as William James said any truth should be.

When we go in search of a modus operandi or a system of beliefs about writing, we find instead pithy fragments, scattered over years and across a range of audiences. Bishop's greatest consistency was her refusal of a systematic means for understanding poetry – a school of poetry or a set of principles to which to adhere. She often made judgments of other writers, but she published very few poetry reviews and almost no literary criticism, dropping her assessments instead into her letters. She enclosed most of what she said about poetry in general and about her own writing in particular in letters to her writer-friends, Marianne Moore, Robert

Lowell, May Swenson, Ilse Barker, and Anne Stevenson. In an exchange of letters with May Swenson, for instance, Bishop worked to articulate poetry's emotion, her own specifically. Swenson wrote that she found "At the Fishhouses" different from the other poems in *A Cold Spring* and "the most *moving*"; she explained her sense of the way Bishop's poetry works:

> Most of your poems (among the 18) are not [moving] – they engage something else than the emotions. What is it? Something else, and something more important. They are hard, feelable, as objects – or they give us that sensation – and they are separate from the self that made them, rather than self-effigies as poems easily tend to be. (24 Aug. 1955, WU)

In characterizing the poems as not emotionally moving she forced Bishop to question the place of thought and feeling in any poem, so as to understand the position of the self of poetry's making:

> I am puzzled by what you mean by my poems not appealing to the emotions. [. . .] What poetry does, or doesn't? And doesn't it always, in one way or another? A poem like "Never until the mankind making" etc. one feels immediately, before one has started to think. A poem like "The Frigate Pelican," one thinks before one starts to feel. But the sequence, and the amount of either depends as much on the reader as the poem, I think. And poetry is a way of thinking with one's feelings, anyway. But maybe that's not what you mean by "emotion." I think myself that my best poems seem rather distant, and sometimes I wish I could be as objective about everything else as I seem to be in and about them. I don'tt think I'm very succesful when I get personal, – rather, sound personal – one always is personal, of course, one way or another. (6 Sept. 1955, WU)

Misunderstanding Swenson's praise of her ability to allow her poetic objects a certain separateness – what Eavan Boland would call her "un-Romanticism" and what she herself had in 1934 called the primacy of the "material" over the "spiritual" – Bishop pursues a slightly different question here, or rather she reformulates her earlier assessment. Turning on Swenson's opposition between the "hard, feelable" object and the emotion, she argues that the objects of the poem must bear the emotion of the self who made them; they and not some externally imposed emotion do the poem's emotional (and intellectual) work. If the poet tries to possess the relationship, or "get personal," she overpowers it.

Describing Bishop's writing in his 1961 *Paris Review* interview, Robert Lowell said that

> In Elizabeth Bishop's "Man-Moth" a whole new world is gotten out and you don't know what will come after any one line. It's exploring.

And it's as original as Kafka. She's gotten a world, not just a way of writing. She seldom writes a poem that doesn't have that exploratory quality; yet it's very firm, it's not like beat poetry, it's all controlled. (347)

He went on to discuss Moore's "terrible, private, and strange revolutionary poetry": "There isn't the motive to do that now" (365). In her letter of response, Bishop brought his two comments together. She quoted him on Moore and continued:

> But I wonder – isn't there? Isn't there even more – only it's terribly hard to find the exact and right and surprising enough, or un-surprising enough, point at which to revolt now? The beats have just fallen back on an old corpse-strewn or monument-strewn battle-field – the real real protest I suspect is something quite different – (If only I could find it. Klee's picture called FEAR seems close to it, I think..) (25 June 1961, HL)

Klee's 1934 *Fear* depicts a round figure with a prominent eye and tentacles ambiguously both engulfing and escaping invasion by an amorphous figure to its right, whose imbedded arrows pointing directly left suggest the irreversibility of the imminent conflict between the two figures.[18] The figures on the canvas articulate hatred and fear; Klee's protest is naked assertion, not special pleading. Here Bishop glimpses the "real real protest" missing from 1960s "revolutionary" verse. In some July 1970 notes toward unfinished poetry reviews,[19] Bishop again articulated her frustration with imposed emotion:

> at the risk of appearing ivory-towerish, cold hearted, reactionary, pro-war, everything wrong – it still must be said – [. . .] when she [Denise Levertov in *Relearning the Alphabet*] starts a poem "Biafra. Biafra. Biafra." one's heart sinks, and not because of the suffering in Biafra, alas. A kind of resentment comes over one, "Oh, I'm not up to feeling that much; I can't . . . " [. . .] When have politics ever made good poems?

Condemning "social conscious" writing in these notes – "so nice, so humorless, so right, so boring" – Bishop speaks to one of her central demands for art and poetry, that it surprise. If one is too convinced of one's own moral truth, Bishop asserts, one can never allow the objects of the poem to do their work of surprising one into feeling or thinking.

Bishop often spoke of that surprise with nostalgia: "If only one could get back to the stage of ignorance, where poems just seemed to happen, with their sense tagging along later –," she mused to Lowell, commenting on the "glazed" effect of Merwin's, Wilbur's, and Snodgrass's technical proficiency (25 June 1961, HL). And again, this time discussing politics in reference to her 1930s and 1940s poems, she wrote, "At the time I was writing the poems I like best I was very ignorant politically and I sometimes wish I could recover the dreamy state of consciousness I lived in then – it was better for my work, and I do the world no more good now by knowing a great deal more" (letter to Stevenson, [Mar.] 1964, WU). She reads the controlling, knowing voice consistently: it is a hindrance to the poem happening. Reaching back to Wordsworthian "trailing clouds of glory" in this nostalgia for aesthetic and political ignorance, Bishop attempts to articulate, over a span of some fifteen years, a pragmatism even Wordsworth's radicalism had not anticipated: The "self-forgetful, perfectly useless concentration" for which she praises Darwin is the most pleasurable element of his thought process; the disorder of his freed-up mind engages a reader more actively than the ordered study he meant to relate (letter to Stevenson, 8 Jan. 1964, WU). In her 1955 discussion of the ways feeling and thought depend on each other, Bishop strikes a middle ground between Wordsworthian faith in poetic recollection of the "spontaneous overflow" and Whitman-like or Ginsberg-like trust in the overflow itself. Bishop reverses Wordsworth's terms and also avoids the "corpse-strewn" "battle-field" of twentieth-century romanticism by embracing the spontaneous emotion founded in her release of a subject she knows well, so that it may discover something she might not have known had she been in fully conscious control.

Bishop criticizes women writers most vehemently for what she considers to be their willingness to shelter themselves from the risks of that potential chaos. The appreciation of domesticity in 1960s and early 1970s women's writing, for instance, does little more than reinforce unacceptable stereotypes, as she complains, again, in her poetry review notes:

> Woemn, unfortunately, seem to stay at home a lot, to write theirs. There is no reason why the home, house, apartment, or furnished room, can't produce good poems, but almost all women poets seem to fall occasionally into the "Oredr is a lovely thing" Anna-Hemspetad-Branch category, and one wihses they wouldn't. Sylvi a Plath avoided this by when she wrote about babies, ovens, etc. – but sometimes one extreme is almost as bad as the other.

Criticizing Anne Sexton for her "simplicity" and her "egocentricity," she closes a letter to Lowell with qualified praise: "I like some of her really mad ones best; those that sound as thought she'd written them all at once" (19 May 1960, HL). Confusion rather than order, a surprising revolt rather than the expected protest, a raw test of values rather than irony – "oh irony, iorny, one is sick of it" (review notes): Bishop asks to see the artist in the midst of his or her struggle, drawing the battles simply and without melodrama, as Klee drew them, so that she, the reader, can also be caught off guard and left pained with unanswerable questions.

While Bishop is consistent in this expectation of writers generally, her specific censure of women writers demands closer attention. Her comments over a range of some fifteen years show greatest frustration with what she saw as women writers' defensiveness, which registered itself in assertions of class privilege. She first articulated her annoyance at female nicety to the Barkers in 1955, in response to a review she was reading about Elizabeth Bowen's *A World of Love*. Her annoyance extends to Virginia Woolf, Rebecca West, and Rosamund Lehman as well:

> It's a fault one almost never finds in men's writing, or if one does in a different form. It is that they are really boasting all the time. There's a sort of intonation of the "She-has-such-a-lovely-home . . . " sort about it. They are secretly pointing out, for you to admire, their beautifully-polished old silver [in the margin she writes, "Well – may Waugh shares it with the ladies –"], their taste in clothes, their intellectual and, frequently, social standing, their husbands, etc. – and ultimately their sexual irresistability . . . (men writers do this last of course, but not in such sly ways) It's the "How nice to be nice!" atmosphere that gets me, and I think women writers must get quite away from it before they ever amount to a hill of beans. I see I've mentioned English ladies – well, there are plenty of American ones, too – Mary McCarthy does it, Jean Stafford less, maybe, but sometimes, Eudora Welty less but also sometimes –
>
> [. . .] I suppose it is at bottom a flaw in reality that irritates me so – not so much of being protected, – you can't blame them for that – but of wanting to show that they are even if they aren't. (28 Feb. 1955, PU)

When, in his response to Bishop's criticism of Sexton, Lowell only slightly qualified his own praise of Sexton's inspiration (12 July 1960, VC), Bishop repeated her old rebuke:

> The Anne Sexton I think still has a bit too much romanticism and what I think of as the "our beautiful old silver" school of female writing which is really boasting about how "nice" we were. V. Woolfe, K. A. P, Bowen, R. West, etc. – they are all full of it. They have to make quite sure that the reader is not going to mis-place them socially, first – and that nervousness interferes constantly with what they think they'd like to say . . . I wrote a story at Vassar that was too much admired by Miss Rose Peebles, my teacher, who was very prooud of being an old-school Southern lady – and suddenly this fact about women's writing dawned on me, and has haunted me ever since. (27 July 1960, HL)

Becoming increasingly aware of class during these years in Brazil, as I will argue in Chapter 5, Bishop recognizes the false sense of protection class privilege offers. As my discussions of such poems as "A Miracle for Breakfast" (1937), "Manuelzinho" (1956), and "The Burglar of Babylon" (1964) should show, Bishop understands class to be a tenuously constructed set of distinctions among people, pierceable by steady analysis but powerful because so craftily resistant to analysis. Whenever her poems do address these constructed divisions, she is careful to demarcate her speaker's place, so that his or her own role in the constructions will not control silently. But here Bishop accuses these women writers of more than simply a defensive and un-self-conscious retreat into their class privilege; it is their "female" means of doing so that most bothers and threatens her. Not only does the superficiality of such female manners make for bad writing, but also the manners lie. These women writers' cowardly adherence to privilege, Bishop asserts, evades the reality of whatever, beneath the defense, they might love or fear. Yet the vehemence of Bishop's tone cannot be attributed alone to her righteousness about these pretensions. Rather, she senses her own writing position to be threatened by these other women writers' transgressions. She had refused in the 1930s to be drawn by Miss Rose Peebles into the privileged pride of an old-girl network; now, if she is "to amount to a hill of beans," she must be all the more attentive to the foibles of women's writing that keep it from being, simply, writing. Better, she insisted throughout her life, invoking "Female Lib-ism," to "be called 'the 16th poet' with no reference to my sex, than one of 4 women – even if the other three are pretty good" (letter to Lowell, 28 Jan. 1972, UT).

The letters to both Lowell and the Barkers, ironically, follow letters praising other women writers. In 1954 and 1955 Bishop revealed to the Barkers an affinity with Sarah Orne Jewett that she mentions nowhere else in her writing. Bishop began to read Jewett perhaps in response to a passing reference by Lowell, who suggested after seeing her Nova Scotia stories, "Gwendolyn" and "In the Village," that she write a "growing-up novel," "what K. A. Porter's childhood stories aim towrds, or a super Miss Jewett" (letter to Bishop, 1 Jan. 1954, VC).[20] In Jewett's prose, in her contemplation of the landscape and its connection to personal history, Bishop saw her own. Specifically recommending Jewett's lyrical Maine novel, The Country of the Pointed Firs, to the Barkers, she writes that the stories that make it up are

> dated now, but still sometimes marvellous stuff and worth reading. I had only read one and I was appalled when I recently read a whole book – I'm sure anyone who read my story ["In the Village"] would think I was imitating her shamelessly – whole phrases, even – it is very strange; I had really never laid eyes on the ones that are like mine. (21 July 1954, PU)

- and it's all so completely true, you know – I wish I could read her without weeping. [. . .] And even some of the more frankly sentimental ones, if they were "translated from the Russian" or something, I'm sure would be world-famous – [. . .] But it was a shock to me to find how closely I'd paralleled things she'd said in spots – I've even had to change some things in two unfinished Nova Scotian stories. (19 Jan. 1955, PU)

The uncanny bond she has recognized here is undermined in her very next letter, which includes the generalized attack on women writers. It is as if, once stated, her identification with Jewett opened her up to the larger suggestion (made now throughout feminist readings of Bishop) that her writing is female in perspective and voice and that she, too, is a woman writer.

It is perhaps no coincidence that when she mentioned Jewett to May Swenson a few months later, she elided any sense of their affinity. Her first mention, following her quotation of a parody of Edna St. Vincent Millay, is merely a passing suggestion to read the book (2 July 1955, WU). When Swenson inquired further, Bishop replied that she was sure Swenson would like it; she had sent a copy to the Barkers, who "are crazy about it and have been telling all their friends" (6 Sept. 1955, WU). Already distant from Jewett, Bishop appears not to have mentioned her again in letters until the summer of 1979, during which she reread Jewett's work in response to a request that she make selections and do an introduction for a new edition.[21] She wrote to Howard Moss that she thought she would turn down the request, because "W. Cather chose the best things yrs. ago, I'm afraid – much of it is very weak" (14 Aug. 1979, NYP).[22] Any bond she had felt with Jewett was long since effaced; Bishop is here the senior poet, contemplating a professional duty.

Bishop responded to Emily Dickinson even more ambivalently and never, finally, dismissed nor embraced her.[23] Bishop returned to read and write about Dickinson's work on numerous occasions in book reviews, letters, and an unfinished poem, which she began in 1955 and worked on again in the mid–1970s. With each return, she revealed anew how unsettling Dickinson was to her. Reviewing *Emily Dickinson's Letters to Doctor and Mrs. Josiah Gilbert Holland* for the *New Republic* (1951), Bishop opens by considering Dickinson's intensity:

> In a sense, all of Emily Dickinson's letters are "love-letters." To her, little besides love, human and divine, was worth writing about and often the two seemed to fuse. That abundance of detail – descriptions of daily life, clothes, food, travels, etc. – that is found in what are usually considered "good letters" plays very little part in hers. Instead, there is a constant insistence on the strength of her affections, an almost childish daring and repetitiveness about them that must sometimes have been very hard to take. (20)

Dickinson was unsettling to Bishop, whose relationships with other writers thrived on precisely the daily details that Dickinson omits. Her intensity, this "almost childish daring," is too much for Bishop, yet it is
extremely compelling. "These letters have structure and strength. It is
the sketchiness of the water-spider, tenaciously holding to its upstream
position by means of the faintest ripples, while making one aware of the
current of death and the darkness below" (21). Bishop's reading of Dickinson's tenaciousness comes closer than anything else I have seen to her
admiration of the revolutionary potential of Klee. Here, perhaps, is the
wholly unarticulated "real real protest."

But Bishop found herself, viscerally, too annoyed with Dickinson to
grant her that power:

> I like, or at least admire, her a great deal more now – probably because
> of that good new edition, really. I spent another stretch absorbed in
> that, and think, (along with Randall) that she's about the best we have.
> However – she does set one's teeth on edge a lot of the time, don't you
> think? (Letter to Lowell, 2 Dec. 1956, HL)

Dickinson is a great poet; Bishop would never deny her that. She was
fully aware of Dickinson's gradual emergence as a central literary figure
by midcentury, her poems in their entirety finally reaching their public
in 1955, when Thomas Johnson published his variorum edition. She was
aware, too, of current critical readings of Dickinson, which included
efforts to place her within a biographical or literary history that could
somehow account for her oddness. She dismissed Rebecca Patterson's
The Riddle of Emily Dickinson (1952), which sought to identify the love
poetry with the supposed lost love of a female lover, Kate Scott:

> These four hundred pages are still many sizes too small for Emily
> Dickinson's work. Whether one likes her poetry or not, whether it
> wrings one's heart or sets one's teeth on edge, nevertheless it exists,
> and in a world far removed from the defenseless people and events
> described in this infuriating book. (20)

What Bishop does not say, either in this public forum or in the more
private one of her letter to Lowell, is that Dickinson's disturbing intensity
does not allow her the professional distance with which other literary
critics take her up, or with which she, herself, was able to put down
Jewett. Nor does it release her emotionally. Something about the tenaciousness she described in 1951 compelled her to continue exploring
Dickinson's power, regardless of whether she understood it. She wrote
to Lowell in 1955 that she was drafting "a complicated poem about
Hopkins and E. Dickinson – after reading that new edition – I am aiming
as high as your Ford Madox Ford one, but have my doubts" (23 Nov.
1955, HL). The poem was to be a double sonnet, nominally about a pair

of caged birds; she wrote their birth and death dates at the top of the page. Whatever she was conceiving escaped her in 1955, and she left this draft in the following rough form:

                    bilocalization
      Feathers are
      they lock together
      unseen   they
      and from each nations' wardrobe   forced
      invented, willed,   proper plumage
      laws of plumage

      nothing so unnatural in nature –
      elaborated   loved and put up with
                          profered   handed a spoonful of stale
        1. Cages are. . . etc   water
        2. Feathers are. . . .

The poem clearly troubled her. She got as far as these Moore-like images of caged birds, unnatural to their surroundings yet somehow tough and stubborn, and then she stopped, apparently, for some twenty years.

Drawn to the problem of the poem enough to pick it up again in the 1970s, she typed another draft.[24] Still unable to characterize her sense of Dickinson's poetry (or Hopkins's, although she had written concisely about him in her published college essay), Bishop tested a few more images:

        . . . peeled withies & a village elegance

      They chose, themselves, their cages, one

        . . . one – the other – made by hand
      peeled withies, cut along the brook –
      (water) chipped Sunday saucer, gold &
      white, of water

      one god divided like (St Elmo's?) fire
      The same god
      & in both   sustained their songs
                            with iron.

      A rusty nail dropped in the cup or saucer

      How they complained!   ?sustained?. . . .
            iron in the stale green(?) water

She followed these lines with notes on the features of feathers and quills: they are "barbs," "norny outgrowths," protectors and weapons. Striking in this later draft is the Moore-like conflation of images – the hand-peeled, homemade cages, the chipped elegance of the saucer, the ambivalent god, the rust in the cup, which both stains and sustains. The poem is all tension and ambivalence; the beauty of Dickinson's or Hopkins's song is inherently tainted by the always present pain. Their pain and their beauty, she suggests, are inseparable. Bishop is herself buffeted by the intensity of these bared emotions. In an unconnected line, between notes about quills and a reminder to herself to include dates, she realizes her defenselessness in the form of a question: "– & spared us next to nothing of their terms?" Decades after Moore's influence on Bishop had faded, her images here are perhaps the closest Bishop's ever came to Moore's characteristic armor, yet she could not complete her characterization of these feathers that are at the same time weapons. Moore could, and, as Bishop wanted to suggest, Dickinson and Hopkins lived the contradiction. She herself, however, was left to sort through fragments of images, void of the ordinary details through which she discovered her insight and her connection, in search of who these writers might have been.

Intimacy with writing and intimacy with the writer were always intertwined for Bishop. She invariably read the journals and letters of writers she cared about; what she loved most about Darwin, as she said in her much quoted letter to Anne Stevenson, were the moments of unself-conscious self-revelation:

> There is no "split." Dreams, works of art (some), glimpses of the always-more-successful surrealism of everyday life, unexpected moments of empathy (is it?), catch a peripheral vision of whatever it is one can never really see full-face but that seems enormously important. I can't believe we are wholly irrational – and I do admire Darwin! But reading Darwin, one admires the beautiful solid case being built up out of his endless heroic <u>observations</u>, almost unconscious or automatic – and then comes a sudden relaxation, a forgetful phrase, and one <u>feels</u> the strangeness of his undertaking, sees the lonely young man, his eyes fixed on facts and minute details, sinking or sliding giddily off into the unknown. What one seems to want in art, in experiencing it, is the same thing that is necessary for its creation, a self-forgetful, perfectly useless concentration. (In this sense it is always "escape," don't you think?) (8 Jan. 1964, WU)

Articulating Darwin's ability to concentrate so hard on detail that he could uncover its strangeness, Bishop describes her own lifelong efforts to query the unknown by reading the materials of her world. She was as drawn to the self-forgetfulness found in details as she was to their accuracy, because precisely at the juncture between these one could hope to be met by the most profound surprise. She particularly loved to accompany another writer whose eye she trusted on such an excursion among the potentially useless. In her copy of *The Autobiography of Charles Darwin and Selected Letters*,[25] Bishop made marginal notations beside homely moments as frequently as beside moments of wisdom. She marked Darwin's repugnance to algebra (18), his comfort in smoking (81), his "pleasure" in his children's sayings (87–8), his inability to hold an argument (94–5), his recognition of his physical decline (152, 158): she marked passages to which she related on a simple, conversational level. Of course, when she found it, she marked a long passage in which Francis Darwin discusses his father's style, wherein "the reader feels like a friend" (106). Throughout her reading library, she marked startling descriptions, such as Coleridge's reference to Newton's fall into a muddy pool, when his black clothes turned green with duck weed (49), Hopkins's definition of an earwig (9), Edward Lear's black-humored juxtapositions – the Indian famine with his large lunch and ill health afterward (66), and Flannery O'Connor's quotation of a long-winded songwriter seeking advice (170). The "heroic observations" she checked or underlined were her means of access to the writer. These relationships were always vital to her, and when she did do "criticism," she allowed them to come to the fore.

Bishop greatly admired Flannery O'Connor, for instance, whose eye for the bizarre detail and whose ability to express that detail in language matched Bishop's own. She asked Lowell, after reading O'Connor's *Wise Blood,* which she considered reviewing,[26] "Don't you sometimes feel green with envy the way she can cram a whole poem-idea into a sentence?" (5 May 1959, HL). Referring to the first section of *The Violent Bear It Away,* she wrote, it is "like a poem – in fact she's a great loss to the art" (to Lowell, 15 Feb. 1960, HL). When O'Connor died in 1964, Bishop wrote a moving tribute to her for the *New York Review of Books* of 8 October 1964. Her article takes the form of a memoir, as much about the relationship between Bishop and her subject as it is about her subject. In interesting juxtaposition, Bishop's piece begins, "I never met Flannery O'Connor, but we had been exchanging occasional letters for the last eight years or so"; the eulogy beside hers, Elizabeth Hardwick's, begins, "Flannery O'Connor was a brilliant writer." Hardwick goes on to discuss O'Connor's work; Bishop traces their connection by letter, by telephone, and through a "cross in a bottle, [. . .] crudely carved, with all the instruments of the Passion, the ladder, pliers, dice, etc., in wood, paper, and tinfoil, with the little rooster at the top of the cross" that Bishop sent O'Connor as a present. She quotes O'Connor's letter of thanks, which ends with blunt delight, "It's what I'm born to appreciate."[27] Within her personal musing, Bishop does not neglect to address what she most admires about O'Connor, the woman and the writer: "Something about her intimidated me a bit: perhaps natural awe before her toughness and courage; [. . .] she lived with Christian stoicism and wonderful wit and humor that put most of us to shame." The phrases she had been testing in her letters to Lowell congealed in her closing paragraph: "Her few books [. . .] are narrow, possibly, but they are clear, hard, vivid, and full of bits of description, phrases, and odd insights that contain more real poetry than a dozen books of poems" (21).

Bishop's personal form can be traced to her first review published in a major journal, "Gregorio Valdes, 1879–1939."[28] She begins that article, "The first painting I saw by Gregorio Valdes was in the window of a barbershop on Duval Street, the main street of Key West" (51). We know we are to be told a story: the first seven pages of the article center on her brief acquaintance with him and his art and radiate outward with the details of his life and death, as she gathered them and as his loving family told them to her. Only on the last page and a half does she do "art criticism." As if mocking the form she has been resisting, she classifies him in a sentence: "Gregorio was not a great painter at all, and although he certainly belongs to the class of painters we call 'primitive,' sometimes he was not even a good 'primitive'" (58). Then, much more interestingly, she reaches behind the classification to bring together Valdes's art and the life she has been describing:

> Gregorio himself did not see any difference between what we think of as his good pictures and his poor pictures, and his painting a good one or a bad one seems to have been entirely a matter of luck.
> There are some people whom we envy not because they are rich or handsome or successful, although they may be any or all of these, but because everything they are and do seems to be all of a piece, so that even if they wanted to they could not be or do otherwise. [. . .] Ancient heroes often have to do penance for and expiate crimes they have committed all unwittingly, and in the same way it seems that some people receive certain "gifts" merely by remaining unwittingly in an undemocratic state of grace. It is a supposition that leaves painting like Gregorio's a partial mystery. (58–9)

Bishop did not really want to penetrate the mystery by analyzing it. Instead, when she taught poets she liked and when she read her friends' work, she responded by discussing the emotional effect and technical effectiveness of the words. As Dana Gioia writes about his experiences in Bishop's classroom at Harvard, "She enjoyed pointing out the particulars of each poem, not generalizing about it, and she insisted that we understand every individual word, even if we had no idea what the poem was about as a whole. 'Use the dictionary,' she said once. 'It's better than the critics'" (92). When friends sent her drafts of their poems or stories to read, she approached them with similar intent. When Swenson, for example, read Bishop's poems, she praised and interpreted; when Bishop read Swenson's, she praised and then got down to the work of the words:

I think HYPNOTIST is very good, & I shd. think the N Y-er would take it quickly, that is if you wanted them to. The first two stanzas are fine. My only objection would be to "a wild child in us cries," which I feel doesn't match the beautiful freshness of the rest of those two stanzas,. "glazes", "delicious snarls", "Throw the Christian chairs," (applause) "Daniel" – I like them all. (This is unforgivable, I know – but could it be "brave child"? – to hitch up with the "bared" later, or isn't that strong enough for you? "Wild child" has been said before, I'm afraid, a good many times.) I suppose that "Stir our teacups" may not be quite right, grammatically speaking, but it probably doesn't matter. "the hearth's stage" is nice, too. But my feeling is that you've said it, by the end of the 3rd stanza – except that the word "terrible" shd. probably be in there somewhere. The reader does "get the idea" in the very first stanza, so it really shouldn't go on too long; amd "confort-ensnared", "langourous", "hunched", "flaring" aren't any of them as real and delightful as the descriptions in the first 2. Forgive me for putting my fingers right in your mud-pie with you – it's a sign I like it, though. The first part has a nice strangeness that I think sounds like you at the best of your form. (17 Mar. 1955, WU)

As Bishop insists, it is not the teacher or critic in her which prompts her to scrutinize a poem's words; it is her delight in the writing itself. Gioia's class "only read poems she liked, and it was a pleasure at Harvard to have a teacher who, however baffled she might be in managing her class, clearly enjoyed the things she was talking about" (93). If one loved poetry, one participated in it.

Just as writing for her was not a romantic recollection of materials fit for poetry's making, reading was not a matter of standing back critically to analyze, as her visceral and imagistic reading of Dickinson – or her inability to complete a single poetry review for the New Yorker – would attest. Bishop nonetheless demanded a great deal from poetry. As she articulated it in her 1934 journal entry about Hopkins and the creation of the spiritual out of the bedrock of the material, Bishop believed consistently – from her college musings through to her 1970s review notes – that achieving one's "real real protest" depended on being faithful to one's facts, one's details "eaten out with acid," and the surprise they yield up for both writer and reader.

In her acceptance speech for the 1976 Books Abroad/Neustadt International Prize for Literature, Bishop likened herself to her sandpiper, "just running along the edges of different countries and continents, 'looking for something'" (12). The two closing stanzas of "Sandpiper" suggest the nature of Bishop's inquiry:

The world is a mist. And then the world is
minute and vast and clear. The tide

is higher or lower. He couldn't tell you which.
His beak is focussed; he is preoccupied,

looking for something, something, something.
Poor bird, he is obsessed!
The millions of grains are black, white, tan, and gray,
mixed with quartz grains, rose and amethyst.[29]

The closing specificity of colors do not answer fully to the vital search for "something" that is inarticulable, some vital protest. The grains of sand can ever only partially meet the terms of "the world." Yet the intense focus on them was Bishop's choice as much as it is the sandpiper's instinctive obsession. As her reviews, her letters about other writers, her reading notes, her responses to friends' writing, and her poetry and prose reveal, focusing on particularities was her means toward insight. At the same time it was a shield from what she calls in her late 1940s and early 1950s notebooks the "fear and embarassment"[30] that come with not having "black, white, tan, and gray, / mixed with quartz grains, rose and amethyst" when one is faced with an ocean. The seeming objectivity of her poems, which won accolades from critics and distanced feminist poets, was actually her most direct route to the center of an emotional insight. "When emotion too far exceeds its cause," as she writes in her first major published poem, "The Map," she does not cease exploring and writing it; rather, she looks for grounding, there, in the printer's words. Bishop's faith in the material to yield up profound relationships among subjects is motivated, as my readings will show, by her personal politics and her sense of poetics. In its dailiness, where its colors are ordinary, Bishop writes her world (and ours); "the roaring alongside [s]he takes for granted," as she says in "Sandpiper," "and that every so often the world is bound to shake."

2

Writing Intimacy

The Map

Land lies in water; it is shadowed green.
Shadows, or are they shallows, at its edges
showing the line of long sea-weeded ledges
where weeds hang to the simple blue from green.
Or does the land lean down to lift the sea from under,
drawing it unperturbed around itself?
Along the fine tan sandy shelf
is the land tugging at the sea from under?

The shadow of Newfoundland lies flat and still.
Labrador's yellow, where the moony Eskimo
has oiled it. We can stroke these lovely bays,
under a glass as if they were expected to blossom,
or as if to provide a clean cage for invisible fish.
The names of seashore towns run out to sea,
the names of cities cross the neighboring mountains
– the printer here experiencing the same excitement
as when emotion too far exceeds its cause.
These peninsulas take the water between thumb and finger
like women feeling for the smoothness of yard-goods.

Mapped waters are more quiet than the land is,
lending the land their waves' own conformation:
and Norway's hare runs south in agitation,
profiles investigate the sea, where land is.
Are they assigned, or can the countries pick their colors?
– What suits the character or the native waters best.
Topography displays no favorites; North's as near as West.
More delicate than the historians' are the map-makers' colors.[1]

It is possible to go to a map of the world and trace the poem's shallows, colors, and names, which, when they are too long, extend into territory

42

they are not naming. It is necessary that we read every Bishop poem at its literal level, because the literal is always and essentially one of the subjects of her poetry. As Bishop told Alexandra Johnson in a 1978 interview:

> My first poem in my first book was inspired when I was sitting on the floor, one New Year's Eve in Greenwich Village, after I graduated from college. I was staring at a map. The poem wrote itself. People will say that it corresponded to some part of me which I was unaware of at the time. This may be true. (20)

Protecting herself from critics' intrusive hypotheses, Bishop turns characteristically to the literal base of her poetry. She would have readily accepted discussions of her interest in travel and in the landscape with regard to this poem, and she particularly praised such a reading by Robert Mazzocco. Assuming, with many other critics, that the poem's closing line is a call to art and a dismissal of history, Mazzocco argues:

> The line seems emblematic of everything about her, then or now. Miss Bishop is the poet of landscapes and seascapes and maps. [. . .] The true tenor of her work, I think, is [. . .] toward measured distances, scales, steps; side-stepping the "vulgar beauty of irridescence," and side-stepping, too, the intimate. (4)[2]

The last line's and the mapmakers' vitality lie not in their sidestepping but in their confrontation with the real. "The map-makers' colors" are barely restrained within the countries' boundaries, the map marking geographic contiguity and difference, even as these countries' cultures and people inevitably spill over the carefully printed edges. Representing overflowing emotion only just contained, these colors are indeed "delicate," fragile, because the fiction of their divisions is so easily exposed, as when demarcating names overrun their boundary lines. Calling attention to this fragility, Bishop undoes her closing opposition as she utters it: mapmakers' acknowledged fictions are not so very different from a historian's reconstructions of historical "fact." The fluid edges and the undermined oppositions of "The Map" are, more accurately, what make it "emblematic of everything about" this poet, who, throughout her writing, examines and reenvisions our constructed definitions of self and other by embracing a "multiple," "contradicted" (de Lauretis), and always relational subjectivity.

Whereas in the preceding chapter I was interested in Bishop's means toward intimacy between herself, as reader or critic, and the writer she was reading, here I explore the ways in which Bishop enacted intimacies among the textual subjects of her early poetry. And whereas a discussion of detail or pragmatic localism assisted my inquiry there, here a different dynamic operates. In this poetry subjectivity is hardly so distinct: if there Bishop sought the surprising but ordinary details that would connect two clear subjects, herself and another, here the complexity of the layered connection becomes central. Subjectivity is at its core relational in these poems: it is layered, contradictory, and blurred at the edges between lovers, friends, or family members. Both for its own pleasure and out of necessity it engages in a continual process of revision and remaking. In this chapter I study poems most expressive of the central relationships of Bishop's early writing[3] – the relationships of lovers, of a daughter with her mother, of a student with her mentor, and of an outsider with his world. Working to understand the nature of Bishop's relationality – what we might, with infant development theorist Daniel Stern, call her subjects' "we self" (see Introduction, note 13) – I examine the ways the poems enact the emotions of these relationships: contented or trustful boundary diffusion, dependency, assertions of independence, aggression, rejection and alienation, playfulness, competitiveness, and the concomitant fear of and desire for reenvisioned forms of intimacy.

Most of Bishop's critics would now consent to a reading of Bishop's early poetry as deeply personal, but they generally prefer to discuss the work of her imagination in these poems rather than the emotions they enact.[4] I make use of Bishop's actual relationships insofar as they offer insight into the emotions of this poetry. Bishop's relationship with her mother is necessarily a conflicted one, because she never knew her as an adult and only for a few troubled years as a child. In Chapter 4 I look closely at some manuscripts of memoirs she began writing in 1934, shortly after her mother's death, about her mother and about her childhood in Nova Scotia, memoirs whose details became central to her 1953 stories "Gwendolyn" and "In the Village." I delay this discussion because Bishop delayed her use of this writing, holding it until it "decayed and fell together"[5] in these stories some twenty years later. Until she was ready to write directly about her mother – or her lovers, as she would increasingly in unpublished work beginning in the 1940s – Bishop's early poetry nonetheless confronts the emotions and confusions of these relationships. To represent her relationship with her mother, particularly in "The Weed," she confronted at its most terrifying the intertwinings of relationality, when the boundaries between subjects become painfully unclear. To represent, on the other hand, the attachment of same-sex lovers, Bishop discovered a range of possible intertwinings that could accommodate the emotions, desires, and insights of what she called an "inverted" vision. She wrote within and against verbal and cultural preconceptions about sexuality in order to discover a language for sameness[6] that does not invoke fear as it dissolves boundaries, but vitally shifts and reshifts them nonetheless. This is not to say that she could always publish

her discoveries. In this chapter I look at some unfinished love poems
that are able to enact same-sex love and sexuality only because they
remained unpublished or were discarded as drafts. To publish a poem
about love was to submerge its gay or lesbian particularities, even as she
was exploring a language of love and sexuality founded, perhaps, in
those particularities.

Both the pleasure and the perplexity of relation in this early poetry,
as in the writing of her mentor, Marianne Moore, find voice in the
complexity of plants, animals, earthy and unearthly creatures, who han-
dily negotiate all emotions. The first poem of Bishop's first book is
representative of Bishop's work: it maps out homely, human intimacies
by means of nonhuman forms, and it explores and reconfigures the terms
of our presumptions, here specifically revising the language of sexual
subjectivity. Like the printer's emotion, sexuality here tests and "exceeds
its cause." A few months before beginning the poem Bishop wrote in
her journal, "Name it 'friendship' if you want to – like names of cities
printed on maps, the word is much too big, it spreads out all over the
place, and tells nothing of the actual place it means to name."[7] Her
depiction of friendship as amoebic suggests just how complexly fused
and confused friends are. "The mapmakers' colors" are one way of
marking boundaries and giving us the fiction of a division, "blue from
green," a friend from her friend. Mapmakers and poetry may offer us
the fiction of form, but neither poem nor map can stop exhuberant
overlapping, "the land tugging at the sea from under," nor would we
want them to. The language of the poem teases; it asks us to consider a
map as it enacts a loving embrace. Bishop was in her early twenties and
in the throes of romance in 1934 and 1935 when she wrote and revised
this poem.[8] Whether "The Map" suggests desired or actual love can only
be conjectured, but in either case the sea lifting the land "unperturbed
around itself" and the bays that we may stroke are sensual, even sexual.[9]

To envision relationship as a haven where partners "spread[ ] out,"
"lie[ ] in," "hang," "lean down to lift," "draw[ ] around," "tug[ ] at
from under," "run out," "lend[ ]" is to constitute sexuality as an intimacy of shared and exchanged subject positions. Bishop's move is radical
precisely because she posits intimacy without a phallus. Her images do
not define a sexuality of contrast, female to male, passive to active or
aggressive, receiving to penetrating, dependent to independent. The
"mapped waters are more quiet than the land is" at the moment of the
poem, but not because they depend on the tugging mapped land for their
activity. We know the constant tidal displacements of both land and sea,
and we can easily imagine the reversal of terms, the ocean tugging at the
beach, the undertow drawing the land. The line following the water's
quietness confirms its subtle power: these mapped waters "lend[ ] the

land their waves' own conformation." Or as Luce Irigaray would put it in closing her own revisionary treatment of gender and sexuality, "You? I? That's still saying too much. Dividing too sharply between us: all" (218). But whereas Irigaray speaks directly of lesbian desire and sexuality in *This Sex Which Is Not One,* Bishop enacts her revision of intimate relations in a poem about land and water, art and history, nature and culture.

Bishop worked the poem (despite her disclaimer in her interview with Johnson) until its structure echoed the map's embrace, disguising within its three-stanza form a feel of doubling. The opening and closing stanzas, tightly patterned octaves, mirror each other as they surround the central unrhymed section; the quatrains within these are even more precise mirrors, since the outside lines of the four abba patterns are identical rhymes. Each of these frames coaxes us inward, structurally re-creating the map's establishment and dissolution of divisions and boundaries. Twenty-seven lines in length, the poem divides invisibly into two overlapping halves, as if embracing in the middle, where "the names of seashore towns run out to sea," structurally as well as thematically. Capable of distinguishing each town from the other and any town from the sea, these names serve instead to dissolve distinction, thanks to the excitement of the printer. Structurally, this centrally posed line of strict iambic pentameter potentially completes both halves of this incomplete double sonnet. The line suggests as it defies form; representative of the poem, it contains as it spills. Keeping her own same-sex love secret and separate from her public life, Bishop invented a language for lesbian love within a poem about a map, land, and water, a love that need not set containing and spilling in opposition.

A year later Bishop published a playful poem, "The Gentleman of Shalott,"[10] imaging a mirror that divides and connects the loving halves of the gentleman's person. The satisfied gentleman is land and sea combined and then halved, so that neither half, once again, opposes the other, and each is, most explicitly, the other's double:

> Which eye's his eye?
> Which limb lies
> next the mirror?
> For neither is clearer
> nor a different color
> than the other,
> nor meets a stranger
> in this arrangement
> of leg and leg and
> arm and so on.
> To his mind

it's the indication
of a mirrored reflection
somewhere along the line
of what we call the spine.

He felt in modesty
his person was
half looking-glass,
for why should he
be doubled?
The glass must stretch
down his middle,
or rather down the edge.
But he's in doubt
as to which side's in or out
of the mirror.
There's little margin for error,
but there's no proof, either.
And if half his head's reflected,
thought, he thinks, might be affected.

But he's resigned
to such economical design.
If the glass slips
he's in a fix –
only one leg, etc. But
while it stays put
he can walk and run
and his hands can clasp one
another. The uncertainty
he says he
finds exhilarating. He loves
that sense of constant re-adjustment.
He wishes to be quoted as saying at present:
"Half is enough."

This hero is markedly different from his namesake, Tennyson's lady of
Shalott, whose attention is drawn as if despite her will from her weaving
mirror to the life out her window, from her shadowed reflections of the
world to the actual, physical forms of her hero, Sir Lancelot, and his
busy town of Camelot. She knows a curse forbids her from such a direct
gaze; her romantic thralldom becomes fatal. Never offering her a third
option – the gentleman of Shalott's option to look at himself – Tennyson
gives his heroine a mirror that reflects only other things – her art or her
lover and the world beyond – though surely she, too, would be reflected
in her weaving mirror if she were to shift her perspective. The gentleman
of Shalott, on the other hand, need not be restless within his reflected

world because he appreciates himself, allowing his own variation to be the entertaining alternative to the world's distraction or confusion.

In this pleasurably narcissistic world, he need not be concerned with definition or subject–object distinction. "Which eye's his eye?" becomes an irrelevant question when both eyes and "leg and leg and/arm and so on" are at once his and his mirrored self's. Love is clearly not love of difference; there is no Lady Lancelot beyond the mirror. But Bishop does give the gentleman of Shalott the option of sexuality constructed as doubling. It is clear that *not* accepting sameness can be a problem: "If the glass slips," he faces only halfness; "he's in a fix –/only one leg, etc." If in "The Map" Bishop's land and water confronted so as to confound cultural expectations of border, form, and difference, this gentleman simply defies them. He is an isolate, though doubled, subject; duplication, not opposition, gives him pleasure, whatever psychological or cultural norms might dictate.

Originally she conceived a love play that was not narcissistic; the gentleman desired to direct love outward but was simply confused about how. After the line that originally read "even thinking might be affected," Bishop tested the following:

> He felt he'd like to hold dearer
> the part not in the mirror
> but one eye cannot discern
> where should he put his love

Perhaps this version seemed too suggestive of a sexuality she could not utter, as she edited it out of two subsequent drafts in the same notebook and all later versions. The final drafts, however, find a way out of the quandary of these deleted lines: the explicit differentiation between self and a similar but separate other demanded by the question of "where should he put his love" becomes a wholly unnecessary one when similarity becomes sameness and when one can in turn appreciate sameness's nuanced flexibility, "that sense of constant re-adjustment." This love, he acknowledges, is not without its risks: if the mirror slips the game will end, as will the walks, runs, and hand clasps, but "uncertainty" itself is part of what "he/finds exhilarating."

He closes by saying that "half is enough," but beyond his assertion is a concern settled only partially by his tone of defiance. He seems to console himself with the knowledge that regardless of how clearly he may view himself, he will never need to confuse himself with the intrusion of another – he need not "meet[ ] a stranger." But which eye, indeed, is his own eye? From which do his own perceptions and judgments derive? Is there such a subjective eye in the first place, or are both eyes so busy mirroring each other that subjectivity dissolves along with objectivity? His "doubt/as to which side's in or out/of the mirror" is playful quandary or climactic union, but, hovering around the edges of such a doubt, annihilation potentially threatens, whether or not a stranger is there to condemn his love. What if he is caught within a perpetual cycle of reflection that reveals he possesses no independent position, no eye outside the mirror? What if the glass slips, and he discovers that without the mirror's necessary completion he is left with half a brain, half a spine, and half a body?

Fear of boundary diffusion and helpless dependency remain just beyond the configurations of relationship in this 1936 poem, which maintains its playfulness through thin, gangly, choppy phrases, whose surface cheer protects it against raw doubt. A few months later in "The Weed," Bishop stripped away that protection, surrealistically exposing a symbiosis that is terrifying.[11] Here the question becomes less How might her subject throw down her gauntlet? than What can she salvage from the wreckage of her confrontation? Yet the poem immediately layers this question: in her most complex examination of the nature of subjectivity, Bishop poses two figures – a weed and an invaded, disembodied speaking voice – who each suggest a range of subject positions.[12] On the one hand, the relationship in "The Weed" appears generational: "A slight young weed" grows through the heart of the speaker, who is at once "dead, and meditating"; a daughter invades her mother's body and struggles to separate from her.[13] Yet at the same time this is a poem about one's relation with one's own creation: the disembodied, divided, and passive speaker repudiates the weed, whose growth within is aggressive and chaotic. Merging some of the central relationships of her own life – her relation with her writing, with her absent mother, and with the newly present, mothering Moore – Bishop engages at its most chaotic the dissolution and shifting of boundaries.

Bishop's mother had died in 1934; by the autumn of 1936 Bishop was deeply involved in her autobiographical project, in which she was unearthing the trauma of her painful childhood memories. As she was keeping this project wholly private, she was looking increasingly to Moore for personal guidance and literary mentorship during the months surrounding the writing of "The Weed."[14] Bishop desired Moore's advice and approval, and Moore was delighted to mother her writer's voice. In turn, Bishop began writing letters of greater honesty, complaining and exposing her dependency. Vacationing with Margaret Miller in West Falmouth, Massachusetts, following her return from Europe in June 1936, Bishop referred vaguely to the horrors of the Spanish civil war, to her reading of several autobiographical works – St. Augustine, Amiel, and Wordsworth – and to her daily reading of Russian Marxist criticism; then she judged her work:

I cannot, cannot decide what to do – I am even considering studying medecine or bio-chemistry [. . . .] I feel that I have given myself more than a fair trial, and the accomplishment has been nothing at all. I had rather work at Science, at which I was fairly good at college, or even something quite uncongenial for the rest of my days, than become like one of my contemporaries – But this is a great imposition – my only foundation is that your interest in behalf of POETRY will lead you to be very severe. (21 Aug. 1936, V:04:30, RM)

Bishop blames her depression on guilt about her social disengagement and lack of poetic output, even as she was drafting four or five of her published poems and a story during these months. If indeed she was returning this summer as well to her memories of her mother, one can conjecture a more direct need for the lap of Moore's mentorship: parent to her writing, Bishop becomes terrified child in it, facing two directions at once, toward a seemingly bad and a seemingly good mother.[15]

Bishop's letters of disillusion prompted Moore's immediate attentiveness. This mother, who worried about her health, accompanied her to the circus, and exchanged odd discoveries with her, began now to take charge of Bishop's creative life. In a letter of 28 August 1936, she requested some writing; Bishop sent "The Weed," "Paris, 7 A.M.," and her first sestina, "A Miracle for Breakfast," along with one of her characteristic apologies: "I realize there are awful faults – one being vague, another an extremely impolite, if true, display of your 'influence'; the sestina is just a sort of stunt" (15 Sept. 1936, V:04:30, RM). Since "Paris, 7 A. M." is the most Moore-like of the group in its abrupt juxtaposition of settings and images, "The Weed" is left as the vague poem, refusing to settle its various subject positions.

Moore returned Bishop's cryptic apology with her own defensiveness:

> The poems are so fine, and dart-proof in every way, – especially THE WEED and PARIS, 7 A.M. – that they shiver my impulsive offers of helpfulness. This exteriorizing of the interior, and the aliveness all through, it seems to me are the essential sincerity that unsatisfactory surrealism struggles toward. Yet the sobriety and weight and impact of the past are also there. The great amount of care, the reach of imagination, and the pleasure conveyed, make it hard for me not to say a great deal; but I fear to make suggestions lest I hamper you. (20 Sept. 1936, VC)

Moore draws back here, as if testing her increased authority in this relationship, but a few weeks later she embraced the aggressive role Bishop had sought, typing and returning her own revision of "The Weed," as she would again on several occasions (MacMahon 142):

> Something may have attacked my nerves and I hope you will not take fright at this overintent analyzing of your work, but just as I was sealing

my letter to Mr. Zabel [editor of *Poetry*], it seemed to me that in two lines, the rhythm did not seem continuous with what went before. If I am trying to disturb an intentional balance of inequalities, or mishearing indubitable equalities, please pay no attention. And I <u>beg</u> that you will in any case send Mr. Zabel a version of THE WEED, the one you typed and signed, or one changed a little, tomorrow or Wednesday. (19 Oct. 1936, VC)

Like a mother dependent on the authority she has assumed, Moore cannot resist correcting Bishop's poem. Like an adolescent seeking advice as she is testing her own voice against a generous, knowledgeable, and overbearing mother, Bishop responded:

I must add my gratitude for all the time you have spent on the WEED. I don't see how you could bear to copy it, the way you did, and I am extremely grateful. I am afraid my ungraciousness appears here the same way it did as regards the story ["The Baptism"]: I sent Mr. Zabell your very superior copy, with "neither" in it and "out of" – both of which I thank you for very much, as for the other suggestions I didn't accept. I am not sure why I didn't, because I make no pretense of comparing my "ear" to your own. I suppose one is very selfish in one's conception of the "picture." I do hope you won't mind. (27 Oct. 1936, V:04:30, RM)

While Bishop was emerging publicly as a poet under the aegis of Marianne Moore, she was trying to explore the range of her own poetic voice. She wanted neither to lose Moore's "influence" and love nor to give over her "conception of the 'picture,'" and her ambivalence is reflected in her shyness about this last word, which she cannot simply tell Moore she has. "The Weed" enacts the ambivalences of such a relationship, as well as the far more problematic and less articulable mother–daughter relationship that Bishop had been facing in her private writing since her mother's death. Overlaying these relationships, in turn, was the conflicted relationship of a writer with her writing. The subject is surreal, the pronouns ambiguous, the poem's sympathies in all positions and none; Bishop renders the emotions of these relationships disturbing.

"The Weed" opens with an uncanny, calm, first-person narration of death and bodily dissolution:

I dreamed that dead, and meditating,
I lay upon a grave, or bed,
(at least, some cold and close-built bower).
In the cold heart, its final thought
stood frozen, drawn immense and clear,
stiff and idle as I was there;
and we remained unchanged together
for a year, a minute, an hour.

Dreaming of death, the speaker's voice separates from her body and becomes, consequently, passive. With disinterest she records the removed pronouns and articles of the now dissociated heart. Modeling her poem on George Herbert's "Love Unknown" (Brown 295), in which the speaker's heart undergoes various brutal punishments until it proves its moral worth, Bishop, too, severs the normal relations between heart and mind. But her poem has none of Herbert's Christian justification. There, dismemberment has a cause; and though the speaker tells his tale of woe as if he has been repeatedly wronged, his soul's italicized voice, strengthened by the voice of God, just as repeatedly helps the heart understand his lapses and his necessary pain. Though his heart suffers for his whole body, his soul and his heart are united in their efforts always to do better by God. Narrated, rather, from the midst of nightmare, Bishop's poem provides no such comforting myth.

We must simply accept her speaker's seeming illogic of time and of pronominal connection: "a year, a minute, an hour" pass with "neither sun nor moon" as guide; "we" signifies the speaker and her heart, a pairing of two subjects that should not, in our logic, separately be animate. But their split signals a vital inconsistency. The speaker is divided and multiple, part observer, part creator, and part victim of the weed's encroachments:

> Suddenly there was a motion,
> as startling, there, to every sense
> as an explosion. Then it dropped
> to insistent, cautious creeping
> in the region of the heart,
> prodding me from desperate sleep.
> I raised my head. A slight young weed
> had pushed up through the heart and its
> green head was nodding on the breast.
> (All this was in the dark.)

If the speaker's is the position of the impassive, helpless mother or the mentor confused about her role, it is also the position of the ambivalent creator, repudiating the chaotic activity inside her, as Robert Dale Parker has helpfully pointed out (7–8). The part of her who thinks and speaks recognizes, though does not feel, the weed's explosive entry; she notices colors and changes in movement, somewhat proud that she sees this much in the dark. Prone and helpless though she is, she does have a creator's convenient access to the intriguing details of this growth and accepts no responsibility for its outcome. She can study this young weed without parenting it or feeling its growing pains; she can even remove herself from her own heart's pain, when it falls victim to the weed's aggression. But such a freedom to observe in the face of pain necessarily produces confusion and self-doubt. Severed from experience, this mother, mentor, or creator is left behind as the activity of creation carries on without her.

We can read in such a light Bishop's effort to understand her mother's position in the family, as she articulated it in her 1936 autobiographical notes: while "we became quite stolidly a family" in the living room together, "Easter," as she calls her mother in these notes,

> never joined in with our feeling for Grandfather's reading. She liked
> Burns, too – once she had asked Grandfather to read "Oh wert thou
> in the cauld blast", but almost always she lay on the sofa with an arm
> across her eyes, her other ~~hand~~ open hanging down so that the white
> hand lay on the floor. Betsy lay across her master's feet feet, occaisionally
> wrinkling up her forehead and rolling up her eyes at me, so that the
> whites showed. (Unnumbered page)

Present but absent, this mother and the speaker of "The Weed" charge the room's emotion with their helpless pain. The equally helpless child can only recognize the wrongness of this mother in the family picture. Or, alternatively, if we place Bishop in the conflicted role of parent-creator of her weed poem, we can read in the speaker's impassivity Bishop's own frustration with her lack of engagement, in her 21 August appeal to Moore, and her effort to enlist Moore's gusto on her poetry's behalf. Moore's subsequent scrutiny indeed seems to shift the responsibilities of creativity from internally conflicted poet to externally demanding mentor. When Moore imposes her expectations, as letters cited earlier show, Bishop can reject and reconsider, in active engagement with an oppositional force. The poem's parent becomes the mentor's child, her creativity now depending not only on her poetic assertions and experiments but on the challenge of defending them.

Whatever the source of these emotions, the weed's insistent growth is a battle for (self-)creation:

> It grew an inch like a blade of grass;
> next, one leaf shot out of its side
> a twisting, waving flag, and then
> two leaves moved like a semaphore.
> The stem grew thick. The nervous roots
> reached to each side; the graceful head
> changed its position mysteriously,
> since there was neither sun nor moon
> to catch its young attention.
> The rooted heart began to change
> (not beat) and then it split apart
> and from it broke a flood of water.
> Two rivers glanced off from the sides,

> one to the right, one to the left,
> two rushing, half-clear streams,
> (the ribs made of them two cascades)
> which assuredly, smooth as glass,
> went off through the fine black grains of earth.
> The weed was almost swept away;
> it struggled with its leaves,
> lifting them fringed with heavy drops.

What seems at first the healthy growth of a weed fully engaged with life becomes a birth metaphor gone awry. Diving headlong into conflict in its urge to grow, the weed breaks the heart in which it is rooted and spills its water, nearly drowning itself in the flooding heart. Only when it has rent all boundaries between itself and the speaker's body does the weed gather its leaves and assert its position. Its fight to be born, to overcome, and perhaps to surpass has testified to the terrible complexity of relationality: whereas the gentleman of Shalott found pure pleasure in his confusion of boundaries, when the question comes home to the primary relations of Bishop's life, her poetry must recognize the potential terror of that confusion.

In the closing lines of the poem, both speaker and weed regroup, the speaker briefly reclaiming the poem's dominant voice in an effort to understand what has just happened:

> A few drops fell upon my face
> and in my eyes, so I could see
> (or, in that black place, thought I saw)
> that each drop contained a light,
> a small, illuminated scene;
> the weed-deflected stream was made
> itself of racing images.
> (As if a river should carry all
> the scenes that it had once reflected
> shut in its waters, and not floating
> on momentary surfaces.)

Giving the speaker a rational perspective for the first time in the poem, one that can sort inner from outer and present from past, Bishop rewrites the mother, mentor, or creator as a separate and reasonable, yet still oppositional force. From that reasoning position, the speaker discovers a means to accommodate her split subjectivity and disavowal of her creation, as she is coming to understand the import of the weed's chaotic rending of boundaries. And now, with a finally viable opponent, the weed can bluntly assert itself:

> The weed stood in the severed heart.
> "What are you doing there?" I asked.

It lifted its head all dripping wet
(with my own thoughts?)
and answered then: "I grow," it said,
"but to divide your heart again."

This creation is forthright. While its source questions, it declares. While
its source seeks justification for the pain of its broken heart, the weed
promises further divisions. Like an adolescent insisting on revising her
mother or a poet revising a poetic order before she can become herself,
the weed asserts her independence with defiance. Were the poem to close
with the speaker's insight into the larger pattern encompassing this conflict, it might have consoled, Herbert-like, even if it could not reconcile
the mother with the daughter or the writer with her writing. Instead,
the weed closes the poem here, suggesting that, if there is any pattern,
it is in the necessary and continuous revision of relationship, wherein
the boundaries can be defined, reshaped, rejected, and embraced by two
equally engaged partners. The more benign effects of Stern's "we self,"
the poem reflects, are counterbalanced by the exigencies of power and
betrayal, dependency and disinterest within any subject (as de Lauretis
argues) and in any pair of subjects. Simultaneously creator, "daughter,"
and daughter of an absent mother, Bishop constructed the painful complexities as she knew them: one must inhabit multiple positions; or rather,
a subjectivity that can envision change, enact it, and not be left amid the
wreckage of its confrontation needs a certain fluidity or flexibility, from
which to negotiate possibilities of revision.

By the late 1940s Bishop and Moore had come to much less conflicted
terms, and when invited to submit something for a Marianne Moore
special issue of the *Quarterly Review of Literature* (Spring 1948), Bishop
could write directly and affectionately of her literary friendship with
Moore. She submitted the poem "Invitation to Miss Marianne Moore"
and a short essay, "As We Like It." The earlier wrestling for control,
which would culminate in their exchange of letters over "Roosters," as
I will show in the next chapter, had by 1948 mellowed to a self-confident
and playful affection between the two poets. In this poem and essay,
Bishop trusted that her own poetic purposes, which were different from
Moore's, could nonetheless articulate her love for her poet-friend.[16] Her
triumph in "Invitation to Miss Marianne Moore" is that it plays fast and
loose with things vitally important to Moore, as it reveals how deep
Bishop's love and respect for her go:

Bearing a musical inaudible abacus,
a slight censorious frown, and blue ribbons,
        please come flying.
Facts and skyscrapers glint in the tide; Manhattan

> is all awash with morals this fine morning,
>   so please come flying.
>
> Mounting the sky with natural heroism,
> above the accidents, above the malignant movies,
> the taxicabs and injustices at large,
> while horns are resounding in your beautiful ears
> that simultaneously listen to
> a soft uninvented music, fit for the musk deer,
>   please come flying.[17]

Moore's metrics, her facts, her morals, her heroism, her awareness of injustices are all swept up by the words, sounds, and fast-moving rhythm of Bishop's poem. Bishop teases Moore, plays with her, but never loses respect for her.

The poem renders deftly what Bishop's essay discusses, as if to match it – Moore's unequaled ability at description, imitation, and verse making. Bishop says near the close of the essay:

> Sometimes I have thought that her individual verse forms, or "mannerisms" as they might be called, may have developed as much from a sense of modesty as from the demands of artistic expression; that actually she may be somewhat embarrassed by her own precocity and sensibilities and that her varied verse forms and rhyme schemes and syllabic logarithms are all a form of apology, are saying, "It really isn't as easy for me as I'm afraid you may think it is." The precocious child is often embarrassed by his own understanding and is capable of going to great lengths to act his part as a child properly; one feels that Miss Moore sometimes has to make things difficult for herself as a sort of *noblesse oblige,* or self-imposed taxation to keep everything "fair" in the world of poetry. (134)

Bishop's definition of "modesty" is a rather strange one, somewhat like her references to Moore's "modestly vain" sense of her own painting skills (*Prose* 128). This modesty accompanies Moore "in a cloud of fiery pale chemicals," "to the rapid rolling of thousands of small blue drums," while "whistles, pennants and smoke are blowing." Bishop describes in poetry and prose here a modesty bursting to show itself off, contradicting Moore in her own claim that "unobtrusiveness is dazzling" ("Voracities and Verities Sometimes Are Interacting"), or rather, simply putting the stress on "dazzling." Bishop, whose poem about Moore dazzles with Moore-like descriptive detail, meets Moore on her own ground. Moore's greatest thanks was to praise her for precisely this:

> Words fail me, Elizabeth:
>   Your magic poem – every word a living wonder – with an unfoldment that does not ever go back of itself, and the colors! beyond compare in

the small blue drums and the mackerel sky and the jelly-colored epergnes. What of your unabashed "awash with morals"! [. . .]
    Alarmingly accurate, Elizabeth, in what you say of the logarithms of apology and the incredible effort of justifying an initial pattern. (24 Aug. 1948, VC)

Pleasurably shocked by Bishop's blasphemy about morals, Moore loved the poem. In her respect for Bishop's poetry and for her insights about her own, Moore acknowledged Bishop as a fellow poet and critic. In her ability to see in Moore the "precocious child" and the "natural hero[ ]" with a long list of charming idiosyncrasies, Bishop also accepted her own poetic and personal difference.

This acceptance involved some dissociation from Moore, which her new friendship with Lowell, whom she had met in 1947, made easier. Writing to Lowell about Moore allowed Bishop to define Moore's work, even judge it, which she never did with Moore directly. In a letter about the *Quarterly Review* issue, she told him that she "can't seem to make much out of Marianne's own contributions ["By Disposition of Angels," translations of La Fontaine proverbs, "Voracities and Verities"], at least not the last one. I think she must be entering upon the prophetic stage or something" (11 Sept. 1948, HL). She wrote him that Moore "showed me quite a lot of the La Fontaine – I just don't know what to think. It all has a sort of awkwardness & quaintness that's quite nice – & sounds very much like her, of course; I'm not sure how much like La Fontaine" (30 June 1948, HL).

Bishop captures both the quaintness and the prophetic in "Invitation to Miss Marianne Moore." Texturing her details about Moore with an equalizing hand, she treats morals and injustices as compellingly and humorously as "the pointed toe of each black shoe" or the "long un-nebulous train of words." When nothing is sacred, everything can be. In a letter of 1 May 1938 (V:05:01, RM), Moore had urged Bishop to discover her "private defiance of the significantly detestable"; here Bishop recognizes Moore's own. Grammatically equating "the taxicabs and in-justices," she shows Moore's ear to be tuned both to the sound of cabs' horns and to the "soft uninvented music, fit for the musk deer." Por-traying Moore's attention, scrutiny, even love for "facts and skyscrapers" and morals alike, she appreciates as she teases Moore about her eccen-tricities, her opinionatedness, her zealousness and exactitude regarding the details of life:

> We can sit down and weep; we can go shopping,
> or play at a game of constantly being wrong
> with a priceless set of vocabularies,
> or we can bravely deplore, but please
>   please come flying.

Bishop knew by 1948 that she could make a poem of Moore, that she could find Moore in language. Years later, after the publication of this poem in *A Cold Spring,* Moore acknowledged the intimate connection between herself and this poem:

> Never could I deserve so lovely a thing. I shall always be trying to justify it. Furthermore, it gives me some standing. Several times this summer I have been ardently received as having been the occasion for it. (29 Aug. 1956, VC)

The poem has somehow become her, as if she has indeed been revised by her protégée. Enjoying this version of herself, she nonetheless reveals sadness that her own poetic moment has passed. She continues: "I really have been writing a line or two, Elizabeth, a 'Come on, Dodgers' sort of ballad. But they are going to lose the series this year, I'm afraid. Roy Campanella pleases me for every reason every day." Though she is still writing, the heroics have shifted: her protégée and her favorite ballplayer give her life its standing.

Writing and publishing love for a mentor was acceptable and fun for Bishop in 1948. But before she could write a love poem, particularly one about a same-sex lover, in terms that would reveal love and not her lover, her poems had to envision the possibility of embracing abberation and inversion, even as the world she was portraying rejected these. Whether or not her early love poems suggest female lovers, as, for instance, "While Someone Telephones" most explicitly does not, they are nonetheless protective of their subject, allusive or underarticulated, as if love itself is abberant and open to the rejection not only of the lover, but also of the world. Alternatively, Bishop approaches love from the perspective of the outsider, in whom she can represent more readily than in the lover our sources of connection. Alone and quite familiar with alienation, the outsider has access both to escape and to profound, imagined forms of intimacy. Repeatedly, Bishop's 1930s and 1940s poetry enacts outsiders' pains, fears, and desires, as it searches for the simplest forms of attachment that might in themselves break the spell of alienation.

One of her earliest poems, "The Man-Moth,"[18] tenderly approaches both alienation and generosity in the figure of an odd, liminal creature, whose compositional history she loved to retell:

> This poem was written in 1935 when I first lived in New York City.
> I've forgotten what it was that was supposed to be "mammoth." But the misprint seemed meant for me. An oracle spoke from the page of the *New York Times,* kindly explaining New York City to me, at least for a moment. (Schwartz and Estess 286)

In the paper she found a typo that characterized New York, she says; through that typo she reveals a creature who is at once a culmination of recognizable opposites, man/nature (moth), man/woman (mother), and an embodiment of difference, "an inverted pin, the point magnetized to the moon." The man-moth scales buildings as an insect or flying creature might, and he feels as a human being does. His grammatical signifiers are male, but he understands the boundaries of his world as female in form: his pin-shaped body reaches from the small shadow, cast by Man "for a doll to stand on," to the light of the female moon.

The lines of "The Man-Moth" are as long and full as those of "The Gentleman of Shalott" are short and skeletal. This creature faces alienation not by turning in to the security of himself but by exposing himself to his readers and judges, who seem so different from him. His cross-species, cross-gendered consciousness makes him aware of the ways in which man ignores his own intuitions, amid his rational, mechanized world. The man-moth registers the moon's properties, for instance, not with anything so calculating as a thermometer, but rather by "feeling the queer light on his hands, neither warm nor cold." He is jarred by man's unsubtle mechanization, by subway trains that start "without a shift in gears or a gradation of any sort." Intuitive and always fearful, the man-moth accepts his vulnerability and his odd necessity.

> to push his small head through that round clean opening
> and be forced through, as from a tube, in black scrolls on the light.
> (Man, standing below him, has no such illusions.)
> But what the Man-Moth fears most he must do

"Man," who opposes the man-moth both as male and as human, is so accustomed to treating his intuited images of danger and pleasure as illusions that he has lost any direct access to the pain or knowledge they might give him.

The man-moth's difference keeps him apart. He lives alone on a moving subway train, where he always sits "facing the wrong way," in terms that echo a notebook entry from the summer during which Bishop composed the poem:

> My friendly circumstances, my "good fortune," surround me so well & safely, & only I am wrong, inadequate. It is a situation like one of those solid crystal balls with little silvery objects inside: thick, clear, appropriate glass – only the little object, me, is sadly flawed and shown off as inferior to the setting.[19]

The man-moth recognizes the danger inherent in the "clear, appropriate glass" that the "I" of the notebook can only internalize. He at least chooses the direction of his seat, opting for this wrongness, as if in doing so to defy it. Always conscious of the threat of the world, he watches it carefully:

> the third rail, the unbroken draught of poison,
> runs there beside him. He regards it as a disease
> he has inherited the susceptibility to. He has to keep
> his hands in his pockets, as others must wear mufflers.

Bishop does capture New York in her rush of crowded, enjambed lines and in the poem's danger, fear, and alienation. But at the same time, pointing bemusedly toward New York as the subject of her poem and toward her odd title as its prime feature allows her quietly to question man's rational thought and to put before us, particularly in the closing lines, the terrible passion of one most exposed to the city's rawness:

> If you catch him,
> hold up a flashlight to his eye. It's all dark pupil,
> an entire night itself, whose haired horizon tightens
> as he stares back, and closes up the eye. Then from the lids
> one tear, his only possession, like the bee's sting, slips.
> Slyly he palms it, and if you're not paying attention
> he'll swallow it. However, if you watch, he'll hand it over,
> cool as from underground springs and pure enough to drink.

Whereas until this last stanza the poem has focused on the man-moth and his tenuous relations with an uncomprehending but unidentified "man," here Bishop triangulates the relationship. In sympathy with that man, we, the poem's human readers, now enter, hypothetically, in the role of the cold examiner who scrutinizes the man-moth and frightens and saddens him one more time. But the tear, which most poignantly attests to his pain, causes a final slippage in the poem's relationships. Bishop gives this tear agency, enabling it to act on behalf of the one who produces it and, as an offered gift, potentially to transform its recipient from a labeled and defined man-object to a subject who can reconsider his or her own responses. Dislodging us from our passivity so that we may recognize our own alienation, our fear of connection, which allows us to stare but has taught us to avert our eye in the face of another's pain, the man-moth offers this "one tear, his only possession." The spell of our difference broken, the tear of this inverted, "wrong" man-moth peels the protective cover off our scientific distance and reveals the potentially gentler, more companionable "you" of the close. The intimacy that the man-moth offers us so vulnerably becomes our responsibility as well. A reader who refuses to "pay[ ] attention" will never feel the touch of the man-moth's "cool," "pure" tear. Bishop's close binds her readers with this potential loss.

An inverted figure closes another poem written in New York the following year. "Love Lies Sleeping,"[20] which surreally juxtaposes early-

morning scenes, ends by studying the upside-down perspective of a figure
ambiguously either dead or visionary:

> for always to one, or several, morning comes,
> whose head has fallen over the edge of his bed,
>   whose face is turned
>   so that the image of
>
> the city grows down into his open eyes
> inverted and distorted. No. I mean
>   distorted and revealed,
>   if he sees it at all.

As if in conversation with herself, Bishop gradually works out the equa-
tion between the inverted and the revealed, while she shows the risk of
assuming such a connection: he may not see at all. The poem's metrics
echo its thematic irresolution. The roughly regular stanzas – two lines
of pentameter followed by two lines of trimeter – are throughout inter-
rupted by tetrameter and dimeter variations. The order of the poem must
be recognized concomitant with the disorder, the water wagon's cleaning
with the "peelings and newspapers" in its path, the preparation of the
evening meal with the cannibalism of our workaday lives – "you will
dine well/on his heart, on his, and his." The poem throughout and the
man's eyes particularly record and reveal the city's underside. Dangerous
as it is, inversion gives insight into order, as it is rejecting its supremacy
and insisting on its flexibility.

In a letter to Bishop, Anne Stevenson suggested that "the man who
'sees' is the man who sees the inverted city as correct." She then asked,
"(Is this also a play on the theory of optics?)" (28 Oct. 1963, WU).
Bishop was fascinated by Stevenson's question, and she offered her own
double-edged interpretation:

> It is odd what you say about "optics" and "Love Lies Sleeping," because
> I was reading, or had just read Newton's "Optics" about then. (Al-
> though again I wasn't aware of this until you pointed it out to me!) (I
> think the man at the end of the poem is dead.) (8 Jan. 1964, WU)

She moved from his seemingly finite close to a discussion of her work
at the Key West optical shop, clearly intrigued by the connection. In her
letter as in her poem, she allows for the possibility of inversion as a
means to revelation. That he does not see because he is dead is challenged
by the vitality of inversion, in the principles of optics and in life. The
risks of being "wrong" – death, the poison of the third rail, desertion,
halfness, morbid penetration – do not stop Bishop from repeatedly engaging subjects whose difference is their modus operandi.

In "The Prodigal,"[21] her best-known work of her Yaddo stay, the begrimed and alcoholic caretaker of a farmer's pigs is an "exile" who has chosen his sty "plastered halfway up with glass-smooth dung." Only if we are willing to enter his inverted world are we able to appreciate the spirit of the dung:

> the sunrise glazed the barnyard mud with red;
> the burning puddles seemed to reassure.
> And then he thought he almost might endure
> his exile yet another year or more.

Bishop shapes the vision in a tight double sonnet that seems directly to contrast the dishevelment of the subject. The outward form holds intact the pain, alienation, and bitterness, and it loads the closing lines with the tension and force of understatement:

> But it took him a long time
> finally to make his mind up to go home.

When one reads the word *home* in Bishop's writing, one is always tempted to shrug and add, as Bishop did later in "Questions of Travel," "wherever that may be." As David Kalstone points out in "Prodigal Years," *home* is rare in this poem, in having no true rhyme; *time* is the only other such line ending. Even when there seems to be a home behind the word, it is not a place to return to, a satisfactory terminus.[22] The prodigal manifests his defiant dismissal of what he interprets as an option to "go home" by embracing, even with lackluster, a life that seems to our world's sensibility inhuman. But as Kalstone, again, suggests, this sty becomes all the domesticity the world of the poem will know. Here there is "the violent mother (the sow that always ate her young) and the loving grandfatherly farmer who seals his animals comfortably in their Ark. One is a child's nightmare; the other, a child's fantasy of security, threats reduced to the faint forked lightnings caught by the pitchforks" ("Prodigal Years" 188). Uncritical because the sty's air is "too close [. . .] for him to judge" and because judging might lead him to repulsion he can ill afford, the prodigal finds a measure of comfort in this life, as well as the companionship he needs.

He does so, we find on closer scrutiny, within a highly irregular sonnet. Occasionally iambic, the lines are as often a mix of trochees, spondees, dactyls, and anapests. Usually in pentameter, they have as few as three and as many as six stresses. The closing line about going home is odd not only because the final word is a return to no rhyme in the poem, but also because the stresses are unconvincing. The spondee that concludes the poem – "go home" – stands in defiance of the sonnet form's iambic expectations. This is a close so overinsistently final that it leads to more doubt. Just as we question the happiness of the "happy, happy love!" in "Ode on a Grecian Urn" because Keats is too insistent in his expression of it, we must realize the notion of home as a wholly unresolved one here. The prodigal's unjudgmental acceptance of the barn's squalor engenders his "shuddering insights" into its subtle emotional shifts, the "reassur[ing]" tones of the sun-reflecting puddles or the "uncertain[ty]" of the bats' flight. Like the man-moth, the prodigal's exile and his vulnerability teach him empathy, even with "the sow that always ate her young." "Home," like the "appropriate glass" that might show off the interior as "wrong," represents here an ambivalent alternative to the rawness and alienation that elicit love.

Bishop did not shift easily from the imagined intimacies of alienated figures to the articulated intimacy of lovers. In part, we can attribute the rarity of love poems in her corpus to her privacy throughout her life, which extended even to her personal correspondences. The most complete record of a romantic relationship in the 1940s can be found in the letters from Marjorie Stevens to Bishop (Bishop's were either destroyed or simply never found). Moving back and forth between Key West and New York from 1938 until 1947, Bishop lived mostly with Stevens when she was in Florida. Stevens's often semiweekly, emotionally intimate letters to Bishop through much of the 1940s were usually turbulent; the distance was always troubling. Bishop suffered repeated asthmatic breakdowns following Stevens's visits to New York, and Stevens expressed constant worry about Bishop's emotional health. Moore's letters to Bishop during these years show concern as well, though their correspondence was much more scattered, since they visited often when both were living in New York. Other relationships can be only vaguely documented: Bishop vacationed in Wiscasset, Maine, with Tom Wanning in May and June 1948 before staying with Lowell and Carley Dawson at Stonington in July. Lowell fell in love with her that summer, and, as occasional letters and poems over the next couple of decades reveal, he never wholly lost that feeling. The facts about whether or not these poet-friends were romantically involved, however, await disclosure.[23] She saw "a great deal of Hyman" Bloom at Yaddo (letter to Lowell, [early 1950], HL). Atop a drafted love poem in her notebook, "Crossing the Equator," she wrote the initials "P. P. H." She was a close friend of Pauline Pfeifer Hemingway, living in her home for a couple of months between other places in late 1948, but the initials were the closest she came to suggesting a love relationship with Hemingway.[24]

Between 1949 and 1951, Bishop published her highly abstract and allusive "Four Poems,"[25] imaging love variously as "the tumult in the heart," as "the great light cage [that] has broken up in the air,/freeing, I think, about a million birds," and as "wasted, wasted minutes that couldn't be worse,/minutes of a barbaric condescension." Whether or

not these poems suggest same-sex lovers, they are nonetheless allusive
or underarticulated, as if to protect against a lurking feature of love – its
possibility of rejection either by the lover or by the world. "O Breath,"
the last of the "Four Poems" but the first published, closes with an
assessment of intimacy true for each of these poems:

> Beneath that loved   and celebrated breast,
> silent, bored really   blindly veined,
> grieves, maybe   lives and lets
> live, passes   bets,
> something moving   but invisibly,
> and with what clamor   why restrained
> I cannot fathom   even a ripple.
> (See the thin flying   of nine black hairs
> four around one   five the other nipple,
> flying almost intolerably   on your own breath.)
> Equivocal, but what we have in common's   bound to be there,
> whatever we must own   equivalents for,
> something that maybe I   could bargain with
> and make a separate peace   beneath
> within   if never with.

Suggesting that the "ambivalent evocation" of the closing lines has something to do with Bishop's attempt, as a lesbian outsider, "to live, and
love, in two worlds" ("Outsider" 17), Adrienne Rich wisely refuses to
argue conclusively about the sexuality of these poems. Bishop's privacy
about her intimate relationships is respected by the surreal imagery, the
rejection of narrative and grammatical cohesion, and the white spaces,
which can only suggest what must be left unsaid. Removing herself
further from the difficult emotions, Bishop encouraged Swenson's, and
decades later Stevenson's, reading of the poems as "mysterious": "Any
meanings you want to attach are all right, I'm sure – the wilder the better.
It should be a sketch for an acute, neurotic, "modern" drama – or "affair",
that's all" (letter to Swenson, 6 Sept. 1955, WU), not to be mistaken,
she seems to assert, for an exploration of the specific matter of love.

Yet "O Breath" is just such an exploration, representing the underside
of the pleasurable boundary exchanging and shifting in "The Map" and
"The Gentleman of Shalott." Here, where the lover's body is realized
as a body and love recognized as love, exchange is rendered ambivalent;
even similarity amid such ambivalence can only be problematic. Love,
in most of Bishop's 1940s and early 1950s poetry, bears with it an
alienation, dependency, and defiance far in their feel from the happy
"equivalents" of "The Map" and "The Gentleman of Shalott." The
"equivocal," which on the one hand holds enormous promise for out-

siders and aberrant lovers, poses on the other as an impossible barrier to love and its articulation.

When Bishop returned to narrative to write about the equivocal inversion in "Insomnia,"[26] published a few months after the "Rain Towards Morning" poems, her tone was both bitter and defiant. She reinvokes the playful mirror of "The Gentleman of Shalott" but refuses her subject easy access to self-love and independence. Love is instead dependency; the mirror's inversion is defensive and unsatisfying:

> The moon in the bureau mirror
> looks out a million miles
> (and perhaps with pride, at herself,
> but she never, never smiles)
> far and away beyond sleep, or
> perhaps she's a daytime sleeper.
>
> By the Universe deserted,
> *she*'d tell it to go to hell,
> and she'd find a body of water,
> or a mirror, on which to dwell.
> So wrap up care in a cobweb
> and drop it down the well
>
> into that world inverted
> where left is always right,
> where the shadows are really the body,
> where we stay awake all night,
> where the heavens are shallow as the sea
> is now deep, and you love me.

The insomnia of the title signals the frustrated tone: this is sleeplessness, not late-night lovemaking. The alienated (and pointedly female) moon is wrong to a world Bishop had identified years earlier by its "thick, clear, appropriate glass," but here she responds with a posture of disinterest: "go to hell."

Bishop had an oddly coincidental dream in the summer of 1935, a few weeks before her thoughts about the appropriate glass, which renders an alienation similar to that in "Insomnia" and a competition not between lovers but between a child and her mother. In her dream a boy, at first, is sledding; mid-dream, he turns into the moon, which, in falling down the slope and through the sky, becomes herself. She lands

> in front of the drive at the house in Great Village. [. . .] My grandmother was standing near me, not paying any attention, not having even noticed that the moon had fallen from the sky. It was early, early morning. She was dressed in black silk, and was holding out in front of her with one hand a small gold watch, worn on a gold chain around her neck. (Notebook, 1 July 1935)

She falls in front of her grandmother, who fails even to notice the tragedy. Her grandmother is preoccupied by her watch and perhaps by her mourning for Bishop's mother, who had died the year before the dream. Significantly, Bishop displaces her need for recognition and approval from her mother to her grandmother; if indeed the black silk represents mourning, Bishop has relegated her mother to a position of competition. Splitting the mother in two, once again, into a needed and a competing figure, this child is left hurt and alone.

In "Insomnia" it is the lover who is split: the moon needs and rejects the world; the "me" desires yet depends on the "you." By italicizing the moon's gender Bishop makes this explicitly a poem about female anger and frustration. This moon conceives of stereotypically female means – coaxing, preening, bitchiness, feigned disinterest, and finally a flight into fancy – as alternatives to the pain of alienation. She lacks utterly the gentleman of Shalott's aplomb, but she refuses to end, like him, alone. Examining contemporary female poetic expressions of anger, Alicia Ostriker argues in *Stealing the Language* that

> the violence, the bitterness, the self-mockery, the sense of absurd entrapment, along with the smoldering nonresignation [. . .], suggest that the secret desire encoded in women's anger poems is a desire to imagine precisely what cannot be imagined within the poems themselves. The stronger the poems, the more emphatically dualistic they are – and the more they convey to a reader that the pattern of dualism is intolerable. (163)

Bishop works anger through understatement. Her touch is light; the poem's angry assertions depend on soft tones, subtle rhymes and metrics, and a lilt of feminine endings; the poem glides into the harsh close with an enjambment. Yet defiance, hostility, and the hatred that is potentially the inverse or reflection in the well of "you love me" lurk behind the lyrical, moony quality of the poem and embitter the moon's effort to "wrap up care in a cobweb."

Of course, the more direct inversion of the closing line is "I love you." The closing line, emptied of its paired opposite, is an expression of longing and loneliness very different in tone from the aggressive stance of "go to hell," yet hearkening back to it, because the spondaic stresses of both lines, in the assertion of the moon's gender and in the call for love, break pattern in their insistence. The poem is ambivalent. Frustration and anger – "go to hell" – erect the barriers to "inverted" love and its incumbent pain; the lover's whisper – "and you love me" – lurks, quietly compelling.

As in her villanelle, "One Art," which reveals only in the closing stanza the greatest loss of the poem, the "you," and, as in "The Man-

Moth," whose closing appeal to "you" is its most vulnerable and most potentially intimate, "Insomnia" delays this painful ambivalence by introducing the "you" and "me" only in the last line. Seeming to offer resolution, the final clause arises as if contextless to fill the poem's void. Yet the clause is, finally, grammatically contingent on the series of conditional clauses that precede it, each of them hanging onto the one above, as if actually on the cobweb in the well. Weighted with contingency, they are moonlike – satellites rather than suns – relational creatures, after all, depending on this equivocal love.

Though she published few love poems during these years, her two 1940s Key West notebooks reveal that she repeatedly took on the challenge of articulating love's frustrations and desires. Apparent in many of these poems is a general malaise she labeled "tact and embarassment" or, alternately, "fear and embarassment" and that she attempted to define further: "EMBARASSMENT – (they'll go together) (of suddenly realizing you're alone with the person you're loving – just 'you two', etc. Usually all yr. thoughts spread out, fan-like, & protect you from that sort of embarassment.)" The image of one's thoughts shielding one's emotions is socially practical but, as Bishop says earlier on the page, "too sad." Once again we can only conjecture whether these reactions were engendered by the conflicting urges themselves toward privacy and toward intimate self-exposure, or whether, when Bishop loved a woman, as she did consistently until the late 1940s and as some of these drafted poems seem to reflect, social censure dictated self-silencing as the most viable option.

The most finished poem about this latter frustration appears particularly to concern the secrecy imposed on lesbian love by a watchful world:

Should rhyme

I had a bad dream,
toward morning, about you.
You lay unconscious
It was to be
for "24 hrs."
Wrapped in a long blanket
I felt I must hold you
even though a "host of guests"
might come in from the garden
at a minute
& see us lying
with my arms around you
& my cheek on yours.
It was warm – but I had to
prevent you

from slippping away
from your body your cheek
from the wound-round blanket. –
            grave dark morning
Thinking of you
a thousand miles away,
how I tried to hold you
with the numb arm of a dream

  in the deep of the morning
            the day coming
that loneliness like falling on
  the sidewalk in a crowd
that fills {   } {   } with shame,   some
            slow, elaborate shame.
the sidewalk rises rises
  like absolute despair[27]

Once again, she wrote "fear & embarassment" at the bottom of another
drafted version of this poem. This is a loneliness and a love that are
embarrassing, like falling, making public what should not be, or so
Bishop characterizes it. The poem cannot sustain the dream's defiance –
putting her arm around her lover regardless of the public perception –
into its waking realizations. Awake, she is left with loss, and with her
distance from her lover that is marked by more than the "thousand miles"
between New York and Florida, Stevens's home. Distance alone would
not make for embarrassment, nor would dreaming that one is holding
one's lover, especially if she is unconscious and needing assistance. Bishop
represents loss of a lesbian lover and the publicity of that loss, however,
as a succumbing to "fear & embarassment," because this loneliness,
particularly in midcentury America, must be kept to oneself. One cannot
write love poetry about it; Bishop never did revise this poem to make
it rhyme, as she had directed herself to do, and she had no intention of
publishing it. It served her, nonetheless, as did her poems of outsider-
hood, as a ground for exploration. If she was to write the poetry of a
different love, one not founded in frustration and alienation or in hierarchies and opposition, she had first to work through the terms of intimacy as she found them.

    One poem in the Key West notebooks rare for its simple positivity
begins with a moment of balanced love:

    It is marvellous to wake up together
    At the same minute; marvellous to hear
    The rain begin suddenly all over the roof,
    To feel the air suddenly clear
    As if electricity had passed through it

From a black mesh of wires in the sky.
All over the roof the rain hisses,
And below, the light falling of kisses.

An electrical storm is coming or moving away;
It is the prickling air that wakes us up.
If lightning struck the house now, it would run
From the four blue china balls on top
Down the roof and down the rods all around us,
And we imagine dreamily
How the whole house caught in a bird-cage of lightning
Would be quite delightful rather than frightening;

And from the same simplified point of view
Of night and lying flat on one's back
All things might change equally easily,
Since always to warn us there must be these black
Electrical wires dangling. Without surprise
The world might change to something quite different,
    As the air changes or the lightning comes without our blinking,
Change as our kisses are changing without our thinking.[28]

The lovers wake up together and feel together the sensations of the storm
and each other. The passion is reciprocal; the images are not mired in
shame, nor in helpless dependency, nor in narcissistic remove. A "we"
and an "us" are perfectly possible and can perfectly represent the mutuality of responses of lovers to an electricity both outside in the storm
and between them in their passion. The closing rhymes of each stanza –
"hisses"–"kisses"; "lightning"–"frightening"; "blinking"–"thinking" –
confirm these relations; the whole poem is set during a waking, rather
than a dreaming, moment. Relationality is wholly benign, as if in thrilling
defiance of the difficulties from within and without that Bishop met
whenever she faced the writing of love. Yet no matter how much she
might rework the details of the poem, she could never publish it, and
that required and hovering silence is intrinsic to the thrill of the poem's
exposure. When "The Map" figured the shared subjectivity of lovers, it
did so safely; when this poem does, it threatens dangerous and forbidden
disclosure. Here she could sketch a bed in the corner of a typed draft,
but at the same time she must relegate the poem to her private notebook.
In perhaps a final irony, Bishop knew that when this and the other
unfinished love poems in these notebooks were seen – when Linda Nemer
would sell the notebooks to a private library – they would command a
fine price. After her death, when the literary world had paid up, scholars
could pore through her thrilling secrets. Until then, she knew, her revisions of sexual subjectivity must remain encoded, "mysterious," as she
wrote Swenson and Stevenson about "Four Poems."

Writing love into a published poem was a process of deleting the explicit, especially the explicitly lesbian, and infusing the particularities of that love into relations among the poem's images. Bishop wrote "The Shampoo" in Brazil several years later but included it as the last poem of *A Cold Spring*.[29] She was by the early 1950s settling into comfortable domesticity with Lota de Macedo Soares. Theirs was an intimacy, the poem suggests, that ranged from the seeming immutability of lichens' growth to the volatility of shooting stars:

> The still explosions on the rocks,
> the lichens, grow
> by spreading, gray, concentric shocks.
> They have arranged
> to meet the rings around the moon, although
> within our memories they have not changed.
>
> And since the heavens will attend
> as long on us,
> you've been, dear friend,
> precipitate and pragmatical;
> and look what happens. For Time is
> nothing if not amenable.
>
> The shooting stars in your black hair
> in bright formation
> are flocking where,
> so straight, so soon?
> – Come, let me wash it in this big tin basin,
> battered and shiny like the moon.

The quiet explosions and proliferation of lichen provide Bishop an opening for representing the complexity of an aging passion. She would again invest lichen with the passion of the poem in "Song for the Rainy Season" and "Brazil, January 1, 1502"; the relationship between rocks and lichen is articulable and publishable. But this love involves more than these "still explosions." It consists, too, of a homier tenderness; it encompasses both the passion and the pragmatics of daily life. When the "dear friend" becomes too impatient with the latter and, as Bishop suggested in draft form, the former – "But you, so voluble, so volatile / by night, by day" – the lover can soothe with a gentle hair wash.

"Lota," Bishop wrote May Swenson,

> has straight long black hair. – I hadn't seen her for six years or so when
> I came here and when we looked at each ooher she was horrified to see
> I had gone very gray, and I that she had two silver streaks on each side,
> quite wide. Once I got used to it I liked it – (19 Sept. 1953, WU)

As it was not in "The Map," the natural setting of this poem is less metaphor for than companion to the relationship between women. Even still, Lota could not appear as Lota in "The Shampoo"; the direct address to "Meu amor," which preceded the last two lines in an early draft had to be removed. This was a poem, finally, to a "dear friend." Bishop's care not to be explicit led May Swenson to respond:

> I like it very much, but can't really grasp it – that is, it feels like something has been left out – but this makes it better, in a way . . . a mysteriousness, although the expression is perfectly straightforward. (14 Sept. 1953, WU)

What Bishop has left out are simply the most obvious terms naming this sexuality. And here, precisely, is part of its revisionary power. This is a sexuality too fluid for demarcation, "spreading" when one least expects it beyond definitions and the borders between lovers. Passions here are sometimes volatile, sometimes quiet, sometimes thoroughly mutual, sometimes seemingly oppositional. Love can be found at any surprising moment, the poem asserts, closing in a very daily sort of intimacy. Here, as in "The Map" almost twenty years earlier, her love poem need not set into opposition sexual spilling and containing, nor the shooting of stars and the encompassing familiarity of the moony basin.

Yet Bishop has brought the lovers into this poem, along with their playful and generous intimacy, and this transgression cost her her audience. Bishop had sent the poem to Swenson in the first place, she wrote, because she wondered if Swenson would see its great flaw:

> It has been turned down both by the New Yorker and Poetry, and although I don't think it's world-shaking, I can't quite figure out why – it seems perfectly clear to me, and rather pretty. So please tell me exactly what you think. (10 Aug. 1953, WU)

Bishop liked the draft she sent to Swenson; she appreciated Swenson's praise of it. When she did publish the poem, she changed only a single verb tense – "look what happened" to "look what happens." Nonetheless, when Swenson again praised the poem after receiving her copy of *A Cold Spring*, Bishop responded that the reception of "The Shampoo" had been consistent silence:

> No one but you and one other friend have ever even mentioned The Shampoo, I don't know why – I sent it to a few friends and never heard a word and began to think there was something indecent about it I'd overlooked. Marianne among others, – She also thought that Insomnia was like a "blues" song – which I wish it were, but I think she meant something rather different and not a bit complimentary! I'm afraid she never can face the tender passion (6 Sept. 1955, WU)

Bishop claimed not to know why the *New Yorker* and *Poetry* had turned
the poem down and why her friends had not responded, except that, as
she suggested sarcastically, "there was something indecent about it."
Although both she and Swenson were living with women, they never
addressed the subject of lesbianism in their letters to each other. Intimate
as were their letters, she would be no more explicit, nor would Swenson
be in her September 1953 letter, about what Bishop has "left out" of the
poem and what she has put in that is a "mysteriousness" not mysterious
enough for some audiences. In terms of its imagery and metrics, its
sound, and its playfulness, "The Shampoo" is similar to the kind of
poem Bishop was publishing and of which friends and editors were
approving throughout these years. Its "tender passion," though, the
rhythms of love that, however discretely, suggest another woman, is a
departure. Very likely this "indecen[cy]" was cause enough for her
friends' silence and the editors' rejections, even though the "dear friend's"
gender is never itself mentioned.

Closing Bishop's second book of poetry, "The Shampoo" ushered in
a confidence about representing her own intimacy that was new to Bishop's writing, yet when she selected poems for *Questions of Travel,* her
first book written in Brazil, she included *A Cold Spring*'s penultimate
poem, "Arrival at Santos," but left out "The Shampoo." Throughout
her early poetry Bishop is ambivalent about representing the tensions,
pain, desire, and passion of intimate relationships. We can attribute to
her shyness and privacy Bishop's setting of these poems in nature, in
fantasy and dream, and among a range of odd characters who articulate
silenced emotions. Or we can explore the options these subjects provided
Bishop in her effort to revise the nature of poetic subjectivity. From her
first major poem forward, she rejected clear-cut distinctions between self
and other, subject and object, mother and daughter, lover and beloved:
normalcy, aberrance, control, passivity, dependence, and assertion mark
all sides of the unhelpful boundaries. Defamiliarizing her poetic subjects
simply allowed Bishop to work the complexities of those intimacies
without baring herself. A man–moth and a pig's caretaker offer ground
on which to explore the emotions of the outsider, his empathy and his
effort toward connection; a map, a mirror, and an electrical storm enact
the passions and frustrations of same-sex lovers; an invasive weed and a
speaker in a stupor give Bishop the language for the terrible boundary
confusion in her own relationship with her mother. A crafted invitation
to Moore lets her play freely with her relationship with her mentor. As
the silence surrounding "The Shampoo" attests, however, Bishop's
friends and editors might relish the beautiful, controlled objectivity of
Bishop's early verse, and they might even be moved by a man–moth's
or a pig's caretaker's inversions, but they were not prepared to accept

an expression of inverted love relations that might reveal their poet. As Bishop was writing her first two books of poetry in the 1930s and 1940s, she was discovering just how much her subjects could lean over into each other's territory, without becoming too possessive, too dependent, or too revealing of their affection, just how much she could revise cultural assumptions without making her poems unpublishable, and just how close her poem's images could be to her own experiences, without seeming "indecent" to her readers. Discovering how to enact the subject in process and in relation entailed for Bishop negotiating among the complex layers of intimacy that constituted any subject. As her poetry of daily, intimate relationships achieves a public dimension, I will argue in the next chapter, it dovetails with her more public poetry, which, despite its embodiment of political concerns in the 1930s and 1940s, sought never to lose sight of its personal ground springs.

3

Turning History Under

In one of her first major "independent" publishing ventures, Bishop sent "In Prison" to *Partisan Review* in January 1938 when they wrote her asking for a story. They were sponsoring a $100 contest, Bishop informed Moore, almost apologizing for story and submission both:

> I finished a story a few days ago which I wanted to send to you to see what you thought of it – but I had just received a letter from the "Partisan Review" asking for a story by February 1st, if possible. I sent it to them and now of course regret it very much and hope they will send it back. My motives were doubly corrupt: they are going to have a $100. "contest" and I thought I should like to try. It is called "In Prison" and is another one of these horrible "fable" ideas that seem to obsess me – (31 Jan. 1938, V:05:01, RM)

Slightly wounded, Moore replied: "It was very independent of you to submit your prize story without letting me see it. If it is returned with a printed slip, that will be why" (10 Feb. 1938, V:05:01, RM). The story did not win the prize but was given special note and published in *Partisan Review*'s March issue.[1] Reading the published version, Moore was both admirer and mentor:

> Never have I [. . .] seen a more insidiously innocent and artless artifice of innuendo than in your prison meditations. The use of immediate experience and of reading is most remarkable, – the potent retiringness, the close observation and interassociating of the circumstantial with the exotic; your mention of the Turkey carpets and the air bubble of potential freedom; the leaves and the inoffensive striping of the uniforms. All this should be ever present consolation to you, I think, for any hard spots in progress; I am much hampered, in fact, in what I say, for fear of spoiling you.
>   On the other hand, [. . .] I feel that although large-scale "substance" runs the risk of inconsequence through aesthetic impotence, and am one of those who despise clamor about substance – to whom treatment

74

really is substance – I can't help wishing that you would sometime in some way, risk some unprotected profundity of experience; or since noone admits profundity of experience, some characteristic private defiance of the significantly detestable. Continuously fascinated as I am by the creativeness and uniqueness of these assemblings of yours – which are really poems – I feel responsibility against anything that might threaten you; yet fear to admit such anxiety, lest I influence you away from an essential necessity or particular strength. The golden eggs can't be dealt with theoretically, by presumptuous mass salvation formulae. But I do feel that tentativeness and interiorizing are your danger as well as your strength. (1 May 1938, V:05:01, RM)

Moore praised the gusto of Bishop's prose and images but was dissatisfied with her moral hesitancy. Though Moore did not specify any political or philosophical agenda – if indeed she had one here – Bishop responded by justifying both her method and her politics.

She thanked Moore for "read[ing] my mind so well" and attempted to explain the aesthetic distancing of her story's vision: "It is the 1st conscious attempt at something according to a theory I've been thinking up down here – out of a combination of Poe's theories and reading 17th century prose!" (5 May 1938, V:05:01, RM). "In Prison" does have the attention to form of "The Philosophy of Composition", which is for Poe in that piece the necessity at the source of creation. It is likely she had Thomas Browne in mind as her seventeenth-century inspiration: the prisoner-to-be chooses for his cobblestone courtyard a "lozenge design" (*Prose* 187), Browne's choice precisely for his quincuncial garden in "The Garden of Cyrus." Like Poe and Browne, Bishop tests theories here about ordering one's creative frame as a means for giving order to one's world.

At the same time she recognized her stalling mechanism, her turn to theory as protection from the "spotted, helter-skelter thing it seems so easy to fall into." Whether or not Moore was indeed encouraging Bishop to stake her claim amid the passionate discussions in the late 1930s of communism, socialism, individualism, militancy generally and the rising fascism particularly, Bishop felt responsible for some such self-assertion. As she continued in her letter to Moore, she was trying to avoid the "short-sighted and, I think, ignorant, views" of poets and thinkers around her who rally to causes and give over their art to them. Rather, Bishop saw herself as often frustratedly perched on the fringes of current political movements, calling herself "a 'Radical' of course," but at the same time complaining of her own "bafflement," "not knowing what stand to take" in the face of the political imperatives around her.[2] Fittingly, Bishop's would-be prisoner opts to "rebel" not under the force of pressures around him but with the force of his own imagination. With a Poe-like tone of self-justification in the face of his reader's potential cynicism, the narrator of "In Prison" records in careful detail his preparations for the imagined, desired imprisonment. Prison, he predicts, will give him the sense of necessity his current "hotel existence" lacks; one must, he asserts, "be *in*"; one's bounds must be clearly defined if one is to have any freedom. This prisoner's freedom, then, would consist of the choices he makes about his reading material, his cell's coloring, decor, and view, and his own position among the prison community. The "commentary" he scratches on the walls and leaves as a "legacy," his dress, and his affects would be his means to mark himself as "just a little different," "rebellious perhaps, but in shades and shadows" (182, 188–9).

Through this narrator, Bishop is able to assert a vital stance of her own. In an essay on Bishop's geography, Jan Gordon discusses Bishop's distrust of "history" in terms that apply equally well to her sidestepping of political stances. Whereas he claims that she simply dismisses history in both "In Prison" and "The Map," I will argue in this chapter that Bishop accepts a history pragmatically redefined, a history whose constructions are understood as flexible and interpretable, as the map's names are. Defining what she means to be "*in*" prison, for instance, she illustrates a South where day laborers toil at menial tasks at the behest of someone in firm power over them; she shows that the only difference between them and actual prisoners is that they "have hung over their lives the perpetual irksomeness of all half-measures, of 'not knowing where one is at'" (182–3). Gordon argues that "in the environment where every intersection is a corner, there is virtually no lineage. [. . .] Since time has virtually disappeared, there is no meaning, save in the shade or the nuance." He sees multiplicity of direction as loss of both direction and meaning (10–13). But the pragmatic vision of the prisoner-to-be and of Bishop is a revision of these terms. Wishing not to take a stand, write an "immortal[ ] poem," rebel overtly or definitively, the prisoner-to-be wants to live a life of inquiry and commentary, where he would play a small but significant role in a much larger reading of life (188–9).

The pressure to be ideological surrounded Bishop in the 1930s, especially, but Bishop spent the period observing and learning from her friends' political positions, particularly those on the Left, rather than claiming her own. At Vassar, as she told Ashley Brown in her 1966 interview, she considered herself a socialist, but she always "disliked 'social conscious' writing." She was bothered by the ease with which Vassar women who knew nothing about social conditions took up the socialist cause: "It was the popular thing" (293). In New York among politically minded acquaintances like Edmund Wilson and Mary Mc-

Carthy and in Europe with Louise Crane, who championed the leftist cause in the Spanish civil war, Bishop remained a reader and observer of political and social stances. Even when the Reich's activities in the late 1930s began to be recorded daily by American newspapers, as were the seemingly worldwide preparations for war, Bishop did not follow the lead of writers and intellectuals around her in condemning militarism or Nazi Germany.

While I read Bishop's neutrality less as a political intention than as a deep, personal frustration, I am at the same time convinced by her poetry and stories that her position at the fringes allowed her to turn the claims of history and politics under so as to explore the individual subjects determined by and intertwined with those world events, but living them daily. If, as William James asserts, pragmatism "stands for no particular results, [. . .] has no dogmas, and no doctrines save its method [. . . , and] lies in the midst of our theories, like a corridor in a hotel" (380), then Bishop's was a pragmatism taken to its ordinary, human ends. Fascinated with the intersections where cultural memories, dreams, or fears, and people in their daily lives meet for brief but insightful moments, Bishop's version of the pragmatic corridor helped guide her poetry through the politicized 1930s.

At the same time, her writing served as potential "commentary" on the political views she was intrigued by: publishing "In Prison" and many other pieces over the next decade in *Partisan Review*,[3] Bishop made a decision to seek out a particularly political audience and to associate herself with writers far more leftist than herself. Bishop's "Unbeliever" and "Quai D'Orleans" were published in *Partisan Review*'s August–September 1938 issue alongside Leon Trotsky's "Art and Politics" and Victor Serge's "Marxism in Our Time." That fall, the magazine underwent a year-long name change, calling itself *Partisan Review: A Quarterly of Literature and Marxism*. Her essay on Gregorio Valdes was published in the same issue as responses by several authors to a questionnaire about the connection of writing to history and politics (Summer 1939). "The Fish" followed Stephen Spender's war chronicle, "September Journal," in the March–April 1940 issue. Like the leaves in the river in "Quai D'Orleans," drifting but always leaving fossils, and at the same time like the observers at the shore, apart from the downward pull of barge and water but caught by their vision, Bishop maintained an ambivalent position, both somewhat removed from and somewhat in the fray of the political and historical moment. Within that doubled position she explored the private consciousnesses and private behaviors that spur and reflect world events – the undercurrents of emotion, the sense of superiority and inferiority, the fear and militarism, and the desire for love and community that motivate ordinary people in their relationships with one another. She sidestepped the ideologies even of the journal in which she published by exploring the private emotions and daily conflicts that undergird them. In this chapter I will explore Bishop's early writing nominally set in a public arena, so as to unpack this relational reading of history, in which all her subjects are personally implicated. When one refuses to isolate a world war from the destructiveness lurking in the unconscious or from the potential warring of lovers in bed, one distorts history at the same time as one revises one's perception of it. Lovers in bed, one might argue, have not slaughtered millions; on the other hand, one might respond, if we do not insist on understanding ourselves where we are, we will not know what is alive, once we have counted the losses of war. Though some of her poems of the 1930s and 1940s border on the sentimental, she trusts that language can make manifest a vitally relational history and politics by recording the ordinary, underarticulated emotions of her subjects.

As she revealed in her "In Prison" letter to Moore, Bishop was for the most part unable to articulate her own pragmatic turning and believed with Moore that her subtlety was instead a lack of commitment. Thus, periodically through the 1930s and early 1940s, she made intentional, self-conscious forays into the public arena. She referred to "A Miracle for Breakfast," about poverty and hunger in the mid-1930s in New York, as her "'social conscious' poem" (Brown 297). In the most famous exchange with Marianne Moore, in which Bishop would overwhelm Moore with her "defiance of the significantly detestable" and which would lead to a vital revision of their mentor–student relationship (Keller, "Words" 422–4), Bishop defended "Roosters" against Moore's attack of its aesthetics, because she felt her message about war was best served by "what (I think) is a very important 'violence' of tone" (17 Oct. 1940, V:05:02, RM). Her effort to write about the situation of African-Americans and Cubans in Key West, which she did in "Jerónimo's House," "Cootchie," "Songs for a Colored Singer," and "Faustina, or Rock Roses," often took on a sense of assignment. Writing to Moore about Auden's *Another Time,* she praised his "Schoolchildren" and "Spain 1937" but wrote that "the 'colored songs' [part of a group he calls "Cabaret Songs"] I want to try to better myself . . !" (14 Mar. 1940, V:05:02, RM). The draft material of a poem about Hannah Almyda, her semi-literate housekeeper, includes many pages of specific, humorous examples of Mrs. Almyda's phrases and habits, crossed out with the word "stiff" written over them. The last draft she was to work on is strictly allusive; a bird building a nest and caring for its young is all that remains to signify the housekeeper. In several letters of 1939–40, especially, Bishop apologized to Moore for not sending any writing, but she was simply dissatisfied with her products. As she wrote in one letter characteristic of this period's slump, "It seems to be so hard to finish anything these days – there seems to be so much that ought to be put into everything one writes, nothing but 'last words' are good enough" (10 July 1940, V:05:02, RM). Bishop felt pressured by the New York leftist intellectual circle from which she could not wholly break, by the war industry in Key West, and by the great poverty there to be a writer in the world.

Though she did write about the war, as I will show, in personal ways, she nonetheless felt that she needed to preface *North & South* with an apology for the absence of war verse. She sent the following request to Ferris Greenslet at Houghton Mifflin:

> The fact that none of these poems deal directly with the war, at a time when so much war poetry is being published, will, I am afraid, leave me open to reproach. The chief reason is simply that I work very slowly. But I think it would help some if a note to the effect that most of the poems had been written, or begun at least before 1941, could be inserted at the beginning, say just after the acknowledgments. I'll enclose a sheet with the acknowledgments and such a note, to see what you think. (22 Jan. 194[6], HL)

The note in *North & South* reads as follows: "Most of these poems were written, or partly written, before 1942." In the wake of a world war that demanded immediate, practical response, Bishop was concerned her readers would not see the integrity, even at times the historically determined integrity, of her seemingly ahistorical verse.

On reading Moore's "The Paper Nautilus" in 1940, Bishop located her own poetic struggle:

> There are so many things in it I'd like to thank you for and praise you for – I admire especially from "wasp-nest flaws – of white on white" to the end. The whole poem is like a rebuke to me, it suggests so many of the plans for the things I want to say about Key West and have scarcely hinted at in "José's House" [her original title of "Jerónimo's House"] for example. (Letter to Moore, 21 May 1940, V:05:02, RM)

The paper nautilus is one of Moore's menagerie of armored animals. The poem focuses entirely on this nautilus's watching and hatching of her eggs within her shell. Their birth is her purpose and the poem opens by making it clear that she has no time for anything but this act of love:

> For authorities whose hopes
> are shaped by mercenaries?
>   Writers entrapped by
>   teatime fame and by
> commuters' comforts? Not for these
>   the paper nautilus
>   constructs her thin glass shell. (*CP* 121)

Moore concludes the poem with the eggs' hatching, in lines that Bishop said she admired especially:

> leaving its wasp-nest flaws
> of white on white, and close-
>
> laid Ionic chiton-folds
> like the lines in the mane of
> a Parthenon horse,
> round which the arms had
> wound themselves as if they knew love
> is the only fortress
> strong enough to trust to. (122)

Bishop echoed Moore, calling her Jerónimo's home his "love-nest" and, alternatively, his "gray wasps' nest," decades before she would close her Brazilian poem "Santarém" with the relationship formed around the wasps' nest of an Amazonian pharmacist. She was especially attracted to these closing lines in Moore's wartime poem, which are invested with not only the paper nautilus's love but also Moore's own. Bishop's effective political poetry of these years works in ways similar to Moore's "Paper Nautilus": intuiting the destructive impulses and selfish ends with which we enact the events of history as well as the compensatory power of love and humor, Bishop creates at the intersection of these impulses.

Differences, however, between Moore's and Bishop's poetry became more and more fundamental during these years. Bishop's poem to Moore – "Invitation to Miss Marianne Moore" – which chronologically follows several of Bishop's people and persona poems, pays tribute not only to their enduring friendship, but also to the distance Bishop has moved from Moore poetically. Moore did not trust her language to embody herself or any person directly. She relied on allusion and always had a paper nautilus or an octopus of ice at the ready. When she did put before her a real person, she turned to his or her effects, the "gray-eyed and straight-haired" Swedish woman's cart in "A Carriage from Sweden" (CP 131) or the layers of quotation of whatever author or public figure she was discussing in her prose essays. Bare language itself was ineffective or dangerous. Understanding poetry's power differently, Bishop was learning to expose human emotions to her innate ability at precise observation. Forcing her way with "bafflement" through her own reticence, taking some unsuccessful risks, she began in the late 1930s to demand that her writing reveal people in their desires, struggles, and pain. She shows in the very frustration of her letters to Moore an implicit trust that writing could have this power.[4]

Bishop's first poetic foray into the arena of poverty and social injustice developed out of personal anecdote and was carefully wrought as a sestina. "A Miracle for Breakfast" reflects Bishop's confusion about her own position as well as her skill at reading an issue of public concern, such as the poverty brought on by years of economic depression, in terms that render both the oddness and the complex power relations of the human dynamic:

At six o'clock we were waiting for coffee,
waiting for coffee and the charitable crumb
that was going to be served from a certain balcony,
– like kings of old, or like a miracle.
It was still dark. One foot of the sun
steadied itself on a long ripple in the river.

The first ferry of the day had just crossed the river.
It was so cold we hoped that the coffee
would be very hot, seeing that the sun
was not going to warm us; and that the crumb
would be a loaf each, buttered, by a miracle.
At seven a man stepped out on the balcony.

He stood for a minute alone on the balcony
looking over our heads toward the river.
A servant handed him the makings of a miracle,
consisting of one lone cup of coffee
and one roll, which he proceeded to crumb,
his head, so to speak, in the clouds – along with the sun.

Was the man crazy? What under the sun
was he trying to do, up there on his balcony!
Each man received one rather hard crumb,
which some flicked scornfully into the river,
and, in a cup, one drop of the coffee.
Some of us stood around, waiting for the miracle.

I can tell what I saw next; it was not a miracle.
A beautiful villa stood in the sun
and from its doors came the smell of hot coffee.
In front, a baroque white plaster balcony
added by birds, who nest along the river,
– I saw it with one eye close to the crumb –

and galleries and marble chambers. My crumb
my mansion, made for me by a miracle,
through ages, by insects, birds, and the river
working the stone. Every day, in the sun,
at breakfast time I sit on my balcony
with my feet up, and drink gallons of coffee.

> We licked up the crumb and swallowed the coffee.
> A window across the river caught the sun
> as if the miracle were working, on the wrong balcony.[5]

Neither of Bishop's two statements about the poem captures the dynamic operating among its members. When writing to Moore, Bishop stated her intentions for "A Miracle for Breakfast" as clearly artistic. It was her first sestina, and she had ideas about what she wanted to do with the sestina form. Though she wrote to Moore that "the sestina is just a sort of stunt" (15 Sept. 1936, V:04:30, RM), when Moore pressed her with criticism of specific words, especially disliking the closeness of the "sun"–"crumb" terminations (22 Dec. 1936, VC), Bishop responded by setting forth her strategy:

> The "crumb" and "sun" is of course its greatest fault. It seems to me that there are two ways possible for a sestina – one is to use unusual words as terminations, in which case they would have to be used differently as often as possible – as you say, "change of scale." That would make a very highly season kind of poem. And the other way is to use as colorless words as possible – like Sydney, so that it becomes less of a trick and more of a natural theme and variations. I guess I have tried to do both at once. It is probably just an excuse, but sometimes I think about certain things that without one particular fault they would be without the means of existence. I feel a little that way about "sun" and "crumb!" (5 Jan. 1937, V:04:31, RM)

Discussing her poem *as* form with Moore, Bishop is highly conscious of the implications of her choices. If the sun's miraculous rising gives substance to the crumb, then the dailiness in the two words together produces an existence beyond either: inexplicably, a crumb in the sun is a mansion.

Such a surrealistic transformation, however, has apparently little to do with Bishop's other statement of intent in her 1966 interview with Ashley Brown: "Oh, that's my Depression poem. It was written shortly after the time of souplines and men selling apples, around 1936 or so. It was my 'social conscious' poem, a poem about hunger" (297). Brown responds by trying to coax her into discussing the surrealist backdrop of the poem, but she has nothing more to say about it. She has earlier in the interview (293) been disdainful of "social conscious" writing, and her tone here flips this poem aside as a representative of precisely that.

"A Miracle for Breakfast" does have its moralistic element, heavy-handed at times. Some of its lines, "his head, so to speak, in the clouds – along with the sun," for example, read like caricatures of the earnest Depression poem.[6] But if the poem has shades of an argument about proletarian hunger in the face of bourgeois wealth and power, it is immediately problematized by the speaker's doubled position. Supposedly beneath the balcony among the hungry, the speaker is at the same time an observer, who can look around and away. Turning toward the river, she sees that another "miracle" is taking place: "One foot of the sun [of Christ?]/steadied itself on a long ripple in the river." Preferring the natural or biblical miracle to the sordid human activity before her, the speaker looks away, here and again in the last stanza. In this respect, she is implicated along with the "miracle" maker, the server of coffee and crumb. She, too, looks over the heads of the hungry, "toward the river" and the sunrise; if her vision – her own imaginatively constructed miracle -- were to occur, it would place her in a mansion, her head perhaps also in the clouds and her "feet up" on the balcony, where she would drink her "gallons of coffee." The title itself makes ironic the Christian allusion: the miracle is not in Christ's walking on the water or in creating the loaves and fishes; it is in the position of power and remove that she achieves, looking away from the hungry.

Yet the position is complicated once again, when we consider the poem's anecdotal origin. Two years before the poem's publication, Bishop recorded what she called "A Little Miracle" in her notebook:

> This morning I discovered I had forgotten to get any bread and I had only one dry crust for breakfast. I was resigning myself to orange juice and coffee and no more when the door-bell rang, I pushed the button, and up the stairs trailed a wary-looking woman, shouting ahead of herself: "I don't want to sell you anything – I want to give you something!" I welcomed her at that, and was presented with a small box containing three slices of "Wonder Bread" all fresh, a rye, a white, and whole-wheat. Also a miniature loaf of bread besides – The only thing I disliked about the gift was that the woman opened the box, held it under my nose, and said "Smell how sweet!" But I breakfasted on manna – (Following note dated 10 Jan. 1935)

She was not starving; she had simply forgotten to buy bread, and orange juice and coffee would have sufficed until she got to the store. Since the Wonder Bread representative appeared just at the breakfast hour, Bishop got breakfast and her stance on high. Her benefactor, though, had warily to climb the stairs, defend her presence, and display her desirable offering for scrutiny. All the power, finally, is Bishop's. To translate this scene into a "social conscious" poem, she divided the roles according to convention: the benefactor looks down upon the hungry. But she preserved for her speaker her own odd doubled position here. Thus conflating the boundaries between poor and rich, hungry and food-bearing, Bishop reveals how slippery power and dominance in fact are.

Educated at Vassar and a tourist in Europe, twice in the midst of the Great Depression, Bishop's own position of privilege gave her access to the duplicity most central to her poem. While she reacted to her situation with guilt,[7] her poem, which she drafted on her return to New York, reveals instead the nature of the power she herself experienced. The man on the balcony, the speaker who gazes at the river, and Bishop at breakfast can redefine reality through their imagination's turnings: power is available to the one who can choose, manipulate, and alter one's perspective. The sestina form itself, whose terminal repetitions offer a continually revised reading of the balcony, the river, and the nature of the miracle, likewise affirms a reality manipulable by the one writing it. Refusing to join the socialist bandwagon, Bishop makes use of a peculiar encounter between herself and a door-to-door advertiser to explore the nature of social power. Secular "miracles" serve and are retained by the wealthy, the powerful, and, in this case, the poet, who can, quite simply, transform reality as they so choose. Bishop does not resolve the seeming contradiction: below the balcony (fourth stanza) there was no miracle; in possession of the mansion and then sitting on its balcony (fifth stanza), there is.

"Paris, 7 A. M." and "The Hanging of the Mouse," also written in New York after her second stay in Paris,[8] have a view of the same courtyard, and their perspectives reflect interestingly on "A Miracle for Breakfast." "Paris, 7 A. M." speaks directly to the potential for altering reality, once one has acknowledged its flexibility:

> It is like introspection
> to stare inside, or retrospection,
> a star inside a rectangle, a recollection:
> this hollow square could easily have been there.
> – The childish snow-forts, built in flashier winters,
> could have reached these proportions and been houses.

"There" is without referent; instead, it accommodates a transposition of present view into childhood memory. The poem goes on to fold the memory into the view, until the snowballs stored beside the childhood fort invest the courtyard with images of war and death:

> Where is the ammunition, the piled-up balls
> with the star-splintered hearts of ice?
> This sky is no carrier-warrior-pigeon
> escaping endless intersecting circles.
> It is a dead one, or the sky from which a dead one fell.
> The urns have caught his ashes or his feathers.

Calling forth what is not-war is just as effective in leading us to picture war here as a direct reference to war might have been.[9] No "carrier-warrior-pigeon" died here, but in war, pigeons (and people), found within a rifle's sight ("circle[ ]"), die. Bishop puts those deaths before us by aligning them with the reimagined child's ammunition. The present winter night's stillness, which has seemed to deaden the pigeon's wing, by the end harbors the nameless war casualty, "a dead one," itself, even though the poem has witnessed no actual fighting.

Almost simultaneously, in *Three Guineas* (1938), Virginia Woolf was broadening the definition of war until it included domination per se. Tyranny, she argues, is far from limited to fascism and Nazism. She turns her attention throughout this polemic to the tyrannies at home, the patriarchal social order that controls women's access to education and the professions. Domestic domination, she insists, is the ideology that fosters a militaristic consciousness and war itself.

Where Woolf positions herself outside the circle of blame, Bishop never fully allowed herself that privilege. Born a generation later and into circumstances that offered her education, travel, and financial independence, Bishop's struggle was not localized, as Woolf's is here, as a male–female one. In a letter to Moore she deferred to an old black woman working for her who "was ironing & she said to me in between solemn things, 'We'll have <u>wars</u> as long as people's <u>hearts</u> is so <u>hard</u>'" (15 July 1943, V:05:03, RM). Although she admitted that she "never cared too much for the [Moore's] war poem, 'fighting, fighting, fighting' etc.,"[10] her sense of the source of war was as ambivalent as Moore's is in "In Distrust of Merits," where she leaves unresolved whether she feels implicated in the war's guilt or removed from it:

> There never was a war that was
>   not inward; I must
> fight till I have conquered in myself what
> causes war, but I would not believe it.
>   I inwardly did nothing.
>   O Iscariot-like crime! (*CP* 138)

The syntax itself is ambivalent. In her shifting of tenses Moore makes ambiguous whether she is pleading an innocence that makes her the more confused about her own fighting role, or whether she is acknowledging a guilt from which past omissions will never release her. Judas's is, after all, not the crime of omission, as is Peter's, but the crime of commission; Moore's poem and her self-implication negotiate the ambiguous intersection between these. The poem does locate, albeit tenously, a source of redemption in righteousness and religious faith: "O / star of David, star of Bethlehem, / O black imperial lion / of the Lord – emblem / of a risen world – be joined at last, be / joined" (*CP* 136). Likewise, Woolf's polemic, *Three Guineas,* envisions a relief from the present state: the "daughters of educated men," who are as yet untainted by male greed and power, have the potential for constructing a different social order. Bishop, however, disallows herself any systematic resolution. Unprotected by a guiding philosophy or set of beliefs, she is vulnerable to sympathy or complicity, even if only momentarily, with each of her poems' voices: there are no positions in Bishop's writing from which she can wholly exclude herself. To measure this is simply to hold up to Bishop's light the opening of Moore's "Paper Nautilus." Nowhere in Bishop's work are there "authorities," "mercenaries," "writers [frivolously] entrapped"; nowhere is there a psyche fully beyond the range of her empathy.

Thus, it is not surprising to discover that the source of "The Hanging of the Mouse," a prose poem about a trap sprung on a mouse at dawn, is her own humorously sadistic act. As she wrote Moore, "I once hung Minnow's artificial mouse on a string to a chair back, without thinking what I was doing – it looked very sad" (4 Feb. 1937, V:04:31, RM). Though wry throughout, the Kafkaesque story is a bleak portrayal of our inability even to understand another's feelings, let alone find means to ease each other's pain. Bishop's crowd of animals follows a tradition of animal allegory that goes back in Western literature through Chaucer's bird characters in *Parlement of Foulys* to classical fables, such as those of Aesop: they are animals barely concealing human traits. They come to the hanging, early, tired, but with a "vague feeling of celebration"; when the mouse is brought in, crying, these animals "tipped back their heads and sniffed with pleasure." Nobody knows what crime the mouse has committed to deserve his hanging. Nor do the animals around the courtyard understand the death sentence, issued from the balcony by the "King's messenger," a bullfrog: his proclamation is in a frog's language, which the praying mantis, the cat, the beetles, the raccoon, and the others do not speak. These animals understand no more readily gestures and emotions. The crowd interprets the mouse's wiping of his tear-filled nose just before the trap springs as a farewell wave, and they are deeply moved by their own interpretation of his action. Likewise, a mother cat, whose appropriate tears have fallen on the back of the kitten in her mouth, enough to make him squirm, assumes her child has had difficulty watching the execution but has had "an excellent moral lesson, nevertheless" (*Poems* 143–5). The humor keeps the tale from seeming moralistic. Though the lack of both satisfactory justification for this death sentence and thoughtful questioning of it may echo the state of law in the increasingly fascist Europe from which Bishop had recently returned, the humor keeps us from judging these animals. They are as "safe" as Aesop's creatures were for him; they are only animals, ignorant and funny. The mouse is only artificial, hung on the back of a chair. Bishop has been a hangman only on a moment's whim. Inspired by the "peripheral vision" (Darwin letter) of her wholly apolitical anecdote and thus revealing our everyday power to oppress and inflict pain, Bishop ends, once again, by registering her "private defiance of the significantly detestable."

War, Bishop shows, infiltrates even more territory than Hitler would have had it do, because it is always "inward." While much of conventional war poetry focuses either directly or through metaphor on the soldiers and victims in the battlefield – or bush, or mined town – and earns our empathy for them there, in the place we, their readers, are not,[11] Bishop refuses the security of a boundary between the war and herself (see also Schweik, *Gulf,* chap. 8). In "Paris, 7 A. M." and in another poem of the late 1930s, "Sleeping Standing Up," Bishop follows Freud and such surrealist painters as Klee into childhood and dream, the unconscious realm where childhood desire and fear return in juxtaposition with adult imaginings, and there she locates war.

Bishop claimed in her 1946 letter to Greenslet at Houghton Mifflin that "none of these poems [in *North & South*] deal directly with the war"; "Sleeping Standing Up,'"[12] if indirectly about war, is a dream poem about more than *the* war:

> As we lie down to sleep the world turns half away
>   through ninety dark degrees;
>   the bureau lies on the wall
> and thoughts that were recumbent in the day
>   rise as the others fall,
>   stand up and make a forest of thick-set trees.
>
> The armored cars of dreams, contrived to let us do
>   so many a dangerous thing,
>   are chugging at its edge
> all camouflaged, and ready to go through
>   the swiftest streams, or up a ledge
>   of crumbling shale, while plates and trappings ring.
>
> – Through turret-slits we saw the crumbs or pebbles that lay
>   below the riveted flanks
>   on the green forest floor,
> like those the clever children placed by day
>   and followed to their door
>   one night, at least; and in the ugly tanks
>
> we tracked them all the night. Sometimes they disappeared,
>   dissolving in the moss,
>   sometimes we went too fast
> and ground them underneath. How stupidly we steered
>   until the night was past
>   and never found out where the cottage was.

The fairy tale of Hansel and Gretel, "the clever children" who devise a (somewhat successful) scheme for ensuring their return home, is the ground from which this dream and this tank derive. Perhaps Marianne Moore put Bishop in the mind of Hansel and Gretel. They appear in "The Frigate Pelican" (first published in *Criterion* in 1934), in the care of a "stalwart swan that can ferry" them home (*CP* 25). Moore's poem suggests that because the swan is predictable, maternal, and stalwart, unlike the daring and carefree frigate-bird, the children will get home. Bishop's dream has a place neither for the frigate-bird's freedom, detailed in the original version in six stanzas later deleted, nor for the swan's generous security. Nothing in Bishop's poem guides the children home nor prevents the dream from becoming nightmare.

The form is tight – rhyme and rhythm are regular – but the poem feels nonetheless unsettling: grammatically and thematically, it seems to move by means of an uncontrolled slippage. The opening recognition of sleep's perspective blurs into dream itself somewhere between the second and third stanzas, where the recalled danger and violence of dream become a reenactment of them. Bishop's inclusive pronoun requires that her reader confront the gap with her, each of us discovering our lack of control and our violence. Though we like to believe there is a distance between the always inherent potential of our doing "so many a dangerous thing" and our actually doing it, Bishop conflates the two in this poem, eliding the hazy present continuous with a past tense of action and forcing us into the armored tank, which had one stanza before been only "ready to go." In the tank we are helplessly out of touch with the fairy-tale resolution of homecoming. "Through turret-slits we saw" the path on which the children would attempt to return home, but in our "ugly tanks" we can only blunder roughshod over the whole scene, trample their tracks, lose their trail, destroy their chance and ours ever to find out "where the cottage was."

We have too much power for our task, or we do not know what our task really is: either could be a comment on world affairs. Rather than make such a comment, however, Bishop chooses simply to set an inclusive pronoun into inclusive settings: the clumsiness of the tank is the frustration in dream when the goal cannot be reached, the hill climbed, the attacker escaped. Reaching back into a simple fairy tale of childhood, Bishop dredges up our unfulfillable desires and our fear that we subconsciously destroy our own access to our desires. We can only steer "stupidly" over the old tracks. "We" subverts "you," allowing her to indict, with no accusatory tone, all people who wield power without intelligence and intuition. "We" also evades "I," Elizabeth Bishop, an adult woman unable to find a home in the late 1930s, moving continuously as if to rub out her traces precisely when she most desires their permanence.

In his 1945 "A Note on War Poetry," which introduces Oscar Williams's anthology of war poems, Richard Eberhart conceives of the states of peace and war in terms similar to the "ninety dark degrees" that reverse day and night in Bishop's poem: "War is another kind of show than the peace show, intractable, profoundly ingrained in man's nature. It is the evil standing up" (19). The "armored cars" of dream would then be, according to Eberhart, Bishop's rendition of the waking nightmare:

> Chaos is present to the poet in war in violent forms. He may recognize in this violence his true element, a reduction to terrible simplicity of what he knew in the heart before. Gigantic objectifications tossed and forced on sky, land and sea only emphasize the essential fact of struggle. Thus, a poet knows war without objective war in the world; it was conflict at the root of his mind that impelled him to the masking of these conflicts in the apparent resolution and order of works of art. In a dialectical sense, all poetry is war poetry. (19)

Or *the* war in which "we" do not take part is inseparable from the war in which we all do. Finding a middle ground in "we" between evasion and accusation, Bishop explores the war where it is in us, in our losses and in our own destructiveness, which ensures those losses.

By 1940, when the war industry was gearing up in Key West, the actual war moved inward on her. Her poetic response was "Roosters,"[3] which relentlessly juxtaposes the dailiness of lovers in bed and the violence of war, undermining any myth of moral righteousness outside war. "Roosters" is skinned of the frames of pastoral harmony and dream. It opens by lurching from bed to battlefield:

> At four o'clock
> in the gun-metal blue dark
> we hear the first crow of the first cock
>
> just below
> the gun-metal blue window
> and immediately there is an echo
>
> off in the distance,
> then one from the backyard fence,
> then one, with horrible insistence,
>
> grates like a wet match
> from the broccoli patch,
> flares, and all over town begins to catch.
>
> Cries galore
> come from the water-closet door,
> from the dropping-plastered henhouse floor.

Real roosters crow here, but since these roosters very quickly take on human characteristics, this poem can, again, be seen within the tradition of animal fable. Yet these roosters are unreliable creatures, posing variously as barnyard animals, personifications, art in the form of weather vanes, and symbols within a Christian allegory of betrayal and redemption. Unsettling any comfortable interpretation, the poem's stanza form and rhyme insist on themselves – twelve *k* sounds, for instance, in the first fifteen lines – and relentless triplets and two-syllable rhymes.

As personifications, these roosters enact human behavior in its jarring extremes,

> where in the blue blur
> their rustling wives admire
> the roosters brace their cruel feet and glare
>
> with stupid eyes
> while from their beaks there rise
> the uncontrolled, traditional cries.
>
> Deep from protruding chests
> in green-gold medals dressed,
> planned to command and terrorize the rest,
>
> the many wives
> who lead hens' lives
> of being courted and despised;
>
> deep from raw throats
> a senseless order floats
> all over town.

The hens are passive, but for their masochistic activity of admiring the roosters who "command and terrorize" them. Admiration and a return in cruelty replace love; courting goes hand in hand with despising. When love becomes an irrelevant factor, power and authority are arranged in "a senseless order." One need go no farther than the barnyard to understand the human relations that make war possible, as Woolf outlined them in *Three Guineas*. But at the same time as she is personifying the roosters, Bishop implicates the human sleepers. They can scold the roosters for waking them, but they cannot extricate themselves from the world into which they are awoken:

> what right have you to give
> commands and tell us how to live,
>
> cry "Here!" and "Here!"
> and wake us here where are
> unwanted love, conceit and war?

"Unwanted love, conceit and war" are as intrinsic to the bed as to the battlefield; except there, enemies and friends are clearly, if artificially, demarcated for the soldier who must honor the distinctions. Though

Mary Magdalen, the roosters' wives, the sleepers, and Christ are beyond
the poem's direct censure, "Roosters" offers no clear means of separating
roosters from humans or love and friends from conceit, war, and
enemies.

The poem refuses to march forth with anger, horror, or disbelief
at insensible war, as the great majority of war poetry does, choosing
instead simple condescension toward fighting cocks. Bishop uses enjambment gracefully to offer the roosters a pedestal, only to shove them
off,

> You, whom the Greeks elected
> to shoot at on a post,

further shriveling their supposed power with sarcasm:

> The crown of red
> set on your little head
> is charged with all your fighting blood.
>
> Yes, that excrescence
> makes a most virile presence,
> plus all that vulgar beauty of iridescence.

She posits a cockfight that concludes in unvictorious death:

> And one has fallen,
> but still above the town
> his torn-out, bloodied feathers drift down;
>
> and what he sung
> no matter. He is flung
> on the gray ash-heap, lies in dung
>
> with his dead wives
> with open, bloody eyes,
> while those metallic feathers oxidize.

While the word "dung" is certainly the rhyme's perfection, Bishop drops
a final irony as conclusion to this section,[14] which opened with sleepers,
perhaps lovers, lying together. The dead cock lies with his dead wives
– they have thrived on this system no better than he – not in love but
in dung.

The ensuing section about St. Peter and his forgiveness by Christ is
marked from the beginning by the cockfight and by World War II behind
it. Most critics, though, have trusted what Lloyd Frankenberg calls the
"forgiving mood" of the close (337). Jerome Mazzaro reads the piece as
a biblical allegory of the "history of man," including his fall and redemption (179–80). Others argue that the stanza break signals a turn
from the world's horror to human forgiveness: "Human beings, after
all, are *not* roosters, for they are able to conceive of salvation" (Stevenson,

Bishop 123); "pain and despair are transcended" (Newman 117). Alicia Ostriker is disappointed by what she sees as a move typical of much of women's writing, calling the end a "withdrawal of a familiar sort" from the opening section's "strong and brilliant parody of male brutality and male aesthetics" (54). But the worlds of the two sections are hardly so opposed, and the roosters are not such clearly interpretable creatures, as Susan Schweik shows convincingly in her discussion of "Roosters." Schweik refutes the developmental reading of this poem by pointing to the range of details common to both sections. The "rooster," she shows, is both a barnyard animal and a craftsman's rendition. If it is a shrieking, parading, and fighting emblem of men in the first section, it is just as much an emblem of the way he betrays his fellow in the second (*Gulf* 223–4).

It is difficult not to hear the tone of sarcasm that pervades the second section as much as the first:

> Christ stands amazed,
> Peter, two fingers raised
> to surprised lips, both as if dazed.
>
> But in between
> a little cock is seen
> carved on a dim column in the travertine,
>
> explained by *gallus canit;*
> *flet Petrus* underneath it.
> There is inescapable hope, the pivot;
>
> yes, and there Peter's tears
> run down our chanticleer's
> sides and gem his spurs.
>
> Tear-encrusted thick
> as a medieval relic
> he waits. Poor Peter, heart-sick.

Christ may stand amazed that his friend and apostle would have betrayed him, but Bishop's bemused tone, which makes the scene seem precious, shows she is not. Nor does she seem to believe in Peter's tears any more than in the rooster-statue's. The Latin explanation for the cock's placement on the column is parody here, not sincerity. If she is indeed convinced, along with the pope and

> all the assembly
> that "Deny deny deny"
> is not all the roosters cry,

then still she offers no assurance that the rooster has anything hopeful to say, leaving any cries he might utter – insults or words of mercy – off the page.

Whatever the roosters cry, the sunrise happens anyway. The third section's description of the beautiful and disinterested sun might distract one from yet alleviates none of the poem's perplexities:

> In the morning
> a low light is floating
> in the backyard, and gilding
>
> from underneath
> the broccoli, leaf by leaf;
> how could the night have come to grief?
>
> gilding the tiny
> floating swallow's belly
> and lines of pink cloud in the sky,
>
> the day's preamble
> like wandering lines in marble.
> The cocks are now almost inaudible.
>
> The sun climbs in,
> following "to see the end,"
> faithful as enemy, or friend.

The broccoli, whose own harsh *c*'s accentuated its role as locus of the rooster's crowing in the first section, is here the source of the sun ray's unfolding. Swallows float here, now that cocks' sounds have faded. With birds as with broccoli, the emphasis has turned from the aural to the visual. The language softens as well, and rhymes are looser. Nine of the fifteen terminal words have feminine endings, and for the first continuous time in the poem only the last syllables rhyme. Where the poem began in intrusive sound, it closes in relaxing sight. But the shift is only one of image and language; it signals neither closure nor transcendence of the poem's conflicts.

In its own refusal "to see the end" of any of the poem's concerns, the conclusion rejects a Christian righteousness with regard to war's depravity. The sun, finally, does not rise up and out of the poem. In its self-contradictory faithfulness, rather, it throws us back into the poem. To know whether one is friend or enemy seems an all-important task. National governments and their soldiers make these determinations confidently and rely on their authority. In its end and throughout, "Roosters" unsettles such a task, repeatedly setting the rooster up and dismissing as political and spiritual symbols that which we have conventionally rejected or relied upon. "To see the end" is, finally, to see how little closure there is, in the face of daily betrayals that cannot help but reflect the war's violation of supposedly sacrosanct values.

Marianne Moore was not so ready to abandon her trust in a higher order that might compensate for the irrationalities of the historic mo-

ment, and her religious faith, as well as her political and social conserva-
tism, often translated into poetic expectations. In 1938 Moore had urged
Bishop to discover her "private defiance of the significantly detestable";
but if the violent structure, tone, and language of Bishop's "Roosters"
represented such a defiance, then Moore would have to redirect this
effort. Praising Bishop's "Pope-ian sagacity," she wrote that her

> justice to "Peeter," and such a crucially enviable consummation as
>
> From strained throats
> A senseless order floats,
>
> are like a din of churchbells in my ears, I am so excited.

Moore had to revise these lines before appreciating them. Bishop's throats
were not "strained" but "raw," and Moore removed what she must have
found an extraneous first syllable, "deep from raw throats." Calling
herself "Dorothy Dix," Moore continued, boldly condemning to erasure
that which did not have the churchbells' ring:

> I think it is to your credit, Elizabeth, that when I say you are not to
> say "water-closet", you go on saying it a little (like Donald in National
> Velvet), and it is calculated to make me wonder if I haven't mistaken
> a cosmetic patch for a touch of lamp-black, but I think not. The trouble
> is, people are not depersonalized enough to accept the picture rather
> than the thought. [. . .] If I tell Mother there is a feather on her dress
> and she says, "On my back?" I am likely to say, "No. On your rump,"
> alluding to Cowper's hare that "swung his rump around." But in my
> work, I daren't risk saying, "My mother had a feather on her rump."
> (16 Oct. 1940, VC)

Revising Bishop's poem and retitling it "The Cock," she returned a
version safe from the violent and disgusting and so different Bishop called
it "your poem" (20 Oct. 1940, V:05:02, RM). Perhaps Moore's greatest
breach is her correction of Bishop's tone. When she reached the St. Peter
stanzas, for instance, she wrote the serious scene of Christian forgiveness
that Bishop had not written, removing the sarcasm so that there really
is a transformation in the rooster's cry:

> Christ amazed,
> Peter, saint, – two fingers raised,
>
> while in between,
> a little cock is seen
> carved on a dim column in the travertine,
>
> explained by "Gallus canit;
> "Flet Petrus" underneath; the pivot.
>
> Yes Peter's tears
> at cock-crow, gemming a cock's spurs.

A new weathervane
On the basilica,
outside the Lateran.

There was always to be
a bronze cock on a porphyry
pillar so that people and Pope might see

that the Prince
of the apostles
was forgiven; to convince

them that "Deny deny deny"
is now [not?]¹⁵ now as it was, the rooster's cry.

Moore did leave intact, perhaps despite herself, Bishop's alliterative series of *p*'s, which call humorous attention to themselves and away from Peter, as they do in Bishop's poem. But for the most part, she removed the sarcasm, the "rattle-trap rhythm" (Bishop to Moore, 17 Oct. 1940, RM), and the overdone rhymes, here as she did throughout the poem.

Bishop accepted only a few of Moore's extensive revisions, explaining her refusal of the rest in the most self-assertive letter of their correspondence:

> What I'm about to say, I'm afraid, will sound like ELIZABETH KNOWS BEST . . . However, I have changed to small initial letters! & I have made several other of your corrections and suggestions, & left out 1 of the same stanzas that you did. But I can't seem to bring myself to give up the set form, which I'm afraid you think fills the poem with redundancies, etc. I feel that the rather rattle-trap rhythm is appropriate – maybe I can explain it.
>
> I cherish my "water-closet" and the other sordities because I want to emphasize the essential baseness of militarism. In the 1st part I was thinking of Key West, and also of those aerial views of dismal little towns in Finland & Norway, when the Germans took over, and their atmosphere of poverty. That's why, although I see what you mean, I want to keep "tin rooster" instead of "gold," and not to use "fastidious beds." And for the same reason I want to keep as the title the rather contemptuous word ROOSTERS rather than the more classical COCK; and I want to repeat the "gun-metal." (I also had in mind the violent roosters Picasso did in connection with his GUERNICA picture.) [. . .]
>
> And I wanted to keep "to see the end" in quotes because, although it may not be generally recognized, I have always felt that expression used of Peter in the Bible, to be extremely poignant.
>
> It has been so hard to decide what to do, and I know that esthetically you are quite right, but I can't bring myself to sacrifice what (I think) is a very important "violence" of tone – which I feel to be helped by what you must feel to be just a bad case of the Threes. It makes me

feel like a wonderful Klee picture I saw at his show the other day, "The Man of Confusion". (17 Oct. 1940, V:05:02, RM)

Bishop mentioned Moore's corrections of this poem and her own defiance in letters to friends over the next several decades. In "Efforts of Affection" she summarized the break: "By then I had turned obstinate" (*Prose* 130). She felt bold enough to challenge Moore over the language and tone of the first section, because the "essential baseness of militarism" was not such a controversial issue between them.[16] The lack of comment about the St. Peter section, which was accompanied nonetheless by an absence of revision in response to Moore's changes there, reveals only that she would not challenge Moore over her Christ. But by insisting that she keep the quotation from Matthew 26:58 intact, she does challenge Moore's vision of the end:

And climbing in to see the end,
The faithful sun is here,
as enemy, or friend.

For Moore, this is only a matter of the sun's – nature's – ambivalence. For Bishop, who quotes the "poignant" biblical lines, Peter's crime is still wholly unsettled, as are the "rattle-trap rhythms," the "sordities," and the uncriminal violences of "unwanted love" and "conceit" that ordinary people enact daily and that seem to blur so confusedly with "war." Bishop's close returns the poem to these daily betrayals, which are not erased by a Christian forgiving or the rise of a new beginning and which cannot be overlooked even while the poem gives its attention to the more urgent violence of war or the more hopeful vision of a sunrise. Bishop's break from Moore regarding one's very ability to convey the nonlinear, unresolved, barnyard or bedroom ordinariness behind the crafted visions of poetry, religion, history, and politics begins here.

By the time she completed "Roosters," Bishop had been working for a couple of years on what she would call her "'tript-itch' of Key West poems" (24 Feb. 1940, V:05:02, RM).[17] As she was writing her poems about Cootchie, Miss Lula, and José (Jerónimo), Bishop wrote letters about them, often with great naïveté, as if blackness itself was a new phenomenon for her. She regaled Moore with stories about Hannah Almyda, Cootchie, and a carpenter – "a 'chieftan' type" (5 May 1938, V:05:01, RM) – who were working for her or her friends. During her periodic stays in New York, her Key West friend Marjorie Stevens kept her abreast of the news with lengthy anecdotes about Hannah Almyda and Faustina. As Bishop also wrote, in her letter about "The Paper Nautilus" (21 May 1940, RM), she was dissatisfied with the poems she was composing about the Key West locals. She was still learning from Moore's ability to embody love or anger in her poetry; but rather than follow Moore's lead into allusiveness, Bishop demanded that these poems confront the emotions of the people behind them. Making increasingly daring experiments in empathy, she gradually discovered ways to voice her subjects' tones and tensions.

She abandoned a poem called "Key West," about a carnival in the "lot of the burnt-out cigar factory," perhaps because it seemed too derivative of Wallace Stevens's ironic remove. A first stanza describes the lights, colors, and acts of the carnival; a second details the people:

> Where six hundred men used to work at rolling cigars
> To fill the boxes with the ornate lids
> That showed a woman with roses in her hair
> And tulle-draped bust, – a woman like her bids
> The citizens to come and see her dancers,
> Guaranteed to wear nothing but feather fans and jewels,
> And a man with the face of an educated ape
> Lures them to see the educated mules.
> While Negro children, who are not allowed,
> Look on solemnly from among the crowd.

Blunt and prosaic, the poem's irony is a heavy-handed barrier separating viewer from carnival characters. Bemused and disgusted subject-observer of a show of exotic objects, Bishop left the poem as an untyped and unrevised manuscript.

Moore apparently criticized Bishop's portrayals of locals – these letters have been lost – as Bishop periodically replied by attempting more accurate characterizations, in defensive response. She wrote Moore, for instance, that "I changed the poem about Cootchie to 'The skies were - - - and the faces sable,' but I am afraid you still can't be forced to admire it!" (14 Mar. 1940, V:05:02, RM). Whereas "Key West" was plagued by a seemingly insurmountable cultural alienation, Bishop set "Cootchie" precisely in the midst of such alienation, so as to explore its effects. The poem is a study in class and racial contrasts; the position of each figure is fixed, the servant Cootchie,

> eating her dinner off the kitchen sink
> while Lula ate hers off the kitchen table.

In these terms the speaker is likewise marked. Her whiteness leaves her necessarily absent from Cootchie's funeral, whose description Bishop quoted to Moore:

> The skies were egg-white for the funeral
> and the faces sable.

The poem recognizes that these divisions are of little help in understanding Miss Lula's loss or Cootchie's apparent suicide by drowning. They offer no access to this lost, long relationship or to the reason for this death. All that there was beyond the racial markers now remains inarticulable:

> Searching the land and sea for someone else,
> the lighthouse will discover Cootchie's grave
> and dismiss all as trivial; the sea, desperate,
>   will proffer wave after wave.

Nature acquiesces in its ignorance and the lighthouse in its indifference; the speaker can only echo, through her perspective of opacity, the alienation that is left to define the relationship between these two women.

Adopting personas in "Jerónimo's House" and three years later in "Songs for a Colored Singer,"[18] Bishop discovered another means of access to her subjects. Here, as if from within their voices, she could project her sense of a culture different from her own. An avid blues follower, Bishop often recorded song titles and lyrics in her Key West notebook.[19] She fantasized Billie Holiday singing her "Songs": "I put in a couple of big words just because she sang big words well – '*conspiring root*' for instance" (Brown 296). While Adrienne Rich criticized the "failures and clumsiness" of Bishop's position, "a white woman's attempt – respectful, I believe – to speak through a Black woman's voice ("Outsider" 17), I maintain, rather, that the songs suggest a mixture of voices, each slightly different and together voicing the alienation fostered by gendered and racial oppression. One hears affinities in these songs with such poetry as Blake's *Songs of Experience,* Gwendolyn Brooks's *A Street in Bronzeville* (1945),[20] or Langston Hughes's poems of the 1930s and 1940s, with the blues of Holiday or Bessie Smith, and with the everyday, overheard banter of neighbors. In the third and fourth songs Bishop seems most intentionally to echo blues and Blake, respectively. The mixture of affinities – white and black, high and low culture – is, I believe, no coincidence. To understand the oppression and the community represented by these poems is to cross various seemingly impassable lines in 1944. Like Brooks's work of the same years, these poems attempt to do so by hearing the connections as well as the differences among ethnicities.

Feisty and humorous, the first two songs portray her subject's self-irony:

> I
>
> A washing hangs upon the line,
>   but it's not mine.
> None of the things that I can see
>   belong to me.

The neighbors got a radio with an aerial;
  we got a little portable.
They got a lot of closet space;
  we got a suitcase.

[. . .]

Le Roy answers with a frown,
"Darling, when I earns I spends.
The world is wide; it still extends. . . .
I'm going to get a job in the next town."
Le Roy, you're earning too much money now.

II

The time has come to call a halt;
  and so it ends.
  He's gone off with his other friends.
  He needn't try to make amends,
this occasion's all his fault.
  Through rain and dark I see his face
  across the street at Flossie's place.
  He's drinking in the warm pink glow
  to th'accompaniment of the piccolo.

The time has come to call a halt.
I met him walking with Varella
and hit him twice with my umbrella.
Perhaps that occasion was my fault,
but the time has come to call a halt.

[. . .]

She is strident and playful by turns, her unbashful rhymes reflecting how basic these problems are: life is unjust for the black woman in the 1940s, stunted by both white and male supremacy. In the first song the singer is trapped by Le Roy's wanderlust, his own desire, which forecloses hers, to reach beyond their poverty. In the second she recognizes her right, only after years of her husband's drinking and womanizing, to escape on a bus that "will take me anywhere." Like a Louis Armstrong trumpet accompaniment to Bessie Smith's blues, both songs have a lighthearted tone that refuses to take itself too seriously, just as they are making the issues of inequity bluntly evident.

Harmonizing the singer's voice with history – the war in the third song and racial strife in the fourth – Bishop ranges from the spirituality of blues to the power of anger in Blake's *Songs* in her articulation of the black woman's story. The third song is a lullaby in a minor key:

Lullaby.
Adult and child

sink to their rest.
At sea the big ship sinks and dies,
lead in its breast.

Lullaby.
Let nations rage,
let nations fall.
The shadow of the crib makes an enormous cage
upon the wall.

Lullaby.
Sleep on and on,
war's over soon.
Drop the silly, harmless toy,
pick up the moon.

Lullaby.
If they should say
you have no sense,
don't you mind them; it won't make
much difference.

Lullaby.
Adult and child
sink to their rest.
At sea the big ship sinks and dies,
lead in its breast.

This lullaby parallels as it opposes the loving, quiet sleep of adult and child to the sinking of bombed ships. Vital to blues is the blurring of singer and song, such that utterance, tone, and beat are elements of both voice and music. Voice and music harmonize each other, repeating, contradicting, and pushing and pulling each other toward realization. Though this lullaby is clearly not blues – most important, it has never been set to music – it reproduces many of the elements of blues: the prolonged notes of spiritual, the twelve-stress stanzas suggestive of the twelve-bar blues construction, the interruption of narrative with (instrumental) tangents that echo and respond to the original call, the return of the first stanza in the last, which is one of many variants of blues closure.[21] Acknowledging the terms of war that cannot be changed – the ships have indeed sunk – Bishop's singer reassesses their impact: the downed ship is a wounded breast, not wholly unlike the adult's on which the child rests, and the war's weapon is a "silly, harmless toy," which warring children should drop. As if with equal and opposite force to nations raging and falling, the song diffuses the rage by domesticating it, dismissing its toys, showing up the impracticality of those weapons by absurdly offering the moon instead, encouraging the child to ignore (white) censure, and embracing him with the alternative of nurturing

love. Down-to-earth and subversive at the same time, as "Roosters,"
for instance, is and as blues and spiritual often are, the lullaby diffuses
as it reevaluates the reality of war, from its tough, well-ballasted position,
for the child on the way to sleep.

While the minor key of the third song is calming, the minor key of
the fourth buzzes out of control:

> What's that shining in the leaves,
> the shadowy leaves,
> like tears when somebody grieves,
> shining, shining in the leaves?
>
> Is it dew or is it tears,
> dew or tears,
> hanging there for years and years
> like a heavy dew of tears?
>
> Then that dew begins to fall,
> roll down and fall.
> Maybe it's not tears at all.
> See it, see it roll and fall.
>
> Hear it falling on the ground,
> hear, all around.
> That is not a tearful sound,
> beating, beating on the ground.
>
> See it lying there like seeds,
> like black seeds.
> See it taking root like weeds,
> faster, faster than the weeds,
>
> all the shining seeds take root,
> conspiring root,
> and what curious flower or fruit
> will grow from that conspiring root?
>
> Fruit or flower? It is a face.
> Yes, a face.
> In that dark and dreary place
> each seed grows into a face.
>
> Like an army in a dream
> the faces seem,
> darker, darker, like a dream.
> They're too real to be a dream.

The song is all confusion; the singer poses insistent questions, obsessively
beating back doubt to root out answers. She does so by mixing an
absurdly simple rhyme scheme (AAAA, with many identical rhymes)
and Dick and Jane repetitions with an exotic narrative of a black army's

birth among leaves. The song echoes the explosive questions of Blake's "The Tyger" –

> And what shoulder, & what art,
> Could twist the sinews of thy heart?
> And when thy heart began to beat,
> What dread hand? & what dread feet?

or of his even more bitter "A Poison Tree," in which the speaker

> waterd it [his wrath] in fears,
> Night & morning with my tears:
> And I sunned it with smiles,
> And with soft deceitful wiles.

Bishop's recognition in the fourth song of the power of righteous, revolutionary anger matches Blake's here. Fear conflates with pride in Blake's lines as in Bishop's; her "black seeds" are neither dew nor the tears of grieving but are the beating, "conspiring" source of a rising black people. The ambivalence in the "The Weed" about whether to admire or fear the new growth resonates here; placing her fourth song at the intersection of these two emotions so as to give her singer the force of both, Bishop tests the gap between cultures. A remarkable poem for Elizabeth Bishop in 1944, the song is necessarily confused because it does not have white confidence that it has mastered the threat of rebellion, nor does it have black confidence in the unshakable strength of its "conspiring root." These seeds do not even have the stability the weed in her early poem had, since that growth took root in a nourishing organ, a heart. The seeds here, which take "root like weeds," must do so from among leaves. The ground is not sure, and the seeds must grow conspiratorially. With a backward glance before closing, Bishop briefly allows the possibility that this is all only a dream, but she dismisses that worry or consolation even before leaving stanza and rhyme.

Jean Pedrick, editor at Houghton Mifflin, wrote to Bishop after seeing "Songs for a Colored Singer" in *Partisan Review* to invite her to submit a book-length manuscript for the Houghton Mifflin Award for a first book of poetry: "There is a fresh quality in the songs, and I think a superb bringing together of the tragic and the humorous in the way life so often brings them together, and poets so seldom do" (22 Nov. 1944, HL). In 1939 and 1940, Bishop had repeatedly submitted manuscripts for a book of poetry and had received publishers' rejections or terms she could not abide in each case. Pedrick's request was a surprise; Houghton Mifflin's award was a financial boon, and it gave her poetry the publicity she needed. "Songs for a Colored Singer," the catalyst to her success, was a daring poem in the 1940s in its insistence that white and black concerns find their common ground, that racial and gendered struggles cannot be isolated from each other, and that as a poet she cannot accept opacity as an excuse for neglecting further inquiry. In her letter of response to Pedrick's request for poems, Bishop wrote that "I am trying to add several more to the group of 'songs' and I hope you will like them, too" (8 Dec. 1944, HL). She did not write another song, and it is hard to imagine what she would have written to follow this fourth, which leaves everything so importantly in doubt.

Rather, Bishop underwent a difficult stretch for the next several years, suffering from asthma, depression, drinking, and the turbulent relationship with Marjorie Stevens. She moved back and forth between Key West and New York, staying in New York, with the ambivalence she always felt toward the city, for longer and longer periods.[22] When she turned again in her poetry to her Key West acquaintances, she did so with none of her earlier sense of assignment. Years in Key West of trying to write people as she knew them and of knowing pain intimately herself culminate in the intensely bare emotion of "Faustina, or Rock Roses."[23]

Three women inhabit the room of this poem, an old white woman dying, Faustina, her Cuban servant, and a visitor who observes and who closes the poem by proffering roses. In the quiet of the deathwatch, the three emerge; "the eighty-watt bulb / betrays us all":

> It exposes the fine white hair,
> the gown with the undershirt
> showing at the neck,
> the pallid palm-leaf fan
> she holds but cannot wield,
> her white disordered sheets
>   like wilted roses.
>
> Clutter of trophies,
> chamber of bleached flags!
> – Rags or ragged garments
> hung on the chairs and hooks
> each contributing its
> shade of white, confusing
>   as undazzling.
>
> The visitor is embarrassed
> not by pain nor age
> nor even nakedness,
> though perhaps by its reverse.
> By and by the whisper
> says, "*Faustina, Faustina . . .*"
>   "*¡Vengo, señora!*"

The detail is so intimate that even as we are looking at objects we see the person who wears or disorders them. Bishop infuses the white sheets and the garments on chairs with the old woman's pain, age, and nakedness; they and not she reveal and, "perhaps," embarrass. The disembodied whisper speaks for the woman, holding all her feelings, as well as the helplessness of empty utterance, in her call to her servant. Faustina comes, "requesting for herself/a little *coñac;*"[24]

> complaining of, explaining,
> the terms of her employment.
> She bends above the other.
> Her sinister kind face
> presents a cruel black
> coincident conundrum.
>   Oh, is it

> freedom at last, a lifelong
> dream of time and silence,
> dream of protection and rest?
> Or is it the very worst,
> the unimaginable nightmare
> that never before dared last
>   more than a second?

> The acuteness of the question
> forks instantly and starts
> a snake-tongue flickering;
> blurs further, blunts, softens,
> separates, falls, our problems
> becoming helplessly
>   proliferative.

> There is no way of telling.
> The eyes say only either.

"Faithful as enemy, or friend," Faustina awaits the old woman's "freedom" and her own. Sinister and kind, she will serve this woman until her end, not out of love, but out of a duty that inspires complaints, but not questioning.

The ambivalence of their relationship binds them in an intimacy that is as powerful an emotional statement as it is a political one. Modifying her statement about the "Songs," Rich concludes about this poem that "I cannot think of another poem by a white woman, until some feminist poetry of the last few years, in which the servant–mistress dynamic between Black and white women has received unsentimental attention" ("Outsider" 18). Reaching through race into the emotions of each woman, Bishop gives us the conundrum in its nakedness. The speaker's questions about freedom and the "unimaginable nightmare" bear no quotation marks; they are the property of none and of each of these women, permeating the room, "becoming helplessly/proliferative." This is not just an old white woman dying, as Cootchie's death is removed from the poet's and our understanding. The questions reverberate in each of these women's hearts and are reflected in "the [unidentified] eyes"; these are "our problems."

The visitor closes the poem with a last rite. She

>   rises,
> awkwardly proffers her bunch
> of rust-perforated roses
> and wonders oh, whence come
> all the petals.

Whereas the ocean could only offer a repetition of meaningless waves in "Cootchie," outside the painful center of things here the rapt attention to rose petals refocuses the poem on the women's intertwining. The titular attachment of crystallized roses to Faustina, the enamel of the old woman's "crazy bed" chipped in the shape of roses, and the "wilted roses" of her sheets resonate in the visitor's "rust-perforated roses." These petals proliferate as the problems do. "The visitor rises" as if to go, with a gesture that whirls her back into the poem's room, from which there is, just as there was in "Roosters," no "end" to "see."

Bishop never did find her niche among the *Partisan Review* crowd, though she sympathized with the Left, because she never could take a consistently political stand. Politics, like history and human interaction, produced for Bishop "helplessly/proliferative" questions, which spread out fanlike into corners, from which they demanded answers that were necessarily partial, continually readjustable, and highly personal. She found it impossible, for instance, when hers was the position of the man on the balcony in "A Miracle for Breakfast," or of the hangman in "The Hanging of the Mouse," simply to condemn the unjust distribution of wealth or the spread of fascism, particularly in the late 1930s before the outbreak of World War II. Even during the war, her poetry located no unimplicated position: we all participate in the creation of Eberhart's "evil standing up"; we all make history. Roosters' violence is much like human betrayal at war and at home; Hansel and Gretel's fairy-tale world must accommodate the vehicles and the mentality of war; white fear and black hope do determine each other and are appropriately sung in the same utterance. Embracing hatred, fear, desire, and love within their historical moment, Bishop turned history under, as it were, exploring through a pragmatism that insists on the local, perspectival nature of historical truth such public concerns as racial segregation in Key West or war in Europe. With the ordinary individual as her subject and intimate emotions as her focus, she located a voice that challenged racial, national, and gender-determined barriers, a voice perhaps unavailable to her, were she to have taken a "stand." She entrusted language with these vital, daily emotions, and, as she articulated decades later in a letter to Anne Stevenson, the surrounding pressure of history "does have a way of taking care of itself [. . .] it will all show itself, one way or another" (15 Aug. 1965, WU). The rose petals in "Faustina, or Rock Roses" represent the delicacy of that trust; when we go carefully, the barest layers reveal themselves. The process, Bishop insists here, as she did in "The Man-Moth," is necessarily inclusive: these are "our problems." We and she are part of this room, never fully removable from any personal or historical action.

4

Gathering in a Childhood

When, at the age of eight months, Bishop lost her father to Bright's disease, she began at the same time slowly to lose her mother to an onset of what would become permanent mental illness. William Bishop seems to have left no scars on the child; he was simply a name out of family history and on the plates of books she had from his library (letter to Stevenson, 5 May 1964, WU). Gertrude Bulmer Bishop, however, who cared for her daughter with the help of her family until she was hospitalized at McLean in 1915, when the child was four and a half, and who attempted several months later to live in Nova Scotia with her parents, now the child's caretakers, left memories so painful that Bishop struggled for years, mostly in unpublished writing after her mother's death in May 1934, to sort out just what was her mother.

Vacationing at Cuttyhunk early in July 1934, the summer after her college graduation and after her twin losing and gaining of a mother, in Gertrude Bishop's death and in the timely meeting of Marianne Moore, Bishop began her memoirs, as I mentioned in Chapter 2, of her childhood in Nova Scotia. She considered the project – her "novel" – in her journal, in a couple of extended entries a year apart.[1] Writing "The Proud Villagers" along the margin in early July 1934, she set forth a plan for a kind of cultural exposé of Great Village dailiness:

> ~~I might speak of~~ the Nova Scotia way of talking – how it sounds, to outsiders, resentful & angry. Swanus will have this way of speaking more than any of the others – harsh and inverted.? The grandmother the only one who shows any affection – & she thinks mostly of herself. She & "I" are the only ones who never show their tempers, too. The heavy cooking and all the black tea – which you think was delicious till you go back to it. Curds for tea – puddings, dumplings, the method of eating ceoreal with a cup of milk at the side.

A year later, living alone in New York City, she recorded the more personal turn these memoirs were taking:

A set of apparently disconnected, unchronological incidents out of the past have been re-appearing. I suppose there must be some string running them altogether, some spring watering them all. Some things will never disappear, but rather clear up, send out roots, as time goes on. They are my family monuments, sinking a little more into the earth year by year, leaning slightly, but becoming only more firm, & inscribed with meanings gradually legible, like letters written in "Magic Ink" (only 5 metaphors).

The only story that survives from this year, handwritten on four pages of paper she used for note taking in New York City, the fall after she graduated from Vassar,[2] offers an entrée into the later stories. Here Lucius De Brisay and his mother travel home over a rain-soaked road, the child clearly tense in the presence of his mother. Bishop took the name from her Des Brisay playmates, who summered in Great Village on their grandparents' farm (letter from Ella Des Brisay to Joseph Summers, 26 Aug. 1983, VC); she chose the child's gender, perhaps, in an effort to distance herself from the emotions she would be exposing; she drew the tense, watchful eye of a child for a mother from the anxieties of her early life, which she would render much more thoroughly in the notes that would follow.

It is impossible to say how much she might have written that has not survived. The next and longest series of notes – some thirty pages[3] – appear to have been written in the fall of 1936, filling the first half of a notebook she would then use for a baroque art class at New York University.[4] In these notes the unarticulated tensions of the earlier manuscripts become realized in raw representations of the always painful family situation. Explicitly and poignantly personal, these manuscripts are entirely unlike the writing she was publishing during the 1930s, the years after her career was launched with the publication of "The Map," whose carefully displaced emotions Moore praised, when she published it in Trial Balances (1935). The early poems and the criticism to date about Bishop's 1930s writing hardly prepare us for what lies behind – story after intimate story about her family, and especially about her mother. There was no place in the waning years of modernism, nor among the sentimental "women's poetry" of Millay, Teasdale, or Wylie, nor even in Bishop's own imagination for the unadorned expression of pain in which these manuscripts indulge. Her greatest censor herself, Bishop dismissed phrases and whole episodes with insistent slash marks, with which she attempted to unsee and unsay what she had just remembered and written.

After writing and typing the forty-some pages, she set the memoirs aside and seems not to have picked them up again until the early 1950s, when, having apparently brought them with her to Brazil, she reworked episode after episode in her stories "Gwendolyn" and "In the Village." Surrounded in Brazil for the first time since childhood with a family and a settled, rural life, amid an air of general effusiveness and affection, as she exclaimed repeatedly in letters, she followed up these stories with a flood of poems, prose pieces, and fragments about her family in Nova Scotia. She published the two stories in 1953 issues of the *New Yorker,* calling "In the Village" her "best story," her "masterpiece" (letter to Barkers, 13 July 1953, PU). She published "Manners" (1955), about her grandfather, "Sestina" (1956), about her grandmother, and "First Death in Nova Scotia" (1962). In a "March ??" 1959 letter to Lowell, she mentioned that she was writing "Memories of Uncle Neddy," though she did not publish it until 1977. She completed but did not publish "Primer Class" and "The Country Mouse,"[5] in which her father is marked for his absence; she drafted as well several stories and poems about her mother, her mother's parents, and her Aunts Mary, Grace, and Maud, beginning the earliest of these in the late 1940s or early 1950s and returning to this material through the rest of her life.[6]

The 1936 series of manuscript notes as well as much of the unfinished 1950s and 1960s family poetry reveal patterns central to Bishop's writing of the intimate, in part by their difference from the work she chose to publish. As Chase Twichell argues in her essay on the narrative movement of Bishop's published poetry, "It's not that the emotion is camouflaged or unacknowledged; rather, it's *written around* as though it were each poem's center of gravity. Each poem has a hole at its heart, a hollow spot" (131). Although I will need to rework her image to accommodate what I see as the relational nature of this writing, Twichell's characterization of this hollow spot is the finest articulation I have seen of the "complex tension between the thing said and the thing unsaid" (Twichell 132) in Bishop's poetry. Indeed, at the revision stages Bishop rejected phrases, images, and whole poems when the blunt and often painful emotions spilled beyond the hollow spots and into the descriptive line. Revising and publishing her memories was a process of decentering those hollows, so that the emotion might be shared by the poem's or story's members, be they animate or inanimate. She sought the objects, sounds, and gestures that might assist her subjects in their mutual rendering of the emotions, "the strangest little details of reality – something real coming along like a piece of wood bobbing on the waves," that "will provide an almost instant relief" from the "embarassment [that] always comes from some falsity," as she put it in her notebook (23 June 1950, VC). Trusting the stability of objects and discovering their great potential to, subject-like, hold her poem's emotions, she could represent love and pain both, for instance, in an almanac and teakettle in a grandmother's kitchen. Giving her objects agency Bishop enacts through them otherwise inarticulable relationships.

A brief return to James's and Dewey's empiricism offers a reading of such a relationship. James spoke, in "Does Consciousness Exist?" of an additive relation, in which, in Dewey's terms, the "mental" and the "extra-mental" objects share their functions and attributes (Dewey, *Darwin* 104; James 172). To consider psychical states or physical objects in this way, as mutual participants in the process of knowing, is to decenter the subject who knows (or fears, or desires). Or, as Teresa de Lauretis would argue in her postmodern reading of gender, that "subject" has always been decentered; rather, recognizing this process helps one inquire into the multiplicitous discourses that speak through or bespeak any relation of subjects.

Here I depart from a reading of Bishop's objects as an Eliotian search for an objective correlative that might render accurately an emotional center, and I likewise depart from David Kalstone's reading of Bishop's detail as a "boundary [...] vibrat[ing] with a meaning beyond mere physical presence," affording "radiant glimpses" into an "element[al]," "primal" world and at the same time into the "inner landscapes" of the psyche (*Temperaments* 22, 26, 32). Kalstone's detail might be seen as part of a Jamesian "halo" of significance (46) that fringes the subjectivity of either the inner or outer landscape; and Eliot's objects, too, participate in a one-way relationship, whereby they serve a clearly central emotion. I am interested instead in the ordinary, relational function played by memories, objects around the familiar rooms, sounds and their resonances, repeated gestures and phrases, and individuals who are themselves composites of one another, in the making and remaking of subjectivity. Each entity is fringed by the others, and consequently each assists in the decentering of the emotional hole. Subject–subject relationships are, then, richly layered meetings in the published family writing, and as we study the unpublished writing we can explore Bishop's process of creating and recovering these connections. She revised self-pity and too-terrible emotion by dispersing them among and intertwining them with the familial details that might participate in their remaking. Particularly when she faced the specter of her mother, whose presence and whose horribly absent existence in the sanatorium were traumatic, she sought in her published writing to decenter the mother–child dyad and discover among her familiar objects and family members a continuity that would make a place for the mother's disconnection. Thus, the hollow spot of emotion Twichell articulates is not intact, historically or spatially, and is no more "written around" than through, against, and between. When Bishop could not find ways to articulate these complex and layered relationships, and particularly when she could not find the details in which to house them, she most often left the work unfinished and unpublished.

Her 1950s personal writing follows an identifiable narrative pattern, ambivalent in its movement between efforts toward settled dailiness and impatience to explore these unknown hollows, "the interior," as Bishop calls it in "Questions of Travel." Her 1960 story "Primer Class" epitomizes such an ambivalence, the child-narrator balancing herself tenuously between the safe and the dangerously unknown. Her grandmother, she says, "had taught me my letters, and at first I could not get past the letter *g,* which for some time I felt was far enough to go. *My* alphabet made a satisfying short song, and I didn't want to spoil it" (*Prose* 4). Perhaps the song is satisfying because it stays home, among "Gammie," "Grandpa," Aunt Grace, and Great Village; it also stops before confronting the possibilities beyond her mother's name, Gertrude, whether or not she was conscious of it. Teased by a visitor into going beyond *g,* she gives up a piece of self-protection, but her brave retrospect allows her to smile back as if at her own childishness: "Once past *g,* it was plain sailing" (5). Reaching to "kiss Grandmother goodbye" (6), however, demands similar machinations:

> My grandmother had a glass eye, blue, almost like her other one, and this made her especially vulnerable and precious to me. My father was dead and my mother was away in a sanatorium. Until I was teased out of it, I used to ask Grandmother, when I said goodbye, to promise me not to die before I came home. (6)

Matter of factly stating her losses, containable because definable, she must guard her grandmother, with whose vulnerability she identifies. Not yet lost but losable, the grandmother suggests to her both domestic stability and the terrible unknowns of death and the sanatorium.

In her important discussion of the domestic and the strange in Bishop's published writing, Helen Vendler argues that "the reserves of mystery which give, in their own way, a joy more strange than the familiar blessings of the world made human" oppose and lead to "the impulse to domestication," the "dream of eternal and undismantled fidelity in domesticity, unaffected even by death" ("Domestication" 43, 47–8). Likewise echoing Robert Lowell's 1947 polarities, Denis Donoghue expresses the double-edged nature of Bishop's impulse as

> the desire to be released from the whole human state – from Yeats's "the fury and the mire of human veins" – and at the same time and with no less force, the desire not to be released but to be held within it. The first part of the desire is pastoral; to be released from time, to sink to rest in elements that have no knowledge of themselves and

> therefore no history: the second part is to live, with all its pain, in time
> and the knowledge of ourselves in time. (278)

If we try to apply Vendler's or Donoghue's definitions to Bishop's unpublished writing, we can see just how important a local and relational
reading is in understanding her process toward these polarities. Often
left helpless with raw emotion or stuck within the security of *g,* this
writing bears witness to the fact that before approaching either of the
opposing dreams, Bishop had to find for her subjects their particular,
often surprising source of grounding. She could only consider tuning
the poem's ear to the inscrutable or the elemental when that ground was
sure, those relationships established.

Bishop first constituted the patterns of her 1950s Nova Scotia writing in
the 1930s project, where she sketched the range of emotions of a child
named Lucius. Discussion of this manuscript, then, will offer a backdrop
for her later, published poetry and prose. Here she wrote the hollow
spots – traumatic memories that she would inevitably write around and
between in order to finish and publish this material.

Early in the manuscript, Bishop records the momentary sensation
when the child nightly rediscovers himself:

> There must have been a minute when the outside was suddenly denied
> its entrance, and the window panes refused to let us out, and flung us
> back at ourselves, glowering. I tried hard to catch it, at first identifying
> it with the minute when the ~~first~~ oil-lamp was lit. We used to sit after
> tea, often, talking for two or even three hours, while it grew darker
> and darker. And I noticed then, that sometimes just before the real dark
> came, and while we were still without the lamp, suddenly we'd all be
> mirrored in ~~grey~~ mist, and grey, deepening to gun-metal. But you
> could never catch the instant when our images, dispersed in air all day
> long, were suddenly gathered in like children at bed-time, and held fast
> on the inner side of the window-pane. I used to look at my worry
> reflection – there I was, and where had I been all day? There was my
> grandmother in the next – window, – where had she been? Here we
> all were at last doubly together. (1)

Representing both Bishop's own attempts at definition in the project of
these childhood memoirs and those of the child, Lucius, this room poised
at the brink of night divides the world inside from that which is other.
Restless in his effort to "catch" and define the moment of this division,
the child recognizes it as both frightening and seductive. Feeling im-
prisoned inside, he nonetheless experiences the release from worldly
daytime activity as a means of security, a gathering in of the family
members in the room, as Bishop would represent it again some twenty
years later in "Sestina."

Significantly absent from this scene of the gathering family is Bishop's mother, whom she names "Easter" in these manuscripts, distancing Gertrude, as she has Elizabeth in her own cross-gendered renaming, from the events of their life together. Gertrude's mental illness confuses the picture of domesticity; this mother does not fit. In a passage I quoted in Chapter 2 for its connection with the speaker's impassivity in "The Weed," Bishop records her grandfather's evening readings of the Bible, especially, and Easter's alien position:

> Easter never joined in with our feeling for Grandfather's reading. She liked Burns, too – once she had asked Grandfather to read "Oh wert thou in the cauld blast", but almost always she lay on the sofa with an arm across her eyes, her other ~~hand~~ open hanging down so that the white hand lay on the floor. Betsy lay across her master's feet feet, occaisionally wrinkling up her forehead and rolling up her eyes at me, so that the whites showed. (Reverse of notebook's front cover)

Unlike her grandmother's "precious" vulnerability, her mother's mystery is impenetrable. Both as a child curious about but emotionally removed from this aberrant parent and as a young adult reminiscing, she struggles to locate a way to understand this absent mother. She finally does so in this passage, as she would again in her 1950s manuscript, "Homesickness," by diverting her attention to the dog's empathy.

Searching again for definition in a later passage, Bishop crossed out most of her effort:

> The hardest thing about it now – the sadness of it must be borne, of ~~course~~ – but harder to do – is to realize that it has happened. Sad things, sudden ~~things, awful things~~ – seem always a minute afterwards, so unecessary, so unreasonable. ~~What I had done before, & have done~~ since, ~~and what has happened to us all – it is understandable~~ if you think about it ~~long enough it makes~~ sense and you feel, ~~{ } like a light~~ moving ~~behind a window~~ pane at night, a certain reason, to it – an illumination. – or like an inscrutable, aloof face, ~~lit up by a smile. But this – what happened to her – throws the picture all off – all out~~ the music all out ~~of key~~ – spoils ~~the answer~~ to every question. Gran, at the end of her life, thought suddenly it had all been wrong – and Aunt Grace could look ahead, thinking whatever came would be all wrong. Just things with an awful gray between. – yet both us. Grandpa thought God might step in between – (4)

This is less a child, Lucius, thinking than an adult working to resolve irresolvable memories. Helpless beside the incomprehensible "it," which stands in for any direct reference to her mother or her illness, Bishop searches vaguely for an image that might clarify her feelings. Finding only that any image is thrown "off" or "out," she ends by addressing doubtfully what her family thought. Besides revealing her grandmother's pessimism, her aunt's invariable contradiction of her grandmother, and her grandfather's trust in God's plan, she resolves none of her own confusions. Bishop did not yet have the knowledge in the 1930s to understand her mother's mental illness in psychoanalytic terms[7] and is left with her childhood frustrations, able only to cross out passages such as this one, with no insight available in their stead. She leaves intact, however, the disconnected fragment, "yet both us," asserting some relationship somewhere, though she does not find the words to elaborate it or even to identify the members of the "us."

In other passages she portrays a child frightened but strangely mature, burdened by an unquestioned responsibility for his mother and recognizing his complicity in a family dynamic gone "wrong":

> In the night she began to cry very gently and complainingly like a good child that's stood all it can. She made little imploring noises, asking someone for something. I sat up & pulled my boots on & took the stick from under the window & shut that, then I sat on the edge of the bed waiting for Aunt Grace. She began to cry louder   Suddenly the door opened & Aunt Grace, holding the little lamp, stuck her head in and said very low: "I guess you'll have to come, Lucius." Maybe she wants you." I took the lamp. We walked along the hall. Just as we got to the door Aunt Grace said, "Oh Lucius – I don't know what to do –" (2)

The entire family, especially Aunt Grace, attempt to act as buffers, shielding Easter from the impending crisis articulated finally as a scream in "In the Village." Easter is the "good child" and Lucius one of the good parents, whose duty it is to look after her. Striking specific lines that mark Easter's childlike behavior and her need for Lucius's support, Bishop perhaps recognizes the wrongness and so denies the memory of a mother depending on the attentions of a child of four or five. Whether or not the episode happened this way, she cannot write this instability.

When the mother is not crying, the child is anticipating her tears, as if the world consists of the one state and everything that leads up to or wards off that state. In a page-long description, Lucius details his preference for dark nights, when "the sky and the silence and the house-full of sleep merged all together," while on starlit nights "the silence of the house separated." Lucius concentrates on nighttime silence, he admits, because it helps ease the tension of "the other noises I was waiting for":

> Those were the nights my feet took to dancing under the quilts, by themselves in the dark. I'd just get off to sleep when my feet would begin to dance and pull me awake again, feeling them. In a cold black ballroom one foot would move up & down, up & down, and then the other. They { } { } – sometimes they lay still and just on the surface they danced on and on. As I listened I tried to pay no attention.

[. . .] My ears would listen, liste, as insistently as my feet would dance, and nothing could stop them. Sometimes ~~Often~~ nothing could be heard. ~~Sometimes she would~~ moon or sob very quietly in her sleep, at long intervals. The silence got to be a third person, a sort of guardian ~~who was keeping her quiet and who's vigilance would be forgotten~~ every now & then. Silence would nod his head in the darkness and my mother would moan. And he'd wake up & all would be still again: The darkness favored my family in some way. (Reverse side of grid 4)

Bishop represents in the child's dancing feet the conflicted relation with his mother. They dance despite him, teasing him into insomnia just as his ears compel him to hear his mother's sobbing. Trying to "pay no attention," Lucius cannot help but listen attentively; writing what he hears, Bishop crossed out what she wrote. She personified silence as the only guardian Lucius can depend on, and then she refused herself that insight. Unless she is censoring her personification of silence, it is the child's desperation for a guardian that must be struck. Such an acknowledgment is too much a transgression of the controlled behavior this child expects of himself.

When she wrote the episodes that found their way into "In the Village," she portrayed Easter's illness explicitly:

> Miss O'Neil picked up a large pair of shears & took hold of the extra cloth, to cut it away. At once Easter fell to her knees and snatched the cloth away from her. "Oh Oh!" she cried, "You hurt me. You mustn't cut it. It shan't be cut. It's mine. ~~It's purple & I got it in~~ New York. No, no take the scissors away. Grace! make her stop, it will bleed. I shall bleed." (5)

Two similar paragraphs later, Aunt Grace asks Lucius to show the seamstress out. Later in the kitchen there are more tears:

> "It is the hand of God," said my grandmother; "the hand of God." Aunt Grace bit her lips, & said don't be silly, mother, Lucius, don't pay any attention. Nobody knows what makes things like that happen."
> "That's what I was saying – Nobody knows – it's God's hand, that's what it is." (5)

This child does not miss a beat. Just as his dancing feet would not let him sleep, something keeps him in the house to hear his mother and then his aunt and grandmother. His repeated urge in this manuscript to escape the emotions surrounding his mother – "My poor grandmother began to cry and wipe her eyes on her apron and of course I got out of the pantry as fast as possible" (8) – conflicts with his ceaseless attentiveness and responsibility both to understand what is wrong with her and to fix it. In both tasks, of course, he fails, and she looms, frightening and uncontrollable.

Lucius's Monday morning trips to the post office, after his mother has gone back to the sanatorium, occupy four pages of this manuscript. His grandmother painstakingly wraps packages for his mother, and he must mail them:

> It is the worst moment of the week and I would do anything to get out of it, but I know that's impossible. It must be done, and{?} of course I'm the right person to do it. All I can do is pray to God I won't meet anyone on the way. (6–7)

Bishop describes in detail his trip to the post office, in which he crosses the river, inconveniently meets and must talk to his friend Dimmy, and finally "shoved the parcel at him [Mr. Johnson, the postman] quickly, address side down, with the quarter on top – then ~~bolted~~ fled" (8). His general ambivalence is localized here: his effort to understand his mother opposes his desire to be released from the alien woman who embarrasses him and competes with him for his grandparents' love. Carrying his mother's packages identifies him with her strangeness, for all the village to see. In order for Lucius to regain a family feeling he must accept his part in the containing of his mother:

> It is very strange that she who'se life always broke ~~in upon our~~ up somehow our other regularities – our mealtimes & bed-times and ways of getting along, should now begin to be { } one of them herself. It's strange that all the wildness and excitement, when we thought we could never do anything in the same way we had ~~before~~, has quieted down, with her, Easter, represented in it by a series of neat, brown-papered boxes. "She may not know," said my grandmother, "but I like to do it." (8)

The family had its regularities and "she" broke these up, the "we" and the "she" clearly demarcated. The intrusive "she," who is carefully not marked as Lucius's mother, leaves, and the family makes of her absence a new pattern. Lucius is caught up for a moment by the irony of the situation, his mother packaged.

With a sense of temporary resolution, the manuscript drops the male persona, referring only to an "I." Bishop tells a humorous story about Aunt Grace and her obsession with throwing things out. She describes rooms the child liked and special toys; she drafts the opening description in "Memories of Uncle Neddy" of her mother's and Uncle Arthur's portraits. The tone of these stories is lighter, more playful, and occasionally humorous. When Bishop first set out to revise the manuscript, these and not the emotionally penetrating stories are the ones she typed. Perhaps the happiest story is an earlier one, which also has its typed revision. Immediately following the dress-fitting kitchen scene, Lucius escapes to meet his grandfather in church. He slides with joy into the

pew beside him, accepting from him a peppermint candy. Guiltily suck-
ing the candy, which goes down "like an icy blast whistling through a
belfry" (6), he is "swept violently together" (TS 3) with his grandfather
in this pleasurable, ungodly act.

Following her last typed story about moths fluttering around the light
of a neighborhood store, her revision continues with her sleeping all
night now that Easter was away and then stops abruptly, refusing to
retell that story. Her manuscript goes on in first-person narration[8] to
detail two of the "endless dreams [that] have come to take the place of
sleeplessness" (13). She records a dream that characterizes, in terms that
defy the neat packages, how elusive the child's mother is to her and how
much anger she holds in her sense of helplessness. She is walking in the
forest with a gun, trying to find "the 'enemy', I was saying it myself"
(13). Suddenly, in the dream, "there were moths everywhere":

> I reached out and touched a log, and the surface of it was made of
> hundreds of them lying folded together, the colors of bark. They flew
> up all around me. I pulled at a bough, and the bough fell apart and the
> leaves were moths. I knew that my enemy had changed into moths and
> the moths were again escaping me by coming out of concealment, and
> disintegrating flying up. The evening walk and my concentration on
> it, with my the gun and my a striding walk, were all disintegrating.
> Easter came into it somehow. I woke up, horrified at the { } with{?}
> all the fluttering, bothersome moths, and just as I woke, so that the
> feeling was neither a sleeping nor a waking one, I became certain that
> the enemy was she. (13–14)

The child grasps something solid – a tree – and its bark is an illusion.
The enemy is elusive, taking on the appearance of a tree's stability simply
as a ploy to escape capture and comprehension. The mother is the enemy.
If the child could, she would hold on to her, or perhaps she would shoot
her, but she cannot even get close. She knows the frustration and anger
of this in an almost conscious state, she says in her recollection of the
dream, between waking and sleep. Bishop did not allow the articulation;
the dream could stand, but the mother's place in it had to be put under
erasure. After a pause of white space, the manuscript ends with a sentence
that might have been a transition between this dream and another story:
"A couple of weeks after that my Grandmother began to get after me
about going down to cut the grass on the family plot in the graveyard"
(14). But she did not tell that story, nor did she develop the connection
between the terrifying dream and the grandmother's request. It simply
stands there, as if to defy the closure of any of this writing.

By the 1950s, when Bishop returned to this manuscript particularly
and her childhood more generally, she was discovering ways to understand her stories differently. Her psychoanalysis in the 1940s, her distance

of time and place from her mother, and some twenty years of reading, writing, and life experience all contribute to the sure voice with which "In the Village" makes use of this raw material. The development was far from smooth, however. Much of the 1950s unpublished writing still struggles with what Bishop accomplishes in her "masterpiece." Much of it never quite locates in the daily objects of her world the subject–subject relationships that might shore the child up or bring the people together. Most of the unpublished writing about the mother does not achieve what seems to be a necessary diffusion of the mother's pain and compensation for the child's.

From its opening passage forward, "In the Village"⁹ admits but de-centers the pain, making the mother's scream communal so that the child need not bear it alone and offering the child sustenance, even pleasure, in her village of profound but homey details:

> A scream, the echo of a scream, hangs over that Nova Scotian village. No one hears it; it hangs there forever, a slight stain in those pure blue skies, skies that travelers compare to those of Switzerland, too dark, too blue, so that they seem to keep on darkening a little more around the horizon – or is it around the rims of the eyes? [. . .] It was not even loud to begin with, perhaps. It just came there to live, forever – not loud, just alive forever. Its pitch would be the pitch of my village. Flick the lightning rod on top of the church steeple with your fingernail and you will hear it. (*Prose* 251)

The scream hovers over the opening, insisting on its presence through its own eternal nonsound and through the narrative's verbal repetition and variation. Even though it issues from the voice of the child's mother at the dress fitting, she is neither its beginning nor its end. It exists apart from her, larger and more permanent.

"In the Village" is about understanding and accepting not the mother, but the scream. Intrinsic to the child's acceptance is her discovery of compensation, both in the relief of her responsibility for the scream and in the pleasurable alternative of the hammer pounding out a horseshoe, matching the scream sound for sound:

> Nate was there – Nate, wearing a long black leather apron over his trousers and bare chest, sweating hard, a black leather cap on top of dry, thick, black-and-gray curls, a black sooty face; iron filings, whis-kers, and gold teeth, all together, and a smell of red-hot metal and horses' hoofs.
> *Clang.*
> The pure note: pure and angelic.
> The dress was all wrong. She screamed.
> The child vanishes.
> Later they sit, the mother and the three sisters, in the shade on the

back porch, sipping sour, diluted ruby: raspberry vinegar. The dress-maker refuses to join them and leaves, holding the dress to her heart. The child is visiting the blacksmith. (252–3)

Whether or not the blacksmith was at work this day, Bishop had not in her early manuscript discovered that his sound could balance her moth-er's, that both sounds infused the village with their difference, and that, oddly, they hovered together over the mother's and child's pain. As the mother drinks raspberry vinegar and the child visits the blacksmith shop, the family's tension eases, "Now it is settling down, the scream" (254). But the process of the scream and its overcoming have changed irrev-ocably the child's position in her story. Embraced by a community pitched to the tones of the scream as she discovers compensatory tones herself, and no longer burdened by the unbearable responsibility of wait-ing for her mother to scream, the child takes over the narrative. Tense shifts from past to present; narrative perspective will shift shortly to the first person (see Kalstone, *Temperaments* 24).

Reconstituting her life during these months of 1916, Bishop writes with a childlike self-possession and serious curiosity, and an adult's ret-rospective humor. The child studies daily events intensely, as if the more she understands the less she will be under the spell of what she does not. She subjects every detail, no matter how seemingly extraneous, to her creative scrutiny, combing the world for clues. As her grandmother and aunt unpack her mother's dresses and china, for instance, she inspects her postcards:

> The crystals outline the buildings on the cards in a way buildings never are outlined but should be – if there were a way of making the crystals stick. But probably not; they would fall to the ground, never to be seen again. Some cards, instead of lines around the buildings, have words written in their skies with the same stuff, crumbling, dazzling and crumbling, raining down a little on little people who sometimes stand about below: pictures of Pentecost? What are the messages? I cannot tell, but they are falling on those specks of hands, on the hats, on the toes of their shoes, in their paths – wherever it is they are. (255)

Concentrating on these other worlds, the child escapes beyond the room being prepared for her mother's return. Similarly, she can leave nothing unnoticed in a village where a mother screams. She is entranced by Nelly's "fascinating" (263) cow flops; she studies the dressmaker, "crawl-ing around and around on her knees eating pins as Nebuchadnezzar had crawled eating grass" (252). She plays words over in her head – "mourn-ing" (254), "vault" (256) – giving them definition by contextualizing them and imagining their depths; she interprets as a serious and grand adventure being sent away from the dress fitting to buy her mother candy. As the scream "hangs over," the child attends to the places of her village – the Chisolm's field, Nate's blacksmith's shop, Mealy's candy store, the post office; all of their various details together enable the child to bear the family emotions.

When her mother is taken away to the mental hospital, the child again accommodates a new pattern, a now weekly mother. Listing the objects in each package her grandmother faithfully prepares for mailing, she marks careful time by beginning a new paragraph for each week's enumeration. As in the 1936 version, the child is embarrassed by her duty:

> I take the package to the post office. Going by Nate's, I walk far out in the road and hold the package on the side away from him.
> He calls to me. "Come here! I want to show you something."
> But I pretend I don't hear him. But at any other time I still go there just the same. (272)

The embarrassment is the same but the resentment is gone, because this child has discovered a ritual parallel to the post office trips "every Monday afternoon" (273). Though Lucius's attempt to stop on the bridge and watch the trout was aborted in the 1936 manuscript by Dimmy's approach, this child can form a present continuous statement: "Going over the bridge, I stop and stare down into the river" (273). The trout, "rushing in flank movements, foolish assaults and retreats, against and away from the old sunken fender of Malcolm McNeil's Ford" (273), are constant, as are the Ford, the tin cans in the river, and her presence on the bridge above them. Together these make up the weekly package, just as the "beautiful pure sound" of Nate's hammer balances the "almost-lost scream," in her sense of the village's sounds.

A passage crossed out and isolated by white space in her 1936 memoirs addresses such compensation:

> ~~When a certain feeling has been built up ( ) a long period of time it creates a space for such feeling~~– a large space which must be filled and ~~as the original excitement or emotion goes away another must come or must be made to come~~ to fill it. ~~Only by a gradual shrinkage can the excitement ever die down.~~
> "If it isn't one thing it's another." (8)

The end of "In the Village" gives closure to the sense that one thing can "fill" the "large space" of another. Here the space is elemental:

> Now there is no scream. Once there was one and it settled slowly down to earth one hot summer afternoon; or did it float up, into that dark, too dark, blue sky? But surely it has gone away, forever.
> It sounds like a bell buoy out at sea.
> It is the elements speaking: earth, air, fire, water.

All those other things – clothes, crumbling postcards, broken china;
things damaged and lost, sickened or destroyed; even the frail almost-
lost scream – are they too frail for us to hear their voices long, too
mortal?
Nate!
Oh, beautiful sound, strike again! (274)

The "it" of the bell buoy and of the elements connotes the sound of
hammer hitting metal, overcoming the scream. At the same time, the
referent still denotes the scream, since the string of "it" pronouns preceding these refer directly to the scream. "Almost-lost" and not "gone,"
we realize, this scream meets the clang in these two undecidable sentences
about neither – about the ocean's bell buoy and the atmosphere's elements. The two sounds blend into each other grammatically, as they
have in fact been blended in memory, the "beautiful sound, strike again!"
matching but not erasing the hovering tones of the scream. Interwoven
with the chips of china, the postcard pictures, and even the objects altogether lost, the vitally conflicting sounds give the mother and child
tl e history, companionship, and compensation of a village of relations.
' he 1936 manuscript's irresolvable attention to the mother's illness and
the child's fear and guilt have been revised for the moment of the published story by these layered subjects and decentered hollows.

In her search for such well-worn objects, the "strangest little details
of reality," Bishop fantasized in her 1935 notebook about a repository
for her life's things. With the same deep regard for the seemingly useless
that she would rearticulate about Darwin some thirty years later, Bishop
mused about her life's details:

Sometimes I wish I had a junk-room, store-room, or attic, where I
could keep, and had kept, all my life the odds & ends that took my
fancy. The buffalo robe with moth-bitten scalloped red-flannel edges,
my Aunt's doll with the limp neck, buttons, china, towels stolen from
hotels, stones, pieces of wood, beach-tarp, old hats, some of my relatives cast-off clothes, toys, liquor labels, tin-foil, bottles of medicine
to smell, bottles of colored water – things which please by their neatness,
such as small lined blank-books, blocks of solder.
– Everything and Anything: If one had such a place to throw things
into, like a sort of extra brain, and a chair in the middle of it to go and
sit on once in a while, it might be a great help – particularly as it all
decayed and fell together and took on a general odor. (Late Aug. 1935)

Whereas in her story "The Sea and Its Shore" (1937), Edwin Boomer's
life work is to assemble and interpret scraps of writing found strewn on
the beach, words are pointedly absent here. More important are the
melding qualities of these objects, their smells, textures, and colors,
which might decay in surprising ways together. Here, amid the array of

combinatory possibilities, the young writer imagines herself sitting in creative anticipation.

Some eighteen years later, Bishop opens "Gwendolyn,"[10] the first of her 1950s memoirs, remembering one winter when, sick with bronchitis, she was given the family's crazy quilt and allowed to play with Aunt Mary's "best doll," who had an eccentric and moth-eaten wardrobe, and with the myriad shapes and colors in her grandmother's button basket and fabric scrap bag. Bishop makes a point of denying any necessary transition between the scene she has just elaborated and "the story of Gwendolyn" to follow (215). But the "general odor" of her almost twenty-year-old "junk-room" has come to fruition: though the button basket and the scrap bag do not reappear in Gwendolyn's story, they help bring to the surface the details of the following summer – Gwendolyn's blocks, the strawberry basket of marbles, the lambs and inscriptions on the children's tombstones, and Gwendolyn's diabetes, her delicateness, her consciousness of death, and her death. The story of Gwendolyn Appletree, the "beautiful heroine" (217), is more precisely a melange of memories from and stories about the particular summer in which she died and the months around it; Gwendolyn's story and all these others simply "decayed and fell together."

Thus, Bishop can wander away from Gwendolyn to describe the village graveyard, where she discovers the details that help her reconcile the concept of death – her own perhaps more than Gwendolyn's:

> I loved to go with my grandfather when he went to the graveyard with a scythe and a sickle to cut the grass on our family's graves. The graveyard belonging to the village was surely one of the prettiest in the world. It was on the bank of the river, two miles below us, but where the bank was high. It lay small and green and white, with its firs and cedars and gravestones balancing against the dreaming lavender-red Bay of Fundy. [...] Blueberries grew there, too, but I didn't eat them, because I felt I "never knew," as people said, but once when I went there, my grandmother had given me a teacup without a handle and requested me to bring her back some teaberries, which "grew good" on the graves, and I had.
>
> And so I used to play while my grandfather, wearing a straw hat, scythed away, and talked to me haphazardly about the people lying there. I was, of course, particularly interested in the children's graves, their names, what ages they had died at – whether they were older than I or younger. (222–3)

In her pleasurable excursions with her grandfather to the Great Village graveyard, the child concomitantly evades and confronts death. The Bay of Fundy, the firs and cedars, the blueberries, her grandfather's love, and the duties they are there to perform give the graveyard, where children like Gwendolyn are buried, a place as vital to the narrator's life as to Gwendolyn's death. Examining the death dates of children she never knew, who had lives comparable in length to her own, she registers the concept of a life span: just as when Gwendolyn's coffin was left frighteningly alone for a minute, propped up against the church, with no one to watch but she (224), she in her life and Gwendolyn in her death somehow complete each other's story.

The "Gwendolyn" graveyard scene suggests several other stories as well. There is the understated, casual love between grandfather and granddaughter and the practical working relationship between granddaughter and grandmother, for whom she picks teaberries despite her inherited superstitions. In the 1936 manuscript, Aunt Grace asked her to pick teaberries, and she cut the grass on the graves with Dimmy. Giving her grandparents these roles in revision, Bishop tightened the intimate circle. Her deep affection for the Nova Scotia countryside also infuses this scene, full and rich whether or not it is peopled. One memory led to another, as she wrote the Barkers (12 Oct. 1952, PU), and in several unfinished poems she took up these other stories, from different angles, including different family members.

She returned to blueberries at the graveyard in two unfinished poems from the mid–1950s.[11] One simply charts the picking of blueberries with her Aunt Maud, with whom she lived from 1918 until 1927, when she began boarding school. The other elegizes Aunt Maud, after her burial in the Nova Scotia graveyard:

> My aunt, you are dead now & live
> I think, only there
> in a tip-tilted graveyard

In different arrangements each time, she developed the graveyard scene:

> with your childhood's river ~~curling~~ quietly curled at your side
> and all of your childhood's Christmas trees ~~now-alive~~ grown much
> > taller
> standing around you. And your parents and grand-parents
> > strange and modest fete
> This was the present they had to give.

She wanted to include the blueberries and tried out a few versions of this image:

> The rain had put
> a finger on each blueberry
> tapped off a spot sky-blue dust –

She never found a way to arrange these memories, but the number of times she wrote somewhat circularly about the "tip-tilted" graves, curling river, Christmas trees, and blueberries, suggests that an elegy about her aunt depended on the precise placement of these objects from their mutual past. Taking Aunt Maud back home to Nova Scotia and viewing her dead, amid these graveyard memories, rather than in the apartment where they lived together, stilled her and left only a greater longing, as Bishop recognized in one draft. Following the line "Your childhood river curls at your side," she typed, "who – maybe even in writing this p epoem/has exercised the same." Seeing her own effort to curl back into the security of *g* at her aunt's side, she ventured in handwritten notes at the bottom of that page to include such un-nostalgic details as

> each chipped damned dish
> you improvised{?} on me
>
> when you talked so much
> to my young deaf dreaming deliberately ears.

Bishop found more fruitful the focus on their life together; a third poem from the mid-1950s celebrates Aunt Maud and Uncle George Shepardson's dilapidated tenement apartment in an immigrant neighborhood north of Boston. After the cold, lonely wealth of her brief life with her Bishop grandparents, which she was to characterize a few years later in "The Country Mouse," this apartment seemed to burgeon with love and noise, in the kind of disorderly meld she had sought in her 1935 notebook. She returned to the subject in an unfinished 1960s prose memoir, "Mrs. Sullivan Downstairs," and in a 1970s revision of the 1950s poem, centering on two canaries, Dicky and Sister, and the household songs.

A happy confusion of noises powers the mid-1950s poem:

> we had time
> on winter afternoons
>
> when the Singer sang; the canary sang eagerly
> and Magee Ideal flashed red & her ~~coal~~,   joints
> [. . .]
> and the water thumped and banged in the long brass pipes
> & the ~~neighbor~~ Irish downstairs were {   } up housekeeping freely
>   din
> we lifted our voices in many a hymn.
>   You took the alto.   straight through the hymnbook –
>
> The pipes and the knobs of the faucets framed us
> in gold & the Jello studded in ruby
> & the stew took on form & joined in the

Though this draft never became a poem, its representation of layered, overlapping sounds is much like Bishop's published writing's attentiveness to the daily things of her world. Marking the sewing machine, kitchen stove, and gelatin with their brand names is not to commodify them but to personalize them: they become subjects acting in the room, alongside aunt and niece, participating in the song and framing the singers. Her interest in the subjectivity of daily objects here once again echoes a passage in her 1935 notebook, written while in France: "I should like to write a series of short, descriptive poems that would give me the same satisfaction as the pictures & descriptions in the old mail-order catalogues. They – the catalogues – must enter prominently into the 'novel.'" She further explores this fascination:

> particularly toy-departments, musical instruments, appliances like trusses & syringes, etc. – filled me with horror – The same effect as the little legs, kidneys, hearts, made out of silver they stick up around the altars in churches here. That an object has an existence strong enough to produce these ghosts, distortions, funereal, engraved – nightmares of itself – with prices & writing underneath – This is very hard to get to the bottom of.

Directly linking the catalogue with the family monuments of her novel in progress, Bishop is intrigued with the sundry nature of her memories, which are so reminiscent of the catalogue's display and with the mystery lingering alive in the objects of both catalogue and personal history. Here and in the junk-room passage immediately following, Bishop suggests how intrinsic these strangely vital objects are to any accurate representation of her family memories. Choosing not to mention the debilitating asthma that kept her home with her aunt in the first place, twenty and as many as forty years later Bishop explored the relationship between aunt and niece, as they discover their mutual pleasure among the kitchen objects.

Writing as often about her Bulmer grandmother, Bishop returned repeatedly to her grandmother's phrase "Nobody knows." Just as she sought in daily objects the metonyms of fellow feeling, she recovered this phrase as the precarious balancing of her grandmother's sadness and resignation. She first used it in the 1936 manuscript, again at the graveyard in "Gwendolyn," and again in "The Grandmothers," a poem about each of her grandmothers (one is called "dear old great-grandmother"), on which she worked in the middle to late 1950s.[12] The poem attempts to represent each – "three average Christian ladies of their day" – through her favorite phrase:

> I had three grandmothers
>
> My day will come.
> We wondered what she meant
> and did it ever come

> Her knee polished   blue-veined
> smelling of oil of wintergreen
> She rose   from the   rocker saying
> <u>Nobody knows</u>
>
> the worst   – the great
>
> and all that she could say
> was <u>Ho-hum. Ho-hum, hum-a-day.</u>
>
> What dismal phrase will come to me?,
>
> Hear myself saying

Each grandmother would have a section, and then she would look amusedly at herself in old age. The task of the poem seems simple enough, but when Bishop began to explore the phrases, her clarity broke down, as did her verse form and handwriting. She began one version with the phrase "but us two," echoing the fragment "yet both us," in her 1936 memoir. Again marking an enigmatic relationship, perhaps a doleful pact between her and her Bulmer grandmother, perhaps an eye-winking one between her and somebody else, Bishop again leaves off the page the exploration of that relationship.

>   but us two.
>   <u>Nobody knows</u> –
>   it was   meant
> Nobody knows// – & nobody knew// what₍they were supposed to <u>know</u>
>
> and ten years after the first one she died, too.

In another draft she followed this line with

> concealing her knowledge – (to the end).

Turning the phrase over and over as she writes, Bishop seems frustrated and fascinated by its resistance. The ghost of the original, her grandmother's resignation, lingers, but it refuses to come to life in response to the phrase's call. Stymied by these resistances, perhaps, the poem remained a draft.

In its 1936 appearance, "nobody knows" how to explain the lifelong family catastrophe of her daughter's mental illness. In "Gwendolyn," the phrase is humorous and has only to do with the effect dead bodies might have on the fertilization of wild blueberries. "The Grandmothers" simply utters and reutters the grandmother's concealed pain. Bishop most explicitly acknowledges her confusion with the phrase in the story she drafted in 1959, "Memories of Uncle Neddy."[13] Nobody, according to her grandmother, knows how to handle her son and daughter-in-law's constant fighting:

"*She* makes the balls and he fires them . . . " Then she would start
rocking, groaning and rocking, wiping her eyes with the edge of her
apron, uttering from time to time the mysterious remark that was a
sort of chorus in our lives: "Nobody knows . . . *nobody knows* . . . " I
often wondered what my grandmother knew that none of the rest of
us knew and if she alone knew it, or if it was a total mystery that really
nobody knew except perhaps God. I even asked her, "*What* do you
know, Gammie, that we don't know? Why don't you tell us? Tell me!"
She only laughed, dabbing at her tears. She laughed as easily as she
cried, and one very often turned into the other (a trait her children and
grandchildren inherited). Then, "Go on with you!" she said. "Scat!"
(*Prose* 241–2)

If, for the child, "nobody knows" represents a Lacanian sort of metonymy that stretches forth in an unreachable desire for the grandmother's and through her the mother's love,[14] for the poet it enacts with
profound accuracy the secrecy and silences that accompanied the love
between grandmother and granddaughter. "Nobody knows" bears the
sadness of the mother's psychosis, but it does not center there, because
it also holds within it a lifetime of the grandmother's memories, doubts,
and acceptances. And, in its repetition, it becomes intrinsic to the child's
very recognition of her grandmother, and to the poet's recollection.

Approaching the relationships buried within the phrase "but us two"
rather than attempting to penetrate the grandmother's mystery, "Sestina," a poem Bishop was drafting within months of "The Grandmothers," reveals in the understatement of diffused tears both this intimacy
and the gap inhabited by the absent daughter-mother. First titling the
poem "Early Sorrow," Bishop writes around and through the sorrow
in this poem renamed for its form. "Sestina" enacts the practical relationship between grandmother and granddaughter, representing their
resignation and continuity in their kitchen objects – the almanac, teakettle, and Marvel Stove:

> September rain falls on the house.
> In the failing light, the old grandmother
> sits in the kitchen with the child
> beside the Little Marvel Stove,
> reading the jokes from the almanac,
> laughing and talking to hide the tears.
>
> She thinks that her equinoctial tears
> and the rain that beats on the roof of the house
> were both foretold by the almanac,
> but only known to a grandmother.
> The iron kettle sings on the stove.
> She cuts some bread and says to the child,

It's time for tea now; but the child
is watching the teakettle's small hard tears
dance like mad on the hot black stove,
the way the rain must dance on the house.
Tidying up, the old grandmother
hangs up the clever almanac

on its string. Birdlike, the almanac
hovers half open above the child,
hovers above the old grandmother
and her teacup full of dark brown tears.
She shivers and says she thinks the house
feels chilly, and puts more wood in the stove.

It was to be, says the Marvel Stove.
I know what I know, says the almanac.
With crayons the child draws a rigid house
and a winding pathway. Then the child
puts in a man with buttons like tears
and shows it proudly to the grandmother.

But secretly, while the grandmother
busies herself about the stove,
the little moons fall down like tears
from between the pages of the almanac
into the flower bed the child
has carefully placed in the front of the house.

Time to plant tears, says the almanac.
The grandmother sings to the marvellous stove
and the child draws another inscrutable house.[15]

Grandmother and granddaughter comfort each other, as did the aunt and the niece, amid the kitchen's sounds and movements; they share a sadness intrinsic to their domestic scene.

Bishop first suggested their kitchen closeness in "In the Village" during the lull between her mother's screams:

> My grandmother is sitting in the kitchen stirring potato mash for to-morrow's bread and crying into it. She gives me a spoonful and it tastes wonderful but wrong. In it I think I taste my grandmother's tears; then I kiss her and taste them on her cheek. (259)

The tears in the potatoes, on the grandmother's cheek, and on the child's lips proliferate all the more in the poem. The sestina form works the house, the stove, the almanac, the child and grandmother, and the tears like therapy or like clay, molding and remolding them, setting them down and resetting them into different contextual relationships. At the same time, since revision must operate within repetition, the entities themselves, the details of this room and these people, remain stable and accountable to one another. The sadness that "nobody knows" how to explain or accept and that permeates the room is met by the almanac's insistence on cyclical, knowable, seasonal fact and by the child's efforts at drawing and knowing domesticity. When she draws yet "another inscrutable house," and when the almanac becomes helpless to the room's season and says it is "*Time to plant tears*," the grandmother, in turn, balances them both by singing, probably her comforting Baptist hymns, "to the marvellous stove."

Thus, for Helen Vendler to articulate the domestic and the inscrutable as, albeit "drift[ing]," polarities ("Domestication" 32), she must overlook the teeming activity of "Sestina's" kitchen, activity that allows domesticity's ease and its trauma to work and revise each other:

> For all the efforts of the grandmother, for all the silence of the child, for all the brave cheer of the Little Marvel Stove, the house remains frozen, and the blank center stands for the definitive presence of the unnatural in the child's domestic experience – *especially* in the child's domestic experience. Of all the things that should not be inscrutable, one's house comes first. The fact that one's house always *is* inscrutable, that nothing is more enigmatic than the heart of the domestic scene, offers Bishop one of her recurrent subjects. (33)

In seeing the house as frozen and the center as blank, Vendler offers no way to read the relations of subjects and objects, which, as much as in "In the Village," enable the process of grieving as they are reinforcing the connections among those remaining. The mother, who perplexes the stove and almanac by challenging domestic order and who prompts the proliferating tears, can overpower neither the bonding of grandmother and granddaughter nor the activity of their emotions among the daily kitchen objects. Pressure-cooker-like, the poem's form repeatedly works the emotions potentially destructive of stable domesticity, and so accommodates them: with every turn of the prosodic pattern the poem confronts one more version of the pain threatening to break through and compensates with its own revision and return. The child proudly captures her mother by circumscribing her within a series of idealistically domestic houses that can accommodate what she cannot fathom about her own. Locating her tears on a man's – perhaps her grandfather's – buttons, she acknowledges their omnipresence as she finds security: allowing somebody else to wear these tears, she can "draw another inscrutable house."

As the poem's objects bear the weight of its subjects' emotions, these crayoned buttons, for instance, acquire their own emotional force. Their simultaneous connection to and distance from the child empower them not only as signifiers of her emotions (they are her own tears, of course, transposed) but also as independent agents of love and pain (they now belong to somebody else in the family circle, who is wearing her pain and protecting her from it). They acknowledge as they are compensating for the absent but hovering mother, and they bind granddaughter and grandmother, for whom the picture is drawn. Like the phrase "nobody knows," the Singer sewing machine, Nate's hammer's sound, and the mother's scream, the objects of "Sestina" both fill the room of the poem with the subjects' emotions and, here particularly because of the form's repetition and variation, meet each other in always renewed combinations that serve to reiterate, diffuse, and compensate for the subjects' pain.

In Bishop's very occasional writing about her father there seems to be none of this pain of loss. He was an absence, someone dead, whose pictures, possessions, and history were to her important inherited artifacts. When Aunt Grace was considering disposing of some of the old family things, Bishop wrote her a pleading letter; she must have them:

> PLEASE do not give away anything! I want everything . . . In fact, I'll get out the letter I had from you just before I left Seattle and go over it [. . .] and see if perhaps there isn't some way you can s hip me some things. I do want to save everything old possible. I had my father's watch repaired in Seattle – Uncle G returned it to me in pieces, you know – face all smashed, one hand misssing, etc. – do you suppose he was in an accident with it, or what? – and now it is runnning perfectly and I do like having it again. I have had my mother's fob watch all these years – had it repaired in N Y only once, I think – and that round glass ball I have – I have so few, but they all look so nice. Here in Rio now I have the old portraits of Uncle Arthur and my mother – (18 Sept. 1966, VC)

There is no extant letter acknowledging receipt of this "everything," so it is unclear what, if anything, was saved. Two years later, when Aunt Grace sent her some napkins her mother had embroidered, she thanked her, wrote about the "family linen" she had had in Key West, and said that she would "love to have [. . .] an old bonnet-basket I remember" (24 Nov. 1968, VC). Her desperate opening tone in 1966 becomes nostalgic by the end of the paragraph. These objects are beautiful, they are useful, and they were her parents'. Amid the chaos of her life in the late 1960s, before and after Macedo Soares's death, these objects offer perhaps more stability than either parent ever could.

When the child-narrator characterizes her father in "The Country Mouse," she represents his place for her within history: "I felt closely related to them all ['the Pilgrim Fathers']: '*Land where my father died / Land of the pilgrims' pride*' – for a long time I took the first line personally" (24). Similarly, his possessions in the story are archaic and solid, producing none of the "horror" of the live items in the mail-order catalogue,

and she moves easily from her dead father's boots to her live grandfather
beneath:

> There was an upright piano, a fireplace with magnificent brass fenders
> and fire tongs, and high on the mantel was a tiny pair of top boots that
> had belonged to my father.
> In the evenings Grandpa sat in the billiard room in a leather chair,
> smoking cigars and reading the newspapers. (*Prose* 25)

Her father's boots remain mantelpiece objects, even less attached to life
in this passing description than are the dead children's tombstones in
"Gwendolyn."

Whereas Bishop left no unfinished manuscripts about her father, she
left most of her writing about her mother unfinished and unpublished.
Remembering this mother, she had at the same time to preserve a distance
with which to discover the stabilizing representative objects. With extremely rare directness she outlined the feelings she had never overcome
in a 1970 letter to Dorothee Bowie, an English department secretary and
friend at the University of Seattle, where she had taught in 1966:

> I was alone with my mother until I was 4 ½ or so – [. . .] and no father,
> as well. But some loving aunts and grandparents saved my life, and
> saved me – a damaged personality, I know, but I did survive.

She went on to suggest the nature of some of the damage:

> My life has been darkened always by guilt feelings, I think, about my
> mother – somehow children get the idea it's their fault – or I did. And
> I could do nothing about that, and she lived on for twenty years more
> and it has been a nightmare to me always. (14 June 1970, VC)

This is, as far as I am aware, Bishop's only written mention of her
mother's incarceration at the Nova Scotia Hospital, where she remained,
psychotic and without family contact, until her death in 1934. But
whether or not this part of the nightmare ever elsewhere reached articulation, it is clear here that it troubled the very remembering of her
mother. As Bishop revealed in "In the Village" and "Sestina," understanding the too painful mother–daughter bond and writing publishable
versions of her memories depended on her discovery of means to diffuse
the mother's emotions and offer the child the continuity of familiars.
Intact, the mother left the child frightened, confused, and, as Bishop
wrote here, guilty; diffused, she is less a mother than a hovering scream
in "In the Village," less a mother than a repetition and variation of tears
in "Sestina."

Bishop began in the late 1940s or early 1950s to write a poem called
"Homesickness," imagining the time before her birth and before her
mother's illness, a subject she would then take up at Yaddo in story

form, using the same title. As late as the 1970s she was revising phrases of the never-completed poem.[16] During these years she also wrote several versions of a poem about a swan-boat ride with her mother in the Boston Public Gardens.

In the prose version of "Homesickness," set in 1899, a family resembling her mother's takes a trip. In early drafts Bishop called the father Lucius MacLaughlin, echoing her 1930s manuscripts' name for herself (in revision she renamed him John MacLaughlin, as if to reserve Lucius). He takes two of his children, Grace and Amos, and the dog, Juno, to visit another daughter, Una (renamed in revision Georgie), who is away teaching school.[17] Bishop explained the scene to Anne Stevenson:

> My mother went off to teach school at 16 (the way most of the enterprising young people did) and her first school was in lower Cape Breton somewhere – and the pupils spoke nothing much but Gaelic so she had a hard time of it. At that school, or maybe one nearer home – she was so homesick she was taken the family dog to cheer her up. I have written both a story and poem about this episode but neither satisfy me yet. ([Mar.] 1964, WU)

The story, however, neither observes nor identifies the schoolteacher, who nonetheless hovers over it, the title signifying her mood and the family voyage approaching but never reaching her. Bishop detailed the clothes, postures, actions, and interactions of a family together, but she broke off each draft before it reached the homesick sister.

The story most closely approaches the emotion of the title in a description of Juno's comforting, maternal presence:

> She had had more puppies than anyone could well remember [. . . .] She had been promiscuous, and yet there was something very settled and domestic in her manner; if she could have talked one could imagine her conversation: cheerful, practical, and tedious, – but a character to turn to with confidence in life's darker moments. Indeed, although she didn't know it, that was exactly why she was being taken on this trip, and among the cloth-wrapped packages under the seat was a large legbone with some meat on it, to be given her when they reached their destination.

Just as the story touches "life's darker moments," it shifts its focus from this enigmatic hint of the daughter's troubles to the quite specific reward Juno will receive for playing her part. The maternal is positively defined here: regardless of her promiscuity, this mother is a practical and cheerful model of domesticity. Gertrude Bulmer, the homesick sister, has no place in the story's description. Further specifying "life's darker moments" might have forced the author to confront her mother; instead, her narrator gazes steadily at the unproblematic canine mother and her reward.

The 1950s drafts of the poem represent the schoolteacher's emotion but reveal helplessness, finally, in their effort to connect this sadness with a larger, off-stage trauma:

remote already & irreparable
Beneath the bed the dog thumped

HOMESICKNESS her tail
================

c. 1900

~~So she~~ put up her hair & went to teach
~~a little~~ from home –
at River Phillips, thirty miles away

The pupils were –

Cousin Sofie –

pan-
The salt pork & the   buckwheat cakes
smelling like frying{?} –

head<u>ach</u>es
the oil lamp – the sloping bedroom
ceiling – in a low tent of sadly
matched wall-paper

<u>Finally</u>
   She missed
her father   her fretful mother &
the jealous sisters –

* The family dog to keep her company.

—   clenched

—

—   sleeping
not even realizing she was weeping
her face   ~~her~~ nightgown   drenched –

It was too late – for what, she did not know. –
already –   , remote,
irrespons<u>ible</u>{?}   (rhyme)   irreparable.
thumped
Beneath the bed the big dog ~~thwocked~~ her tail.

The incomplete phrases at the beginning and near the end of the draft, particularly the repeated "already," suggest an effort to reach back from present knowledge of the trauma to its source. If she can only reenact the scene with careful detail, she might understand this woman's irreparable remoteness.

Whereas this 1950s version combs the room with its attention, the 1970s notes turn directly to the bed on which the schoolteacher lies:

Beside the bed, or on it –
or die,
     where later I was born. and I cried, too – ?
     where later I was to be born & cry –
          weep –
She cried but tried.   to say her prayers
Frantic &   Juno licked her ears.
Concerned – frantic "   "   "   "

     And this was how it all began?
Or had it started earlier?
Beside a bed, or on one,   where we weep

or die   where later   I was born –

This draft is a vital exception to Bishop's tendency to revise by diffusing the painful center. Between drafts the details of the room and the family members that peopled it have faded and the bed has risen in significance, its ghostlike presence somehow bearing the connection in pain between mother and daughter. Focusing as directly as possible on the confusion of birth, death, and madness that engulfs this pair, Bishop returns to the rawness of her 1936 writings. Unable, as she was there, to extricate her birth from its seeming inseparability with her mother's madness, she leaves this draft as painful enigma.

Bishop probed the confused connection between herself and her mother again when she studied the memory of her mother's swan bite in the Boston Gardens. There are three extant versions of a poem,[18] in addition to the published mention of the ride in her 1952 *Poetry* review of Wallace Fowlie's *Pantomime*. In the review she discusses the event as the kind of reality missing in Fowlie's "idealization[s]":

> As I read his book I could not help making comparisons between Mr. Fowlie's early impressions and my own. My own first ride on a swan boat occurred at the age of three and is chiefly memorable for the fact that one of the live swans paddling around us bit my mother's finger when she offered it a peanut. I remember the hole in the black kid glove and a drop of blood. I do not want to set myself up as a model of facing the sterner realities of swan boat rides in order to discredit Mr. Fowlie's idealization, – but there is remarkably little of blood, sweat, or tears in Mr. Fowlie's book. (Schwartz and Estess 282)

Here she makes the scene objective; Bishop, the adult reviewer, looks back at a frightening but distant memory of childhood. The various versions of the poem likewise reenact the day when child and mother were in Boston together, but they find none of this objectivity.

                              meddle
                              model{?}

        Swan-Boat Ride   paddle –
        ~~Ballad-of-the-Swan-Boats~~
                    where the live swan paddles
dead water
* pontoons & pedals   peanut –
    my mother's hand
proffered a peanut from the bag   (?)
Ungracious bird –   Ungracious, terrifying bird!
Afloat, afloat   suspended
the whole pond swayed
                    descended
madness & death
I saw the hole, I saw the blood.

                    set (designs)
The flower beds (in the same patterns)
– the State of Massachusetts seal

        the State House Dome –
        its thinly crusted sun.

                    ambiotic flood –

The child faces a terrifying thought: perhaps her mother's "madness &
death" began here in this bloody hole; having witnessed this biting, she
herself is irrevocably linked to this horror.[19] As if to avoid the very
thought, her eyes dart wildly away from the terrible hole, scanning
instead the pond, the flower beds, the state house dome. It seems very
important here to mark personal boundaries; it is "my mother's hand";
"I saw" it. This child must keep herself from being "suspended" in or
"descend[ing]" to her mother's place. In the uncorrected spelling error
that ends the draft, however, the fear arises once again: suggestive of
amniotic fluid, this "ambiotic flood" leaves the connection between a
mother's madness and a daughter's birth wholly unsettled, as they were
most explicitly in her 1970s draft of "Homesickness."

    The fear, repulsion, and particularly ambivalence of the child's re-
sponse in "Swan-Boat Ride" find their counterpart in the typed version
of the poem, which makes every effort to ensure neutrality and control.
The narrating child firmly if not defiantly separates herself from her
mother, who is in this draft in pieces, depersonified, defined as the events
in which she acts and the parts of her clothes and body that do the action.
Yet Bishop ends this version with an irresolution different only in its
tone from that closing "Swan-Boat Ride":

    A mother made of dress-goods
    white with black polk-dots,
    black and white "Shepherd's Plaid."

A mother ~~of a~~ is a hat
balck hat with a black guaze rose   gauze rose
falling half-open

A long black glove
the swan bit
in the Public Gardens

Hair being brushed at night
and brushed
"Did you see the spark?"
Yes, I saw the spark
and the shadow of the elm
outside the window
and

A naked figure standing
in a wash-basin shivering   half coruched
a little, black and white
in the sloping-cieleing ed bedroom
with the strioed wall paper

A voice   heard still
echoing
far at the bottom somewhere
of my aunt's on the telephone –
coming out of of blackness –   the blackness all voices come from

The snow had a crust, they said, like bread –
only white – it held me up but it would not hold her
she fell through it
and siad snhed go home again for the snow-shoes –
  and I could slide in shine and glare while she
stepped wide
on the

What is this mother? this version asks; of what does she consist? In terms similar to those of the child Vardaman in Faulkner's *As I Lay Dying* – "My mother is a fish" (79) – Bishop opens with a picture of her mother not in but as the fabric of her clothes. Her revision in the fourth line is telling. This is not a mother "of" anyone, but a mother disconnected and definable – "a hat," or at least more akin to the stillness of a hat than to the vitality of the one who puts it on and takes it off. Here Bishop most explicitly questions the dichotomy between subjects and objects, or between people and the things that participate in the making of their subjectivity. Whereas John Dewey shook loose the bounds of subjectivity so as more broadly to define empiricism, Bishop radically shifts the terms here, rendering her mother an impassive object and giving her attendant objects all the activity of the poem. Having throughout her career freed her subjects and objects to interact in flexible relations with one another, Bishop takes but a short step to this reversal. With the mother fixed, the child can focus on the glove and not on the mother wearing it; the glove, and not even the mother's hand, is bitten. Constituting the mother as her material terms, the child staves off the chaos, as the child of the 1936 memoirs felt it her duty to do.

In linked but separate moments, the mother is hair, a crouched and naked figure, a voice: Bishop attaches participial verbs to the synecdoches, giving them actions without requiring that these representatives of the mother act directly. The question we assume issues from the mother's mouth, "Did you see the spark?" stands alone, without a speaker. It is heard, nonetheless, since it is answered by the child's thought, disengaged one step further, not even reaching articulation. In this limbo of partial persons, the biting scene loses its violence. Disconnected though these images are, in the sense that they convey neither a human being in control of her parts nor a single event in which she acts, they do have a certain cohesion: the child sees or hears each scene, actually or by implication. They are parallel entities, all pendant on an almost articulable whole in the child's mind, not chaotically discharged as were the images of "Swan-Boat Ride." Finally, however, this version, too, becomes helpless to the mother's enigma. The snow emblematically holds the child up, "but it would not hold her" mother, who leaves the poem in search of snowshoes. As if Bishop was aware that the snowshoes would not help, or as if awaking from a dream that had to end, because its conclusion might be too terrible, she left off here, before giving the mother a chance to return.

A few years later she closed her published poem "First Death in Nova Scotia"[20] amid similarly alienating, cold snow. There, reexploring a child's death, as she had done in "Gwendolyn," her child-narrator can once again meet her subject on equal terms. Here, as there, the room's details give the death a continuity, and, belonging to the live family in the room, this child, too, has the security to pose the difficult questions. She does not quite believe, for instance, the stable fictions she and her family have been posing regarding "little cousin Arthur's" death. Arthur does not belong among the entourage of royalty whose likenesses adorn the walls above his open coffin:

> The gracious royal couples
> were warm in red and ermine;
> their feet were well wrapped up
> in the ladies' ermine trains.
> They invited Arthur to be
> the smallest page at court.
> But how could Arthur go,

clutching his tiny lily,
with his eyes shut up so tight
and the roads deep in snow?

Whereas Vendler asserts, about this poem and Bishop's poetry generally, that Bishop's subjects seek not only to domesticate the unfamiliar but inevitably to achieve "some assurance of transcendent domesticity" in defiance of the awful, lurking unknown ("Domestication" 36, 48), I argue that this child-speaker is caught in a far more ambivalent position. Sympathizing with Arthur's coldness in this "cold, cold parlor," as she could not with her mother's alienation, she closes by transposing herself with him beyond the wake and onto the dark, fascinatingly and dangerously inscrutable "roads deep in snow." Resisting the safer alternative –

"Come and say good-bye
to your little cousin Arthur" –

she strains to see down these unknowable roads on behalf of Arthur, whose eyes are shut. Whereas her mother's madness confounded her absence, so that looking into the hollow of one forced the child into the other, here Arthur's death, awesome as it is, is not terrifying. With troubled doubt and bravery both, this child inevitably gazes into the darkness of her closing question mark. When Bishop tried, however, in her 1970s draft of "Homesickness" to approach directly her mother's void, she was left with all the chaos of her earliest efforts at exploring her family hollows.

Bishop left unfinished a 1970s poem about her grandfather,[21] which brings into focus many of the issues raised by her 1950s and 1960s personal writing. Returning to snow and the strangeness of dream and beginning where the "mother made of dress-goods" poem and "First Death in Nova Scotia" end, Bishop follows her grandfather into death:

FOR X GRANDFATHER

How far north are you by now?
– But I'm almost close enough to see you:
under the North Star,
stocky, broadbacked & determined,
trudging on splaying snowshoes
over the snow's hard, brilliant, curdled crust...
Aurora Borealis burns in silence.
Streamers of red, of purple,
fleck with color your bald head.
Where is your sealskin cap with ear-lugs?
That old fur coat with the black frogs?
You'll catch your death again.

> If I should overtake you, kiss your cheek,
> its silver stubble would feel like hoar-frost
> and your old-fashioned, walrus moustaches
> be hung with icicles.
>
> Creak, creak . . . frozen thongs and creaking snow.
> These drifts are endless I think; as far as the Pole
> they hold no shadows but their own, and ours.
> Grandfather, please stop! I haven't been this cold in years.[22]

This is the last of four extant drafts. In it, she finds most ʾarly her own position in relation to her dead and beloved relative: she trudges along behind him, almost reaching him, imagining their touch. He is strong, and he asserts his place among the elements. There is room for humor, in his coat with frogs that he left behind and in her twist on the cliché about going out in the cold without enough on. This grandfather walks on snowshoes, and they hold him up; the North Star illuminates him; the stars play their colors against his capless head.

The poem only gradually reached this intimacy, whereby she is "almost close enough to see" him. In the first draft he acts and she watches:

> So far north you are by now –
>   under the north star
> strong and broad, I see you
> trudging on splaying snoe-shoes
> on the briiliant snow-crust   over
> with your back to me.

By the second draft, she had changed the opening statement to a question, "And How far north are you by now?" suggesting in her first word a poem in medias res and transforming her speaker into a participant who actively searches for her grandfather. Simple vision becomes vision in motion:

> Under the North Star,
>   almost   determined,
> stocky, ~~strong~~, broad-backed (I'm ~~finally~~ close enough
>   to see you), trudging

Not yet decisive about where she is on his path, she first "finally" and then "almost" sees him; yet, in either case, she is moving with him. Bishop also revised what was in the first draft her grandfather's alienating posture and her passivity in relation to it. In this second draft the broadness of his back became simply one adjective in a descriptive series. By the third draft, she deleted the series altogether,

> (But I'm almost close enough to see you.)
> Under the North star, determined,
> trudging on splaying snowshoes,

conflating herself and her grandfather by leaving as ambivalent whether she or her grandfather, or both, are trudging determinedly. Her title's revisions reflect similarly the changing nature of their relationship. In this order she tested the following:

ForMy Grandfather   W. B.
    died 1927?
    FOR W. B.   (Ask Phyllis –   ) dates?[23]
    (Died 1927? 1928?)
    A
    FOR ~~MY~~ GRANDFATHER   ~~FOR ONE OF MY GRANDFATHERS~~
    FOR X̶ GRANDFATHER

The date becomes unimportant, as do his initials; precise identification gives way to relationship. By leaving out all of her choices of articles in the last title, she in one breath names him for an audience, "Grandfather," and addresses him intimately, as if saying, "For You."

The penultimate line, which until the fourth draft read, "they hold no shadows but their own, and yours," tells its own story of alienation and relation. Whether the "ours" of the last draft is an unmarked revision or a typo, it leads Bishop most poignantly to her closing cry. This is their experience together. Bishop did not simply stop this journey through beautiful but terrible coldness, as she stopped the dress-goods poem about her mother or as she ended "First Death in Nova Scotia," with the relationships left unfinished. This poem attains closure in its recognition that these subjects cannot abandon each other; the "I" must experience the pain through and through. The last line's revision from "Please, Grandpa! Stop!" to "Grandfather, please stop!" suggests that this is not simply a child crying out helplessly to her grandfather. The more controlled utterance gives it an urgency and a power that matches in its considered resistance her grandfather's stocky determination.

Her revisions of this poem follow the patterns of much of her personal writing throughout this period. She revised self-pity by discovering an object to stabilize an emotion – a broad back to replace a back turned to her. Though often unsuccessfully, she worked to affirm subject–subject relations whereby the people and the objects of her writing compensate together for the pain in their midst. She attempted to revise the threatening mother–daughter symbiosis, which she describes so rawly in the 1936 manuscript, by decentering its potentially terrifying emotions and diffusing them around the room or around the village, so that none must bear the responsibilities of "madness & death" alone. Serving as both participants in the family's emotions and independent agents of love and pain, the familiar objects, gestures, and sounds of Bishop's published writing offer domestic stability, as they are testing the inscrutable. The mother's chaos and disconnection in the swan boat and dress-goods poems testify to the importance for Bishop's published writing of a relational subjectivity: preserving the mother in isolated, containable moments in the second version of the poem may serve to stop the chaos of the first, but it offers neither security nor the terms for poetry's making. Dispersing the mother's and child's hollow spots of emotion among the poem's animate and inanimate members, as she did in "In the Village" and "Sestina," Bishop provided the writing and the child with the compensation they needed to explore the tones and shades of these hollows' depths. Bishop's representation of her family monuments depended, as her progression of titles toward "For Grandfather" reveals, on an intertwining of the intimate and the objective. Constituting family relations, relations between land and sea, or relations among parts of the different world she encountered in Brazil, as I will show in the next chapter, Bishop kept in tension seemingly polarized efforts to discover the bedrock of g as she was exploring beyond it. Amid Brazil as among her family, she created the domesticating stories – the royal court and the careful artist Jack Frost who make sense of "little cousin Arthur" – as she was peering curiously at difference, at the boy's death and the impermeable snow.

5

Confronting Brazil

When Bishop began to write about the Brazil that had become her home, she did so with the conflicted voices of a self-imposed exile not of and not apart from her subject. The position pressured issues with which her writing had dealt since the beginning of her career. Always feeling, as she told Elizabeth Spires, that she had been a guest in her family's houses (75), she was most concretely here a foreigner, a guest, an observer-writer-translator of a culture not her own. Yet from her first few months, as she wrote repeatedly to friends, among the effusive affection of her Brazilian friends and acquaintances she felt so much at home that she found her writing returning home to Nova Scotia. The concepts of home and not-home were foregrounded for her amid this oddly coincidental social geography. What was difference? what foreignness? what inside and what outside? Was it ever possible to reach "the interior," for which she sets off in her first Brazilian poem, or was the culture's interiority finally as inscrutable as her mother's or grandmother's would prove to be, during the same years of poetic inquiry? Would what she called her "double point of view" ever offer an intimacy with Brazil, or would the inbreath of her empathy interfere with her knowing the other? Bishop worked these questions in her writing about Brazil, much of which she never finished, perhaps because she never found satisfactory answers.

While the political and postmodern approaches of Gayatri Spivak and Clifford Geertz help me in this chapter to understand Bishop's confused subject position in Brazil, their concerns, especially those of Geertz, can be traced to an American pragmatism questioning, in the first decades of the century, what it is that goes into our knowing of things. As John Dewey articulates it in *Experience and Nature*:

> Reverie and desire are pertinent for a philosophic theory of the true nature of things; the possibilities present in imagination that are not found in observation, are something to be taken into account. The

features of objects reached by scientific or reflective experiencing are important, but so are all the phenomena of magic, myth, politics, painting, and penitentiaries. The phenomena of social life are as relevant to the problem of the relation of the individual and universal as are those of logic; the existence in political organization of boundaries and barriers, of centralization, of interaction across boundaries, of expansion and absorption, will be quite as important for metaphysical theories of the discrete and the continuous as is anything derived from chemical analysis. The existence of ignorance as well as of wisdom, of error and even insanity as well as of truth will be taken into account. (20)

Politicizing such a reading, Gayatri Spivak argues that even when the elements of observation are seen in their multiplicity and even if we are willing to question the relative positions of the "subject" who observes and the "object" observed, as Dewey does if only in the grammatical shiftability of his terms – *"the odor knows the rose"* (*Darwin* 88) – and as Clifford Geertz does in his anthropological work, finally, we reach only rarely if at all to the subjectivity of the observed subaltern. As Spivak has shown in her essay on subaltern studies, the sort of opacity Bishop experienced, despite her willingness to embrace a "double point of view," is intrinsic to our efforts to retrieve a "subaltern consciousness." We can finally only chart "subaltern subject-effects" that are "part of an immense discontinuous network [. . . of . . .] politics, ideology, economics, history, sexuality, language, and so on." The intertwining of these yields what might appear to be a subject but is in fact only a "metalepsis, or the substitution of an effect for a cause."[1] The interior of this country Bishop had just met was as befuddling as was the source of her mother's mental illness: unless she could trace each of the variously entangled strands that together might retrieve a subject from the subject effects she was inevitably misrecognizing, she could not know the Brazil she meant to write.

Bishop was first an American, who never abandoned her primary literary, political, and personal allegiance to things American, even as she embraced her Brazilian home. She kept in constant contact with her first country through journals, newspapers, and an exchange of letters with more than a dozen regular correspondents. She wrote letters home about her frustration with the tide of American politics, expressing her hopefulness about Adlai Stevenson and disgust with Eisenhower (to MS, 16 July, 10 Nov. 1956, WU) and her anger over what she saw as the Kennedy administration's wrongheaded relations with and representation of Brazil (to MS, 9 June 1961, WU; to RL, 11 Oct. 1963, HL). In 1961 she corresponded with Arthur Schlesinger, on Lowell's urging, about being a cultural attaché in the American Embassy, though nothing came of it (to RL, 15 June, 20 Aug. 1961, HL). She wrote several impassioned letters, including one to the editor at *New Republic* (30 Apr. 1962), refuting misleading and erroneous representations by the American media of Brazilian events (to Barkers, 16 Nov. 1955, 4 Sept. 1961, PU; to RL, 14 Sept. 1961, HL). Yet when she wrote "From Trollope's Journal," her poem denouncing Eisenhower's Washington (to RL, 18 Nov. 1965, HL), she located the criticism in the voice of a foreigner, Trollope, at a foreign time, 1861. She was an American in self-imposed exile, reading about and watching her country from a distance.

Accepted as an American intellectual into the Brazilian elite in an overtly class-oriented social system, Bishop befriended the country's political and literary leaders; her insight into Brazil was from the beginning framed by her friends who were her guides into Brazilian language, culture, family dynamics, and sociopolitical perspectives. Although she often claimed to hate and so to avoid argument, she also held increasingly strong opinions about the workings of the Brazilian government. In the 1950s Brazil was run by "the Vargas gang," as "antigetulistas," including Macedo Soares and Bishop, called Getúlio Vargas and his protégés, particularly Juscelino Kubitschek and João Goulart. Bishop explained political events to the Barkers, especially after Vargas's suicide and during Kubitschek's early months as president (15 Apr., 27 Oct., 16 Nov. 1955, PU). In 1961 Bishop began researching the geography, history, economics, arts, politics, and sociocultural concerns of Brazil for a Time–Life volume. Although she wrote her friends caustically about the editors' bowdlerization of her text, she had the opportunity to read about and travel extensively in Brazil on Time–Life's expense account.

By 1960 Bishop had already become increasingly politicized. She wrote Lowell and the Barkers that she and Macedo Soares were overjoyed at the election of Jânio Quadros as president, though his term was short-lived, and of their friend Carlos Lacerda as governor of the new state of Guanabara, the capital of which was Rio de Janeiro (to RL, 6 Oct. 1960, HL; to Barkers, 28 Dec. 1960, PU). Lacerda, who had entered politics as a young journalist during the Democratic National Union's attempt to block Vargas from becoming president in 1950, was one of Brazil's most virulent antigetulistas; his tenure in office was constantly volatile. From him, Bishop had a biased but nonetheless an insider's understanding of Brazilian power politics; she recorded in a letter to the Barkers, for instance, Goulart's supposed involvement in a smuggling ring and his wife beating (5 Sept. 1962, PU). Lacerda appointed Macedo Soares commissioner of a huge landfill park, the Parque do Flamengo, being planned in Rio, a position that moved her and Bishop to Rio and away from their quiet life on the mountain. As Macedo Soares was discovering how difficult it was to get anything done amid a government of sexist and corrupt co-workers (to Barkers, 4 Mar. 1961, 2 May 1963, PU), and as

Lacerda was relying on Macedo Soares more and more, even using the
Samambaia house as a hideout during an assassination attempt by Goulart
men (to RL, 11 Oct. 1963, HL; to Barkers, 14 Oct. 1963, PU), Bishop
became involved in politics in a way she could not control, as she could
her participation in Vassar socialist activity in the 1930s.

Amid various attempted coups, a threatened state of siege, and finally
the 1 April 1964 "revolution" – the deposition of Goulart by the military
– which Macedo Soares spent barricaded inside the governor's palace,
Bishop was caught in her self-imposed exile's bind, desiring to cut herself
clear from the turmoil yet drawn to and implicated by her position in
Brazil. She wrote of her predicament to the Barkers:

> I want to get away badly these days – I feel like those moments I've
> jus been watching on the beach when two waves going at angles to
> each other meet and an immense confusion of helpless ripples and foam
> and upheavings result... Lota wonders how we keep corresponding,
> Ilse, and I think – besides the fact we both like to write & get letters –
> perhaps it is partly because we are both exiles in a way, even if voluntary
> and cheerful ones – (2 May 1963, PU)

> Oh God – poor Brazil – my feelings are so mixed. I read in an Eng.
> review of Fellini's "8 ½" that it was about someone – artist – who "was
> stuck because he was feeling too many things at once" – and realized
> that describes my state of the last two years exactly. The necessary
> elimination, sequestration, concentration, etc. have been harder &
> harder. (14 Oct. 1963, PU)

The very fact that she is an American with the ready option to get away
makes her exile's position all the more conflicted. She stands amid the
clashing waves not through necessity but through painful affection.

After the revolution and accession of Castelo Branco, Bishop summarized her opinions about events of the past several years for Anne
Stevenson. She discussed the corruption of Kubitschek and Goulart, the
misconceptions of the American press, both from the Right and the Left,
the unjust comparisons between Joseph McCarthy and Lacerda and then
between McCarthy and Branco, of whom she approved, despite his
leadership of a military takeover; she criticized the shortsightedness of
Brazilians in general over matters economic and social. As if spent, she
closed by reaffirming with tired pride how much in the middle of things
she was:

> You see, unfortunately (I often think) I am very much involved in
> politics here because of Lota. – It is such a small society and her family
> has been prominent in diplomacy etc for generations. [...] She is
> working at his [Lacerda's] request, and I suppose we are for him (he's
> running for President, and I hope wins) – in spite of many reservations,

and his obvious faults. – This is a part of life I never would have had much of an idea of if I had stayed in the U S and just paid my taxes and voted, and never had come within miles of any of the real leaders. (5 May 1964, WU)

Holding intact the contradictions of the 1963 letters, Bishop here romanticizes her position inside, a month after the revolution, when she had renewed hopes for Brazil. "In spite of many reservations," she loves this country. Earlier in the letter, however, she devotes several paragraphs to the details of the several-month European vacation for which she and Macedo Soares will leave in June. She is "involved," and she "get[s] away."[2]

Over the two decades Bishop lived in Brazil, she played the course from tourist to resident to exile, not always in this order. Her writing of these years reflects both the opacity and the clarity with which she attempted to define the relations of the place, its people, and herself among them. Her early letters from Brazil record her fascination with the vagueness and the blurring. In a letter to Moore about the Brazilian mail, Bishop's attention is diverted by her world on the hill at Samambaia:

> I don't mean to complain about the mails – they are part of the really lofty vagueness of Brazil, where no one seems to know quite what season it is, or what day of the week, or anyone's real name, – & where a cloud is coming in my bedroom window right this minute. (3 Mar. 1952, V:05:04, RM)

The cloud imposes itself on the room, her imagination, and this letter. Interrupting the discussion of Brazilian laxity, it embodies the strange otherness of the country, in Bishop's recuperation. As newcomer, Bishop is intrigued with whatever might surprise her next. In her early 1950s tourist poems, her speakers address outsiders' alienation and self-protection, as well as their curiosity about the relation they might have with the difference surrounding them.

As Bishop became settled into a daily life that included not only the frustrations of the mails and the sweeping beauty of her view of clouds and flowering trees, which she described in letters each spring, but also the extreme poverty in the slums near Rio as well as the overt sex and class discrimination everywhere, she began to seek ways to define her often clashing impressions. In the mid–1950s, after spending three years writing the tones of rural Brazil as she translated The Diary of "Helena Morley," her poetry became increasingly alert to the economic, racial, and gendered structures that configure speakers and subjects. Writing the relational subjectivity of Brazilians required acknowledging these structures as well as her own framing devices, as she does most poignantly in "Brazil, January 1, 1502," where her speaker participates in the power politics of knowing, having, and controlling the unknown.

Bishop did explicitly confront such issues as child and infant mortality, poverty, crime, Brazilian inflation and corruption, and exploitation in the mines, despite her assertion that she was "always opposed to political thinking as such for writers" (Brown 293). These poems and travel writings, however, consistently position her speakers at various degrees of unacknowledged remove from their subject, and she finished and published none of it. In the best of her poetry and in her translations, on the other hand, Bishop locates the points of conversation between an outsider's insight and a Brazilian familiarity. Translating, or creating a "new" poem founded in an interaction between two writers' perspectives and voices, Bishop extended her own range of political and cultural concerns by working with poems more confessional or more political than her own writing. Here, within the intimate dialogue between the Brazilian poet's voice and her own, Bishop discovers her "double point of view."

Bishop's early Brazil poems, "Arrival at Santos" and "Questions of Travel,"³ make most conscious the tourist's lack of such a dialogue:

> Oh, tourist,
> is this how this country is going to answer you
> and your immodest demands for a different world,
> and a better life, and complete comprehension
> of both at last, and immediately,
> after eighteen days of suspension?

Folded into the tourist's babble in "Arrival at Santos," these voice-over lines of self-judgment reveal her "suspension" between the expectations of home and the details of here, the not-home that she cannot really see, except in the irrelevant terms of home. Yet even as she poses the question, the tourist cannot begin to address it, when before her lies so much to judge and define.

> Finish your breakfast. The tender is coming,
> a strange and ancient craft, flying a strange and brilliant rag.
> So that's the flag. I never saw it before.
> I somehow never thought of there *being* a flag.

She judges the world seen from the vantage of a world already known and personifies places, "self-pitying mountains, / sad and harsh," in her myopic duty as tourist to see things. Reinforcing in her rhyme scheme the heaviness of the tourist's imposition, Bishop breaks the words that refuse to rhyme:

> Miss Breen is about seventy,
> a retired police lieutenant, six feet tall,

with beautiful bright blue eyes and a kind expression.
Her home, when she is at home, is in Glens Fall
s, New York. There. We are settled.

The break's misplaced sense of the precise mirrors the tourist's, who is most keenly attentive to that which is easily known, in this case, fellow traveler Miss Breen, soap, and postage stamps. She is protected from the unknown by her xenophobia, which allows her to ignore it or spout preformed opinions about the difference of this place, about

the unassertive colors of soap, or postage stamps –
wasting away like the former, slipping the way the latter

do when we mail the letters we wrote on the boat,
either because the glue here is very inferior
or because of the heat. We leave Santos at once;
we are driving to the interior.

The thrill behind the fear in "First Death in Nova Scotia" becomes here an eagerness dulled by jadedness. Prosy to the point of awkwardness, this is no equator equivalent of cousin Arthur's lyrical and solemn "roads deep in snow"; Brazil's wild and, in 1952, little traveled interior is simply the next stop on this boat trip around South America. As if thumbing through the pages of her brochure until she reaches the day for "the interior," the tourist blithely ignores the self-scrutiny that pervades the poem.

Bishop begins "Questions of Travel" with similar terms of judgment,

There are too many waterfalls here; the crowded streams
hurry too rapidly down to the sea,

but this tourist is fully aware of her double-edged position:

Is it right to be watching strangers in a play
in this strangest of theatres?
What childishness is it that while there's a breath of life
in our bodies, we are determined to rush
to see the sun the other way around?
The tiniest green hummingbird in the world?
To stare at some inexplicable old stonework,
inexplicable and impenetrable,
at any view,
instantly seen and always, always delightful?
Oh, must we dream our dreams
and have them, too?

Figuring us all in her "we," as spectators of natural and human difference, Bishop questions as she participates in our insatiable curiosity, our dreams, and our demands to see the inexplicable otherness of a world not ours: while the tourist "listen[s]" to, "stare[s]" at, and "ponder[s]" difference, the poem's images engage with that world, creating the beauty as they describe it:

> But surely it would have been a pity
> not to have seen the trees along this road,
> really exaggerated in their beauty,
> not to have seen them gesturing
> like noble pantomimists, robed in pink.
> – Not to have had to stop for gas and heard
> the sad, two-noted wooden tune
> of disparate wooden clogs
> carelessly clacking over
> a grease-stained filling-station floor.
> (In another country the clogs would all be tested.
> Each pair there would have identical pitch.)

In a rhetoric of negativity reminiscent of Wallace Stevens's "The Snow Man," Bishop exhibits the loss that would come of not traveling and questioning one's travel. One might never become aware of difference and likeness, or the intricate detail of any ordinary thing. Yet in contemplating what might never have been seen, the poem's rhetoric – its proliferating similes, metaphors, and personifications – offers a way to see, rich with its own distinctions and relations. While the uncomprehending tourist watches a strange play, the poem's noble pantomimists converse with nature and its roadside trees: the poem seductively positions before us less the place potentially unseen than the imagination's characterization of it, superimposed with memories of things not there at all.

The poem's close questions directly the role imagination plays in any perceptual act:

> – And never to have had to listen to rain
> so much like politicians' speeches:
> two hours of unrelenting oratory
> and then a sudden golden silence
> in which the traveller takes a notebook, writes:
>
> *"Is it lack of imagination that makes us come*
> *to imagined places, not just stay at home?*
> *Or could Pascal have been not entirely right*
> *about just sitting quietly in one's room?*
>
> *Continent, city, country, society:*
> *the choice is never wide and never free.*
> *And here, or there . . . No. Should we have stayed at home,*
> *wherever that may be?"*

Whether we should have "stayed at home" – a phrase she tested in five different places in one early draft – depends on whether we can separate home and not-home, familiarity and difference, or whether, finally, there is no alternative to our marginality, no home or society that can be known, apart from the one our imaginations co-create.

In his inquiry into the authorial role of the anthropologist, *Works and Lives,* Clifford Geertz pursues a parallel set of questions for the tourist's academic soulmate, the ethnographer: we cannot "get round the un-get-roundable fact that all ethnographical descriptions are homemade, that they are the describer's descriptions, not those of the described" (144–5). Instead, we admit

> that the writing of ethnography involves telling stories, making pictures, concocting symbolisms, and deploying tropes. [. . .] The strange idea that reality has an idiom in which it prefers to be described, that its very nature demands we talk about it without fuss – a spade is a spade, a rose is a rose – on pain of illusion, trumpery, and self-bewitchment, leads on to the even stranger idea that, if literalism is lost, so is fact. (140)

"Squatter's Children" and "Manuelzinho," two poems written within months of "Questions of Travel," study Macedo Soares's gardener and his family, as if through them further to approach an interior. Bishop's representations of the Brazilian poor attempt to challenge as they inevitably end by confirming Geertz's "un-get-roundable fact": Bishop's imagination steps in to fill the gaps left by what Spivak articulates as the subject effects' interference with access to any subaltern subject. When all else fails, Spivak might have added in ironic recuperation of Dewey's words, "the possibilities present in imagination" (*Experience* 20) become not just one among many aspects of our knowledge; rather, they attain supremacy, filling in for what we cannot know. "Squatter's Children," Bishop's ethnographic exercise, which she first published in a São Paulo journal,[4] opens with the speaker's recognition of her distance from her subjects:

> On the unbreathing sides of hills
> they play, a specklike girl and boy,
> alone, but near a specklike house.
> The sun's suspended eye
> blinks casually, and then they wade
> gigantic waves of light and shade.

Although the speaker's distant perspective finds them almost unrecognizable as children, her imagination's figurations and the sun's give them movement and character. Ambivalent, however, about whether to trust those figurations, she looks again and reconceives her description:

Clouds are piling up;
a storm piles up behind the house.
The children play at digging holes.
The ground is hard; they try to use
one of their father's tools,
a mattock with a broken haft
the two of them can scarcely lift.
It drops and clangs. Their laughter spreads
effulgence in the thunderheads,

weak flashes of inquiry
direct as is the puppy's bark.

With the sun's distorting brightness now covered by clouds, she sees detail. But vision is selective; the mattock, not the children, comes into focus. The mattock whose haft is broken, the entity most distinctly seen and heard in the poem, is recognizable, actual, a working, or in this case ineffectually working, means to insight into the family. Like the Maggie Ideal in her aunt's kitchen or the blacksmith's hammer, the broken mattock clangs and the family responds in laughter. But as soon as the speaker returns to represent the children, literalism fades and her imagination returns to fill in the tones of their laughter, blending their sounds with the thunder as she had their forms with the sun. The poem reveals how thin is the boundary between ethnography and artistry, how closely related discovering and creating the unknown.

Bishop had admired and collected primitives from the days of her Key West acquaintance with Gregorio Valdes. She invoked the form years later in notes during her 1960 trip on the Amazon:

> Strecthes were lined with tables outdoors – a few benches – a great deal of cooking going on, adding to the blue smoke – bright oilcloth table cloths, cafezinho cups all arranged, upside down, Men sitting eating dinner – almost no women in these places – and the bright shirts, white pants, thatched ro ogfs – & wierd-looking foods – all very mch like Brazilian primitive painteings)

Here she scans a living scene and sees in it a painting; "Squatter's Children" is itself a verbal primitive, exaggeratedly visual and aural.

But Bishop chooses not to end the poem with the stormy portrait. She returns to what was in draft form the broader "human voices" and in the poem a capitalized, intrusive "Mother's voice, ugly as sin," who

keeps calling to them to come in.
Children, the threshold of the storm
has slid beneath your muddy shoes;
wet and beguiled, you stand among

the mansions you may choose
out of a bigger house than yours,
whose lawfulness endures.
Its soggy documents retain
your rights in rooms of falling rain.

Rejecting both the ethnographer's and the artist's distance, the speaker closes by uttering her subjective response. The mother's voice is "ugly" to the speaker's ear; in her perception the children have been betrayed by the economic and legal systems. Rather than pretend she can simply listen to the mother's terrible calls, she steps in and speaks for them all. Preaching to the children and perhaps to their parents and to the poem's Brazilian and American audiences, the speaker formally reprehends the children's place in the rain.

Bishop published "Manuelzinho" the following month,[5] writing the Barkers in June that "I've earned so much money off the poor little man now I feel guilty every time he comes to the kitchen door with a bunch of monster radishes" (5 June 1956, PU). She admits here that representing this man's life in two poems, the second of which is quite long, is tantamount to converting it to dollars: the New Yorker pays a hefty per-line fee. "Manuelzinho [Brazil. A friend of the writer is speaking.]" establishes in its subtitle an inquiry quite different in nature from "Squatter's Children." The poem's conversation will be among the speaker, the "writer"/auditor, and the reader, over and against the enacted relationship with Manuelzinho, which is as if on display:

Half squatter, half tenant (no rent) –
a sort of inheritance; white,
in your thirties now, and supposed
to supply me with vegetables,
but you don't; or you won't; or you can't
get the idea through your brain –
the world's worst gardener since Cain.
Tilted above me, your gardens
ravish my eyes. You edge
the beds of silver cabbages
with red carnations, and lettuces
mix with alyssum. And then
umbrella ants arrive,
or it rains for a solid week
and the whole thing's ruined again
and I buy you more pounds of seeds,
imported, guaranteed,
and eventually you bring me
a mystic three-legged carrot,
or a pumpkin "bigger than the baby."

The speaker disarms us with her ready acknowledgment of Manuelzinho's poverty and his employment on her land.[6] She progresses by anecdotes, warm, amusing, and condescending, combining criticism and a Brazilian *abraço,* or hearty embrace, in the same utterance. Her heart goes out to him as she watches him running barefoot in the rain

> all over my property,
> with your head and back inside
> a sodden burlap bag,
> and feel I can't endure it
> another minute; then,
> indoors, beside the stove,
> keep on reading a book.

The poem requires us to be of two minds: since we have insight into the poor man's pitiable state solely through the speaker's affectionate dismay, we smile with her – it is a funny poem, and she is a funny woman. Our postmodern consciousness intact, however, we reprove the situation and her (and our) lighthearted discomfort with it. The "gap" Geertz locates "between engaging others where they are and representing them where they aren't" (130) necessarily imposes itself on our reading of this poem, whether or not it did on Bishop's 1956 *New Yorker* readers. Bishop's conflicted tone opens the way to our hesitation:

> Immediate confusion.
> You've left out the decimal points.
> Your columns stagger,
> honeycombed with zeros.
> You whisper conspiratorially;
> the numbers mount to millions.
> Account books? They are Dream Books.
> In the kitchen we dream together
> how the meek shall inherit the earth –
> or several acres of mine.

> With blue sugar bags on their heads,
> carrying your lunch,
> your children scuttle by me
> like little moles aboveground,
> or even crouch behind bushes
> as if I were out to shoot them!
> – Impossible to make friends,
> though each will grab at once
> for an orange or a piece of candy.

The "writer" catches us between the voices. She capitalizes Dream Books for our benefit; we, too, are invited into the eye-winking exasperation. But arranging her friend's stories so that the impossible gap between speaker and subject repeatedly troubles the poem, she never allows us to feel fully comfortable with our position in this triangular relationship. Opposing "Squatter's Children's" distanced and then preachy tone regarding poverty as a systemic betrayal of individuals, this speaker's interior monologue addresses Manuelzinho individually and familiarly; she blames not society but himself for his failure at arithmetic and his children for their fear. We who know him least of all may argue the politics of her purse, even as we are won over by the effusiveness of her spirit. She loves him, perhaps self-consciously and condescendingly, but she loves him. Recalling her laughter at his brightly painted hats,

> Unkindly,
> I called you Klorophyll Kid.
> My visitors thought it was funny.
> I apologize here and now.
>
> You helpless, foolish man,
> I love you all I can,
> I think. Or do I?
> I take off my hat, unpainted
> and figurative, to you.
> Again I promise to try.

In an early draft Bishop wrote,

> I apologize here & now
> >& take off my hat (unpainted) / to you.
> But, can't you change?

Though privately she might wish he and all of poverty and ignorance would just "change," publicly, as revision would have it, she considers her responsibility to him. She will not resolve the problem of class distinctions; she will not worry over her inability to communicate with him; she will not pretend she is not better educated, her hats figurative rather than literally and badly painted. She will only resolve to love him as she laughs with us, who will know how to read his stories. Bishop, the "writer," refuses to condemn that position, even as she leaves us the opening, through her poem's contrived conversation, to challenge the nature of this representation.

Moore called the poem one of her best (9 June 1956, VC); Lowell compared it to "In the Village." He said, more specifically:

> This last poem and your long wonderful Nova Scotia story both give themselves, as though you weren't writing at all, but just talking in a full noisy room, talking until suddenly everyone is quiet. (29 Dec. 1955, VC)

He mentioned "Manuelzinho" in his next letter as well: "Liked your Brazilian man better than ever in the New Yorker – the most feminine of character sketches with you and Lotta both speaking through each other" (18 June 1956, VC). Unwittingly in his praise of the poem Lowell characterizes accurately the poem's casual demonstration of Spivak's "subaltern subject-effect." Although the poem's affection tempers such an interpretation, the Brazilian man is indeed known only through the lively perceptions of Bishop and Macedo Soares. Reaching his interior would demand a different sort of inquiry altogether, one about which she would not feel "guilty."

Making such an attempt four years later in a persona poem, Bishop wrote "The Riverman" after reading Charles Wagley's ethnography, *Amazon Town*.[7] Perhaps discovering in Wagley's ethnocentric academics her own relative intimacy with Brazil, Bishop undertook to write the riverman's dream. She paraphrased extensively from the facts and stories in Wagley's book but intuited the emotional force of the *sacaca*'s wisdom and the water spirit's lure:

> I got up in the night
> for the Dolphin spoke to me.
> He grunted beneath my window,
> hid by the river mist,
> but I glimpsed him – a man like myself.

The riverman narrates his story in a mostly regular trimeter, whose lulling rhythm lyricizes the prosiness. Indian, "primitive," as Wagley informs Bishop (2),[8] but a person "like [her]self," the riverman and his writer are similarly curious to know a life they glimpse from the outside, much like the speaker of Bishop's 1947 poem, "At the Fishhouses," who opts for "total immersion":

> I went down to the river.
> I heard the Dolphin sigh
> as he slid into the water.
> I stood there listening
> till he called from far outstream.
> I waded into the river
> and suddenly a door
> in the water opened inward,
> groaning a little, with water
> bulging above the lintel.
> I looked back at my house,
> white as a piece of washing
> forgotten on the bank,
> and I thought once of my wife,
> but I knew what I was doing.

Wagley tells the story of Satiro, a minor *pagé,* or spiritual healer, training himself until the day he possesses the powers of a *sacaca,* the greatest of healers. First, he must learn to travel underwater, where he might be honored with a *maracá* (rattle). He must obtain a "virgin mirror" with which to "see his spirit companions without danger to himself" (232). Just as Wagley's matter-of-fact tale telling makes possible Bishop's intuitive journey into the riverman's feelings, so the stabilizing forces of the riverman's whitewashed house and his wife, who "slept and snored," permit his daring voyage, naked, beyond them.

Entering the water the riverman drinks *cachaça* and smokes green cheroots with others who are, presumably, likewise testing their powers. In this smoke-filled underwater room he meets the great serpent, Luandinha, who will be his river spirit and whose language

> I understood, like a dog,
> although I can't speak it yet.[9]

Not only language but pure, unmediated knowledge of another's spirit: this is all the riverman requires and all Bishop would need in order to be conversant with Brazilian difference, or so the poem humorously suggests:

> I need a virgin mirror
> no one's ever looked at,
> that's never looked back at anyone,
> to flash up the spirits' eyes
> and help me recognize them.
> The storekeeper offered me
> a box of little mirrors,
> but each time I picked one up
> a neighbor looked over my shoulder
> and then that one was spoiled –
> spoiled, that is, for anything
> but the girls to look at their mouths in,
> to examine their teeth and smiles.

Paraphrasing Wagley closely here but adding the detail of the girls' smiles, Bishop exposes in its prosaic humor the mystical dream of pure, direct intercourse with another. The riverman does not, of course, find such a mirror; he crosses the last barrier between his safe world and the magical dangers of the *sacaca* only in dream:

> Godfathers and cousins,
> your canoes are over my head;
> I hear your voices talking.
> You can peer down and down
> or dredge the river bottom

but never, never catch me.
When the moon shines and the river
lies across the earth
and sucks it like a child,
then I will go to work
to get you health and money.
The Dolphin singled me out;
Luandinha seconded it.

Shifting from the lyricism of his dream to the stunted prosiness of his
promise, the riverman is of two worlds – the *pagé* under the sea and the
poor godson, cousin, and husband of a snoring wife, who wants to make
good for his family. Or the riverman and Elizabeth Bishop are of two
worlds, their prose and lyric overlapping, their desire for clear-sighted
access to a compelling mystery similarly thwarted by the limitations of
their own perspective.

Bishop did go to the Amazon that spring, and she considered it one
of the two most important trips of her life (the other was her 1972 visit
to the Galápagos). She wrote Howard Moss that she was "living to go
back there again":

> Last night I dreamed there was a narrow road that began at Tierra del
> Fuego and went straight north, and I had started to walk it, quite
> cheerfully. – A large primitive stone coffin was being carried on mule-
> back alongside of me, ready for me when I gave out – the mule driver
> had a toothache. (I can't understand that part.) (10 May 1960, NYP)

She dreamed that she was undertaking a trip from the southern tip of
the continent north to the Amazon by foot, fully aware that the journey
would leave her buried amid the primitive. She was not afraid of the
prospect, but "cheerful"; the mule driver, and not she, was in pain. Or,
rather, if both people represent her, her dream is a meeting of the exotic
and the prosaic in her own nature – the river that "lies across the earth /
and sucks it like a child" and the work that "get[s] you health and
money."

Neither Bishop nor Macedo Soares liked "The Riverman." Bishop
cautioned several friends that she had written it before her trip on the
Amazon and that she was drafting a much better Amazon poem.[10] Its
inauthenticity bothered her; "if one thinks of it as a sort of fairy-tale
maybe it's all right" (letter to Swenson, 26 Dec. 1960, WU). Discussing
her planned book of prose with Ashley Brown, she said that "I'd like
to make Brazil seem less remote and less an object of picturesque fancy"
than it is generally seen (302). The Amazon of "The Riverman," which
she constructed out of her own alienation from the place, could only
foster, she feared, such a fiction of remoteness.

In "Brazil, January 1, 1502," which precedes "The Riverman" in writing and publication by a few months,[11] she puts perhaps her greatest pressure on the questions she had raised initially in "Arrival at Santos" and "Questions of Travel," the poems that surround "Brazil, January 1, 1502" in book form. Namely, if our perceptions govern our constructions of the other, are we inevitably guilty of appropriation; or can we, rather, distinguish stages of uninnocence? The poem crafts and frames nature, in its own fantasy-making activity, as preface to its larger concern with the possession and domination of the paradisal setting. From the beginning the perfectly constructed poetic images implicate the writer, as well as the Portuguese conquistadors, who have penetrated the Brazilian wilderness, and the reader, whose gaze belongs to the communal "our eyes" now looking:

> ... embroidered nature ... tapestried landscape.
> – Landscape into Art, by Sir Kenneth Clark

> Januaries, Nature greets our eyes
> exactly as she must have greeted theirs:
> every square inch filling in with foliage –
> big leaves, little leaves, and giant leaves,
> [...]
> and flowers, too, like giant water lilies
> up in the air – up, rather, in the leaves –
> purple, yellow, two yellows, pink,
> rust red and greenish white;
> solid but airy; fresh as if just finished
> and taken off the frame.

> A blue-white sky, a simple web,
> backing for feathery detail:

The land is beautiful, available to explorers and poets for framing and reconstituting. It is difficult to tell, as the epigraph from Clark suggests, where nature's display and the imagination's constructions meet, where the "blue-white sky" ceases to be just sky and becomes "backing for" the "feathery detail," chosen and arranged by the poet.[12] The act of appropriation only gradually becomes apparent. But when "Sin" rages among the "five sooty dragons" – fantastically enlarged lizards – near the "massy rocks," and when lichens are "threatened [...] by moss / in lovely hell-green flames" and are in turn "attacked above / by scaling-ladder vines," nature's patterns begin to bear an oddly human imprint of morality. Bishop so frames a natural violence, whose hell is cooled by its mossy green and whose sin is no nastier than a lizard in heat, that it nonetheless presages human forms of violence:

> The lizards scarcely breathe; all eyes
> are on the smaller, female one, back-to,

her wicked tail straight up and over,
red as a red-hot wire.

Just so the Christians, hard as nails,
tiny as nails, and glinting,
in creaking armor, came and found it all,
not unfamiliar:
no lovers' walks, no bowers,
no cherries to be picked, no lute music,
but corresponding, nevertheless,
to an old dream of wealth and luxury
already out of style when they left home –
wealth, plus a brand-new pleasure.
Directly after Mass, humming perhaps
L'Homme armé or some such tune,
they ripped away into the hanging fabric,
each out to catch an Indian for himself –
those maddening little women who kept calling,
calling to each other (or had the birds waked up?)
and retreating, always retreating, behind it.

We hear in the Christians' Mass echoes of nature's "moss" and "massy rocks" and return in their postchurch rape of the forest – and its women if they have their way – to the theme of the sooty lizards. But whereas the male lizards act instinctually in response to the female's instinctual tail's flare, the Christians, shielded by religious and cultural hegemony, quite intentionally raid the home they have newly appropriated, in order to ferret out its "brand-new pleasure."

As the poem makes clear, however, the Christians' aggression is only the last and perhaps the most insidious of a series of appropriations, arranged by the poet's tapestry work. Bishop's is a pointedly female nature – "she must have greeted" the Portuguese explorers just as she did Bishop, and through her, us – so that we each become a participant/voyeur of female lushness.[13] The correlative adverb opening the third stanza so orders the poem that if we have been drawn in by the poem's beauty or seduced by the lushness of nature's "Sin," we are at the same time implicated by the colonizer's sexual violence of the close. Just as Bishop found no removed, authorial position from which to judge her world in her late 1930s and early 1940s poems about war, there is no position apart here. Bishop so charges both the instinctual activity of nature and the purposive aggression and fearful retreat of human beings each with the sense of the others that even the framer-poet who has drawn the parallels ends by leaving all in an uncomfortable suspension. Cornered like the lizard, the Indian women finally neither retreat nor are captured; colonization and victimization are hardly so historically simple. "Calling, / calling to each other," the women's voices are the last heard.

Perhaps they confuse the conquistadors enough to escape this time, but perhaps they do not; closure here would make simply moralistic the complex problem of how we possess one another.

In the first extant draft Bishop had not conceived a necessarily male–female conflict. After Mass the Christians in this draft

> went tearing their way into that fabric
> after the maddening little Indians.

She suggests separable acts of possessive violence, toward the female[14] – nature and lizard – and toward the native population. Representing in revision the "ripp[ing] away into" a population at once native and female is more in keeping with the history of the Portuguese invasion of Brazil, as Bishop would represent it in *Brazil,* where she quotes Pero Vaz de Caminha, the scribe of Pedro Alvarez Cabral's flagship, as he discourses on an Indian woman: "'She was so well built and so rounded and her lack of shame was so charming, that many women of our land seeing such attractions, would be ashamed that theirs were not like hers.'" Bishop follows this with her own assessment:

> The Portuguese had always been romantically drawn to women of darker races; they had long taken Moorish wives and Negro concubines, and there were already many Negro slaves in Portugal. In Brazil it was only natural for them to become eager miscegenationists almost immediately. (27–8)

Here Bishop records in polite sarcasm the sexual exploitation of Brazil's women; in the poem she faces the greater complexity of any such appropriation. Implicating herself in the process[15] but refusing any fixed definitions, she charts the stages and nuances of uninnocence, from the natural to the imaginatively projected, from the poetically framed to the politically appropriated, and from the never wholly victimized to the never wholly victimizing.

Frustrating closure further, the poem's conception seems to have little to do with its political force. Rather, four years earlier Bishop discussed, in terms the poem's opening would refine, the colors and textures of the Samambaia spring:

> This is the most beautiful time of the year here – [. . .] there are purple, (two shades) pink, bright yellow, pale yellow, and white flowering trees – gigantic ones, the pink ones always hang with gray moss – the mountains really look amazing, like a tapestry – sorry to be so unoriginal but they do, a brand new tapestry, maybe – plus lots of streams of water glittering down them, and <u>all</u> the butterflies – one variety only in March – enormous, limp ones as big as this page (really) – a pale, pale, irridescent blue. (Letter to Barkers, 23 Mar. 1956, PU)

Apologizing for her cliché, she repeats it, nonetheless, in a letter thanking Lowell for his praise of the poem:

> I am so glad you liked the New Year's poem – I think it is a bit artificial, but I finally had to do something with the cliché about the landscape looking like a tapestry, I suppose – And it does now in February, too – the Lent trees are just starting to come out all over the place a wonderful purple – and the pink and yellow trees are beginning, too – I have some more poems, too, of dubious value. (15 Feb. 1960, HL)

Lowell had written her that "your poem is one of your most beautiful, I think – wonderful description, the jungle turning into a picture, then into history and the jungle again, with a practical, absurd, sad, amused and frightened tone for the Christians" (4 Jan. [1960], VC). He is right that this poem is powered by the jungle's incarnation as history and vice versa, but his sympathy with the Christians misses Bishop's satirization of them, and he says nothing of the women's fear. In her response Bishop shows, simply, her refusal to take on his sexual politics, or to argue her own. Even if Bishop had been able to articulate in a letter the slippage in the poem from natural to human and historical structures of power, she would not have corrected Lowell. Nor would she have acknowledged in a letter that the tapestry she apologizes for is, in her poem, one of a series of gendered and framed images vulnerable to being "ripped away." Instead, she writes him as she wrote the Barkers about the beautiful spring, while she allows her poetic subjects to test and retest the complex problematic by which we co-create in our effort to know the other.

If she used the framing device in "Brazil, January 1, 1502" to include nature among the violable and to challenge her own and her reader's roles, she uses it quite differently in her ballad, "The Burglar of Baby-lon."[16] The Burglar's burglaries and murders are finished before the poem begins; nature is not always potentially rapable but already "stain[ed]." The ballad frames the consequences of violence – the Burglar's death watch – with an interpretation of its social origins – the poverty where it festered in the hills of Rio.

> On the fair green hills of Rio
>   There grows a fearful stain:
> The poor who come to Rio
>   And can't go home again.
>
> On the hills a million people,
>   A million sparrows, nest,
> Like a confused migration
>   That's had to light and rest,
>
> Building its nests, or houses,
>   Out of nothing at all, or air.

> You'd think a breath would end them,
> They perch so lightly there.
>
> But they cling and spread like lichen,
> And the people come and come.
> There's one hill called the Chicken,
> And one called Catacomb;
>
> There's the hill of Kerosene,
> And the hill of the Skeleton,
> The hill of Astonishment,
> And the hill of Babylon.

While the frame sets the reader and writer apart from the scene, our "you" interpreting the poor's "they," Bishop carefully located her place as observer in a foreword to the 1968 publication of this poem as a book:

> The story of Micuçú is true. It happened in Rio de Janeiro a few years ago. I have changed only one or two minor details, and, of course, translated the names of the slums. [. . .]
> I was one of those who watched the pursuit [of Micuçú] through binoculars, although really we could see very little of it: just a few of the soldiers silhouetted against the skyline of the hill of Babylon. The rest of the story is taken, often word for word, from the daily papers, filled out by what I know of the place and the people. (Unnumbered page)

The ethnographer's position here is double, as it was not in "Squatter's Children." Set apart from the poem, this foreword recognizes most bluntly Clifford Geertz's claim that any observation, description, or analysis of "there" is also, necessarily, a reading of "here."[17] Thus, her position among the wealthy on their balconies matters. Likewise, her education, her newspaper reading, and further research "filled out" Micuçú's story.

The massive *favelas,* or slums, perched on the hills of Rio have the sticking quality of lichen, despite their seeming impermanence, or so Bishop reports it here and in *Brazil.* The poor had come from the Northeast to the city to find work, Bishop wrote in *Brazil,* and could not "go home again." In 1962 the slums had 700,000 inhabitants, out of Rio's 3.3 million (*Brazil* 56). These *favelas* "stain" the hillside with their shacks built of any available material, their crime and disease, and their lack of sewage and water. Bishop understood the problem as deeply connected with the almost total lack of education in this large population. A letter to May Swenson became a long "lecture," she admitted, in her frustration over a servant's premature baby's death: far too many Brazilians were ignorant about prenatal and infant care (2 Feb. 1962, WU). The *favelas,* she said in *Brazil,* had some of the highest rates of infant mortality (11).

As she wrote Swenson, everyone loved children to distraction, but "it seems to take two or three generations for people to learn anything" about the nutrition and medical care they need. Little had changed, it seemed to Bishop, since the days of *The Diary of "Helena Morley,"* when a neighboring family refused to see a doctor, trusting that the family cure of rose water would clear up a film collecting in their infant son's eyes. The boy went blind (*Diary* 210–12). Not only was Bishop a binoculared Rio homeowner looking down upon Brazilian poverty, but she also served as grandmother to spoiled, badly nourished children on sometimes a daily basis, attempting to remediate what she saw were the glaring flaws in the servants' and Macedo Soares's adopted daughter-in-law's parenting.

In Micuçú's "auntie," Bishop portrays the genuine confusion. Trying only to do her best, she does not know what went wrong:

> "We have always been respected.
>   My shop is honest and clean.
> I loved him, but from a baby
>   Micuçú was always mean.

> "We have always been respected.
>   His sister has a job.
> Both of us gave him money.
>   Why did he have to rob?

> "I raised him to be honest,
>   Even here, in Babylon slum."
> The customers had another,
>   Looking serious and glum.

Auden-like in its blunt presentation of character, this ballad is reminiscent of his 1930s ones. The auntie's questions are genuine; Micuçú's badness is not entirely his fault: the poem's social frame offers a liberal humanism through which to read his fate.

Just as the poem seems to set us in a safe position of removed observation, however, it challenges that very position. As Geertz, again, argues: "The pretense of looking at the world directly, as though through a one-way screen, seeing others as they really are when only God is looking, is [. . .] itself a rhetorical strategy, a mode of persuasion" (141). Midway through the poem Bishop foregrounds that very act of seeing, drawing the parallel between Micuçú and his newly made audience. Micuçú's supposed difference from the "you" of the opening frame – those who may watch, understand, and explain him – dissolves.

> Rich people in apartments
> Watched through binoculars

As long as the daylight lasted.
  And all night, under the stars,
Micuçú hid in the grasses
  Or sat in a little tree,
Listening for sounds, and staring
  At the lighthouse out at sea.

And the lighthouse stared back at him,
  Till finally it was dawn.
He was soaked with dew, and hungry,
  On the hill of Babylon.

[. . .]

He saw the long white beaches
  And people going to swim,
With towels and beach umbrellas,
  But the soldiers were after him.

Far, far below, the people
  Were little colored spots,
And the heads of those in swimming
  Were floating coconuts.

[. . .]

Women with market baskets
  Stood on the corners and talked,
Then went on their way to market,
  Gazing up as they walked.

The rich with their binoculars
  Were back again, and many
Were standing on the rooftops,
  Among TV antennae.

It was early, eight or eight-thirty.
  He saw a soldier climb,
Looking right at him. He fired,
  And missed for the last time.

He and they watch and await his death; he and they see the other as
"colored spots" or as "silhouette[s]." Tucking into his more mundane
observations the likeness of the ugly morning to "a raw egg on a plate"
and the ocean swimmers' heads to "floating coconuts," Bishop distributes
the activity of description. Micuçú is an observant murderer, with time,
like the rich, to stay and watch. In a draft of the poem he directly
reciprocates their gaze:

> ~~He saw the~~ Binoculars on rooftops
> or he ~~saw the people-on-roofs~~
> and ~~penthouses looking up~~

In revision, however, he exchanges a look with only the lighthouse and the death-giving soldier. All other observation is partial, shadowy, imaginatively colored in where it is incomplete.

The poem does not close with the death of the burglar-murderer, whom she carefully notes "never raped," after testing the more alliterative but apparently inaccurate line "he'd robbed and he8d raped." His particular crimes and death emerge from and lead back to his aunt's sad confusion and the *favela*'s squalor. Reporting on two more burglars being sought in Babylon, the poem closes as it began. The parallels between the burglar and the rich have faded as such insights inevitably do, so that the easier voice of liberal humanism can return to mark the "fearful stain" on the landscape. The "double point of view" that Bishop always sought gave her a way both to frame the poem and to undermine the frame's very perceptions, as she intuited Micuçú's death from her rooftop.

In most cases, however, when she attempted to deal directly with political or social concerns in her poetry, the results were unsuccessful. She wrote, occasionally revised, but did not publish several moralistic, empathic poems. She speculated, for example, about the slaves who worked the mines in "A Trip to the Mines – Brasil," which in its second draft began:

> The slaves, the slaves have disappeared
> in all their thousands, millions, even.
> That came, in black and broken waves,
> from Angola, from   have they hid
> Where could they hide so many graves?
> Where can their graves be   (hidden)

She wrote about inflation and about the extravagant expense of building Brasília, the new capital, in "Brasil, 1959":

> The radio says black beans are up again.
> That means five hundred percent
> in the past year, but no one quite believes it.
> [. . .]
> And meanwhile far inland
> a fairy palace rises
> a fairy palace small, impractical
>
> rises upon a barren field of mud
> a lovely bauble, expensive as a jewel

She wrote about poverty in general, in "Capricorn": "And the poor never freeze/they just starve," and about a poor baby in a poem called "A Baby ~~Found-in-the-Garbage~~":

> Wrapped in the very newspaper
> whose ~~headlines~~ she would make that day,   front page

> newborn, she lay,
> quite quiet.

This poem melodramatizes the ride to the dump – "where the buzzards and the poor join forces" – that the baby, found, was spared. Bishop did not resist writing the kind of intentionally political poem she most criticized in interviews. Nor did she attempt here, as she did in her published poems, either to listen to her subjects' voices or to place her own. But because she published none of these earnest poems, her publicly stated principles regarding such poetry were effectively served.

In Vargas's suicide (1954), perhaps the first political event whose details Bishop knew with some intimacy, she found a subject for "a report in verse & prose":

> This is a day when truths will out, perhaps; –
> leak from the dangling telephone ear-phones
> sapping the festooned switchboards' strength;
> fall from the windows, blow from off the sills,
> – the vague, slight unremarkable contents
> of emptying ash-trays; rub off on our fingers
> like ink from the un–proof-read newspapers,
> crocking the way the unfocussed photographs
> of crooked faces do that soil our coats,
> our tropical-weight coats, like slapped-at moths.

Now that Vargas is gone we can recognize what is dust, dirty ink, and ashes; now, the poem closes, we may affirm what is still of value: "At eight two little boys were flying kites." Bishop's dedication of the poem to Carlos Lacerda, who was active in Vargas's demise and who would remain an oppositional force in Kubitschek's government, placed her squarely into position within a polarized Brazilian political sphere. Though she made scattered revisions, she chose to publish neither the poem nor the humorous prose notes, which were based on a newsreel of the crowd's effusive farewell to the "(moderate) dictator":

> A long long look deep into the eyes of a Negro girl, glistening blankly.
> Women sobbing in each others arms. Then the women start fainting.
> [. . .] And There's the Wreath. ~~by god~~. How did it get here? Now it's
> over at the right – no – it's fallen behind – no there it is, tipping up up
> on a crest. But it neve never tips over. It is a patented life-preserver.
> It is as bouyant as the coffin. The coffin reaches the plane door – the
> worst moment – tipping and swaying, almost writhing, push and pull,
> they get it in somehow – the camera heaves a sigh.

With irony and hope, mockery and earnestness, Bishop entered the political fray, though privately, since she published none of this writing either in Brazil or in the United States.

When she considered the charged issue of race relations, however, her

principle regarding the separation of overt politics from poetry became
conflicted. By the end of a verbal battle with a Brazilian critic of her
New York Times essay, "On the Railroad Named Delight,"[18] she resorted
to invoking her poetry in the service of her politics. Bishop found the
theories of Gilberto Freyre, the Brazilian historian, persuasive, as her
notes toward *Brazil* indicate. Miscegenation of the Portuguese and their
slaves had integrated Brazil from its early days; because distinct races
were difficult to trace by the twentieth century, race relations were, he
argued, relatively unproblematic. Central to such theories was the notion
that contemporary race relations were in Brazil an un-self-conscious issue, lacking the tension they had in the United States and elsewhere.
Despite her acknowledgment in *Brazil* that all of the upper class was
white and all the blacks were "second-class citizen[s]" (114), Bishop
believed that the un-self-conscious interaction of racially different individuals offered the only first step toward revision of race relations. She
attempts to represent the harmony between blacks and whites in Brazil
by closing her *Times* article with a description of a billboard that

> showed a young Negro cook, overcome by her pleasure in having a
> new gas stove, leaning across it toward her white mistress, who leaned
> over from her side of the stove as they kissed each other on the cheek.
> Granted that the situation is not utopian, socially speaking, and that
> the advertisement is silly – but could it have appeared on billboards, or
> in the newspapers, in Atlanta, Ga., or even in New York? In Rio, it
> went absolutely unremarked on, one way or the other. (86)

Willing to overlook the display of racial stereotyping, Bishop is impressed
by the seeming spontaneity of the billboard's represented kiss and by the
unconsciousness of passersby to it. She allows what she calls the "easy
mingling of races," in an unpublished letter to the editor of the Brazilian
newspaper *Correio da Manha,* to supersede the concern she registers for
the women's social situatedness; it does not bother her that no one noticed
that. As she argues in this letter, written to contest Fernando de Castro's
accusation that her article is anti-Brazil and racist:

> The fact that no one in Rio even commented on the advertisement, for
> or against, that I know of, I took as a clear and beautiful demonstration
> of the fact that Brazil has reached an advanced and highly civilzed stage
> of racial integration.
> [. . .] I do believe that the better aspects of race-relations in Brazil
> are unconscious; that is exactly why they are so good. Alas, – it will
> take us many generations, in the U S A, to reach that state of uncon-
> sciousness, before the unselfconscious acceptance of people of all shades
> of color becomes second nature with us, – and we still have much

> bitterness and violence to go through before we achieve it. (5 Mar.
> 1965, VC)

As her final defense, she cites her own poetry, expecting it to serve as empirical evidence for her position on race relations. She suggests that Sr. Castro "get someone to read him a poem I wrote over twenty years ago. It is number IV of a group of poems called SONGS FOR A COL-ORED SINGER. It is a prophecy, or a prayer, that justice will eventually triumph for the Negro in the USA." Asserting as direct polemic the "meaning" of that powerfully allusive poem, Bishop catches herself between the two positions she characterizes in *Brazil:* "The upper-class Brazilian is usually proud of his racial tolerance, while the lower-class Brazilian is not aware of his – he just practices it" (114). As an educated American, she was closer to the former group; as a poet, she embraced the latter, whose spontaneity, however, she reified when she tried to argue it as a social principle.

When she discussed Brazilian art, she similarly reified as she appreciated the folk. Dividing her discussions of folk and high art into two chapters in *Brazil,* she proposed the titles "The Unselfconscious Arts" and "The Selfconscious Arts." The Time–Life editors rejected her titles, choosing "Graceful and Popular Skills" and "A Merited Respect for the Arts" to mark their own opposition between skill and art. Bishop's distinction, and the liveliness of her writing in the former chapter, reflect her own preference.

She was fascinated with folk culture, and especially with the Brazilian samba, about which she wrote in *Brazil,* at length in the *Times* essay, and in letters beginning in 1954. The samba epitomized spontaneity, in Bishop's conception of it, defining for her the Brazilian spirit:

> As Lota just remarked "This is a country of loucos" a band went by playing sambas – we all rushed to look o er the terrace and there was a small band, two small trucks, and a scattered group of ladies & gents dancing like crazy and throwing colored leaflets all over the streets q they're dressed like butcher-boys, more or less – white coats and caps – Negros – and on their backs embroidered in big red letters (and painted on the trucks) CASAS DA BANHA – that is, "Houses of Lard" – the attractive name of the cheapest chain-store grocery . . . All the trolley cars and traffic held up, of course, but all very gay. (Letter to Barkers, 28 June 1963, PU)

In another letter to the Barkers she described a performance by samba singer Clementina de Jésus, giving full and lively detail of the homemade, household instruments and the raucous dance and song (15 Dec. 1964, PU). She sent Swenson a samba record, translating the slip-cover text for her. Occasionally she sent translations of lyrics, when new sambas came out:

> They always cover world news – but this year's crop isn't too good –
> "Ay, mulatta, your love is terrific//it's an explosion – pum/20 megaton
> – pum//Because of you/I am going to/Disintegrate – pum//etc...
> "Life is beautiful/Let's go with life//While they go to the moon/We
> have the moonlight in the street"/ – However – everything is lost
> without the original rhymes, and the music, most important of all –
> (Letter to Swenson, 24 Mar. 1963, WU)

Bishop admired their bluntness and, as she wrote in the *Times* essay, their "honest reaction" to events (85). They were un-self-conscious artifacts, emblems of the particular political/cultural moment, and she lamented the sudden interest of the "young rich," for whom "slight subversiveness is considered chic":

> Ironically, what may prove to be the real kiss of death to the spontaneity
> of the samba is that the young rich, after years of devotion to North
> American jazz, have discovered it. A few years ago only the very few
> Brazilians, mostly intellectuals, who cared for their own folk-culture
> took the samba seriously, or went to the rehearsals of the big schools
> up on the *morros*, the hills. This year, crowds of young people went,
> one of the symptoms, possibly, of a new social awareness since the
> "revolution." And some of this year's crop of songs show a self-
> consciousness, even a self-pity, that is far removed from the old samba
> spirit. (86)

For the purposes of her own writing, she nostalgized political ignorance, yearning to "recover the dreamy state of consciousness I lived in then [in the 1930s and 1940s] – it was better for my work, and I do the world no more good now by knowing a great deal more" (letter to Stevenson, [Mar. 1964], WU). Like a protective anthropologist, she, one of the "intellectuals," discovered the samba in its "old samba spirit" years before; now she wishes consciously to preserve the un-self-consciousness of this art.

The conflicted nature of her position amid but outside a culture, reading it and at the same time filling in the gaps with tropes of her own making, gave her poetry incisive power. The same conflicts, however, left much of her travel prose aimlessly descriptive, and at its worst, narrow-minded and judgmental. When she set out with the intent to describe the poor and primitive cultures she met traveling through the jungles and on the rivers of Brazil, the vast distance between her and her subject overwhelmed her. During her 1967 trip down the Rio São Francisco, which was her most devastating in terms of the poverty of the area, she translated passages from *Quatro Rodas,* a Brazilian touring journal, about the towns, people, and sights. Some of her interactions with that text are the most interesting of this writing:

> Itacarambi, Morrinho, (300 yr old church) end of S F in Minas – Manga – bandeira ntes gold and jewels (where are they all, anyway?) With each miner, the town" changed its name Thus, when they decided to raise dogs (WHY? – but remark on how remarkably sweet and docile all those mongrels seemed to be – with wide, hand-made home-made leather collars – the 2 puppies in B J de L – etc.) it was called "Manga dos Cachorros; in the cattle phase, Manga do Armador (?) and after-wards, later, Manga de Santo Antônio, when the marriage para those bandas was difficult (???) (Chateaubriand has a fazenda somewhere around here – he apparently made a sensation by pumping water from the river to irrigate – they do it futrther down, certainly, now, and it seems like th simplest solution of all for the region, to ignorant me)
>
> Now comes Bahiha. A wind springs up (it certainly does) "from Bahia" the sailors say.

This is safe. She is engaging in history and anecdote; there is a conver-sation here among the touring book, her other reading, and her "real" experience of this trip downriver. When she leaves the safe territory of the books and the boat, on which most of her own notes center, and ventures ashore, her writing instead bears a tone of pity or disgust. Describing a scene on a village square at nightfall, she does not know what to feel about a child she sees sitting there,

> in rags, her very thin legs folded buddha like and – absolutely alon e in the praça in the dark, in the river-wind. I went over to her. [. . .] I tried to talk to her but she looked frightened – at the same time, she automatically held out her hand to beg. Her parents must have gone off to find a place to stay or something to eat – well, who knows. I put a conto – tucked it down inside her filthy little shirt – [. . .] I left her there, a little silent scrap awaiting God knows what.

The scene is too painful, Bishop, the tourist, too helpless. Bishop, the writer, could only record her actions and her pity. She did not include this episode at all in her revised version. On the next page of her notes, she wrote with amazement and disgust about the lack of hygiene:

> Everyone dabbling in the Rio constantly – washing clothes (how they get them clean is beyond me) [. . .] I watched o ne tiny naked boy – 6 or 7 – washing a whole woodeon dish-pan of dishes – plates, cups, frying pans, all – one after the other – half way through washed himself, then went on. – And the water is filthy Lots of fish – some of the crew have lines over the side all the time – I have lost all interest – in fact it was after the fish the 2nd day that I developed this dysentery.

When she revised these notes, she laundered her own focus, discussing at length the supersensitivity of Brazilians to cleanliness, despite the quality of the water they wash in. She edited this boy out altogether. Most of her revised version is about the boat on which she traveled and the other tourists. Beginning the revision with pleasantries – "Like any cleanly travelling American citizen, the morning after I got to Salvador, State of Bahia, Brazil, I did a bit of drip-dry laundering in my hotel room and hung it about on coat-hangers, shower-curtain rods, and window-fastenings" – the trip itself defied her project of writing casual travel literature. She could not and did not finish. It is as if she has gone too far: having immersed herself in the "interior," she loses the balance that keeps her world and the world she is confronting in tension, the kind of tension on which her Brazil poems so skillfully perch. It is perhaps no coincidence that Bishop's trip down the Rio São Francisco coincided chronologically with Macedo Soares's most difficult stretch, a few months before her suicide. What Bishop encountered was not about being a "cleanly travelling American citizen," and her fragmented drafts suggest that she was not prepared emotionally or artistically to do more than embrace what she experienced with pity, or reject it.

Her prose writing about her trip on the Amazon, a trip she dreamed about and wrote about in letters for years afterward, remains as well the fragmentary notes of a tourist: she briefly describes the towns at which they stopped, the pictures she took, the crafted items for sale, and the people. With tourist-like distance from and desire for the exotic, Bishop says about the town of Orixininá:

> Vey pretty children one little girl one of the prettiest children I've seen in years – long hair pale tannish skin and greenish tan eyes – wide sweet face, blue dress with yello edging – we wanted to take her home to Mary – some little boys – marmalucos narrow, dark faces, small sharp features, one handsome and looking exactly like one of these primitive ex-voto wood heads with balackeyes –

The girl is adoptable by Bishop's white, American friend;[19] the boy looks "exactly" like a piece of primitive art. The author of this writing is indistinguishable from the American tourist abroad stereotyped in her first Brazil poem, "Arrival at Santos." We do not know what she planned to do with this Amazon prose nor whether she did in fact revise it for her prose book, as she revised her impression of the Amazon in her late introspective poem, "Santarém.

Bishop referred to her project of a book of prose frequently over the years. She first mentioned it in a letter to Anny Baumann (11 Nov. 1955, VC) and characterized it for the Barkers in 1956: "Sort of stories, sort of travel sketches – before I know too much about the country and get afraid to say anything. It is rather hectic and surrealist – but so is Brazil – and fun to write" (26 Jan. 1956, PU). Ten years later she was no longer thinking of the country as surrealist, but she was still engaged in the project. She told Ashley Brown in her 1966 interview, "It is tentatively called *Black Beans and Diamonds*. It's to be a combination of a travel book, a memoir, and a picture book. I am quite interested in photography. I'd like to make Brazil seem less remote and less an object of picturesque fancy" (302). That year she received a $12,000 Rockefeller fellowship for research and travel, and in 1978 a $21,000 Guggenheim for this and two other projects (see Chapter 4, note 6). In 1973 she wrote Howard Moss that she had "masses of Brazilian material and probably several 100 pages of my long-procrastinated book on Brazil on hand" (18 Dec. 1973, NYP). Hundreds of pages of prose about Brazil have never been found; unless one includes her drafts toward *Brazil,* the extant material amounts to a few dozen pages.[20] We must discuss the prose with these gaps fully in mind; nevertheless, a pattern does emerge. When Bishop saw Brazil with a guide, when her own perceptions interacted with those of a Brazilian familiar with the place or the event, her travel writing was insightful, witty, and more often finished. She characterized that interaction in the introductory note she drafted for her prose book in the words I have been quoting throughout: "I was lucky to spend most of these years in the company of Brazilians and to see society from a double point of view – perhaps in that way ~~with more three-dimensionally~~ than a travelr or tourist would have seen it, or the Brazilians themselves."

Her "Trip to Vigia" is lively, confrontational, and introspective in precisely these terms; she begins both rough and final drafts with an introduction of her and her companion's guide: "The shy poet, so soiled, so poor, so polite, insisted on taking us in his own car."[21] Tourism becomes conversation. They first view the river, for instance, at the home of a Dona Sebastiana, through the poet Ruy's affection for it: "Ah! the water here is a *delicia,* isn't it, Dona Sebastiana? It's the best water, the only water, from here to Vigia. People come for miles to get water here. Wait till you try it" (*Prose* 116). Bishop invests her description with Dona Sebastiana's pride and Ruy's praise:

> It really was a beautiful river. It was four yards across, dark, clear, running rapidly, with white cascades and deep pools edged with backed-up foam, and its banks were a dream of the tropics. [. . .] It made up for a lot, and Dona Sebastiana was proud of it. José Augusto and the little boys went wading. The thin dogs stood in the water, and gulped at it, then looked back at us over their shoulders from *their* river. (117)

The river may be lovely, but it is also "*their* river." Ruy, Dona Sebastiana, her family, and pets have offered her their perspective from which to see it. The essay progresses by means of such dialogic moments. Earlier, during one of the car's recurrent breakdowns, they stop at an almost empty store. Juxtaposing her first impression with her corrected one, Bishop remarks, "The store had been raided, sacked. Oh, that was its normal state" (114). Whether or not she actually commented and Ruy actually explained the store's bareness before her eyes scan it in the succeeding sentences, her essay constitutes the two levels: beyond her observation is conversation; beside the tourist's ignorant stare is a Brazilian's experience and his pride.

Likening the church in Vigia to "a sacred bull, a great white zebu" (118), she recognizes the hurt Ruy will face if she and her companion do not like it. The dynamics between them – his desire for them to like it and their reconsidered response – comprise the dialogue of this visit, local and tourist each meeting the culture of the other:

> Smack in the middle was a blue-and-white bandstand. It was hideous, but because it was so small it didn't spoil the effect at all – rather as if these absurd offerings had been laid out on the ground in front of the great, indifferent, sacred white zebu. The dark green mango trees were dwarfed by the church. On either side the little old houses were tile-covered with Gothic blue-and-white, or yellow-and-white, tile-covered *azulejos*.
>
> Ruy watched us. But we liked the church very much and said so. He looked greatly relieved. The church danced in the light. (118)

Listening, criticizing, imaginatively projecting, appreciating, simply describing: the conversation between Ruy's pride in this place and her tourist's eye directs and redirects her utterance. Saying what she sees in anticipation of his reaction allows her to see further and to complete her picture. Like Gregorio Valdes's art, Vigia is at the same time the way into a relationship. Bishop awaits the "mystic moment," at which her friend, M, will begin to address Ruy in the second person (112), as eagerly as she does any other element of the trip. Whether her fellow subject is an actual guide or a guidebook with which to banter, Bishop's writing becomes most engaged in its topic when her voice meets another's.

The meeting ground is perhaps most evident in her translations. Bishop's own discussions of translation pose questions somewhat different from my own. When she justified her choices of poems to translate, she invariably mentioned how well the particular poem went into English.[22] She believed that faithfulness to the rhyme, meter, and poetic intent of the original was essential to a good translation, exhibiting this imperative in a several-page lecture to Lowell, after reading a draft of his book of translations, *Imitations*. Criticizing him not for doing "Free translations," exactly, but for making "changes that <u>sound</u> like <u>mistakes</u>,. and are open to misinterpretation," she prefaced her specific corrections with a self-assured apology: "If you will forgive my sounding like the teacher of

French 2A, I'll give you some examples" (1 Mar. 1961, HL). In her letters Bishop made translation sound like a task she fulfilled as best she could for the benefit of the original poet. After listing some translations she had done and planned still to do, Bishop wrote Swenson, "Then I think I'll have dome my duty for Brazilian letters for some time" (30 Dec. 1963, WU).

Representing translation as a service she performs, Bishop submerges her own engagement in these intimate relationships between the perspectives and voices of two writers. Yet she considered her translations intrinsic enough to her body of poetry to include sections from João Cabral de Melo Neto's long poem and three of Carlos Drummond de Andrade's poems in her 1969 *Complete Poems*. Through Bishop's voice, then, on those pages, come leftist utterances in poems like Cabral de Melo's *The Death and Life of a Severino*. In the *Diary* and in one of Drummond de Andrade's most moving poems, "Travelling in the Family," Bishop participates in the grappling with and reliance on family. Clarice Lispector's story, "The Smallest Woman in the World," pushes "Brazil, January 1, 1502" beyond its end, as if they are in fact companion pieces. Whether or not she knew the writer she was translating, the relationships that the translations enact, the dialogues in which they participate, are intimate.

Writing about *The Diary of "Helena Morley,"* May Swenson captured Bishop's position as translator perhaps more accurately than Bishop could:

> Keeping within the mind of this youngster so consistently in order to choose the right expressions in another language – making it build in interest to the end – that proves great power on your part. You've made it a delicious book – one probably alone of its kind. [...] You can feel in the book that the translator had great fun doing it, too – that's a big part of the reader's enjoyment. (27 Mar. 1958, WU)

Swenson recognizes not Bishop's self-effacing faithfulness to a text, but her "fun," which matches "Helena Morley's" own. For Bishop, doing Brazilian translation meant, especially in the case of the *Diary*, embracing an entire world, immersing herself in a culture and language not her own and, for the duration of some three years on that project (1954–7), making it hers.

The "fun" is perhaps most evident in the *Diary*, which she began as a way to teach herself Portuguese (letter to Lowell, 30 Nov. 1954, HL). Over the years of translating into English the adolescent diary of Senhora Augusto Mario Caldeira Brant (Dona Alice), or pseudonymously, "Helena Morley," Bishop wrote regularly to her friends about it, as if writing about a new and preoccupying friend:

It is a wonderful, fearful book, I'm sure – she's NOT a nice child, but it's all so real it gives you the shivers – I don't think I'm exaggerating. (Letter to Barkers, 12 Nov. 1954, PU)

I went to Diamantina [Helena Morley's village] for six days. [. . .] It's a wonderful little place, really, – tiny, god-forsaken, eaten up with the passion for finding diamonds in every brook; 5,000 ft high, the highest town in Brazil, and with wonderful crisp, clear air; and NOTHING there, just nothing – a sea of crazy steel-gray rocks. There are 17 churches, toy-church size, one on every little corner almost. (Letter to Swenson, 10 May 1956, WU)

Then I started the introduction and fussed and fussed over it, trying to get everything just right. Burton went to Diamantina in 1861, and as usual he is endlessly talkative, and absolutely accurate about everything . . . he is amazing, and I bet his passion for exactitude and information drove his Brazilian friends mad! Then just as I got it done and would probably have written you a long letter I did something you may have seen in the paper – got the Pulitzer Prize – to my astonishment. [. . .] Well, it's been very nice and lots of fun. (Letter to Barkers, 5 June 1956, PU)

Awarded the Pulitzer for *Poems: North & South – A Cold Spring*, where she had only begun in the last two poems to consider the tones of Brazil and had not yet returned home to Nova Scotia, Bishop's writing by 1956 was fully engaging both worlds. She began working on the *Diary* shortly after the publication of "In the Village"; as she was nearing its completion, she began her prose book about Brazil, and she returned to her childhood in Nova Scotia, in published and unpublished writing. In 1955 she urged Lowell to write the childhood memoir that found its way into *Life Studies* (20 May 1955, HL); through 1956 and 1957 she immersed herself in Ernest Jones's three-volume study of Freud, reexamining, as she wrote the Barkers (28 Nov. 1957, PU), the psychoanalysis she had undergone in 1944. The diary of an adolescent girl living in a Brazilian mining village near the turn of the century posed itself at the juncture of Bishop's intense return to childhood through her writing and reading, and her immersion in Brazil as traveler and chronicler.

In Bishop's introduction to the *Diary*, Helena Morley's story becomes hers. She describes visiting Diamantina, meeting the Brants, being invited to "'suck fruit,'" "in Helena's very phrase" (xxiv), with an eighty-year-old friend of the Brants and inspecting the houses, churches, and the diamond mine that figure in Helena's diary. Bishop describes as if she knew them Helena's grandmother, her overbearing Aunt Madge, the children at school, and Helena, switching into the present tense to make Helena all the more immediate: "She is greedy; sometimes she is unfair to her long-suffering sister, Luizinha [. . .] She is obviously something of a show-off and saucy to her teachers; but she is outspoken and good-natured and gay" (xxvii). This introduction's tone echoes that of her letters about the *Diary:* Bishop likes Helena immensely, and she wants her affection to be catching.

The diary itself is Helena's account of daily, family life, humorous and uncensored: "I'm going to write down here what I did to her [Luizinha], and not be ashamed, because only the paper's going to know" (54). She gets angry at her relatives, she pities them and laughs at them, always expressing her necessary guilt, as she tells the uncharitable story. She reveals as well how close she is to her family, especially her grandmother: "It seems to me that she's the mother and mama's the grandmother. I tell grandma everything I think; if I'm happy I tell her and if I'm mad I complain to her" (63). When she puts into her grandmother's mouth the phrase so characteristic of Bishop's own grandmother – " 'This one's going to give me trouble; nobody knows ["ninguem sabe" (*Minha Vida* 180)] what she wants' " (*Diary* 132) – it is difficult to separate the Elizabeth Bishop whose English words these are from the Helena Morley who wrote them some sixty years before. Bishop had been puzzling out that phrase for years and would return to it shortly in "The Grandmothers" and in "Memories of Uncle Neddy."

Helena is forthright, knows her own mind, and rarely sees a reason not to express it:

> If they gave me Diamantina to run the last thing I'd start here would be a Post Office. [. . .] Papa says it's all politics, just to give people jobs. But wouldn't it be better if instead of a Post Office they put in streetlamps for us, so that on dark nights we wouldn't have to walk slowly for fear of falling over a cow? And put in water-pipes? Wouldn't they be more useful, too? Nobody's going to die without a letter, but the water from Pau de Fruta, which runs uncovered, has killed lots of people who might be alive today. (196–7)

Like her, Bishop was commonsensical and unsentimental. She offered similar suggestions or "lectures" in letters of the early 1960s. But unlike Helena, she was shy as a child, the "Country Mouse" who avoided any confrontation not forced on her by family circumstance. Helena was surrounded by a large and sometimes stiflingly loving family; with and about them she was challenging and direct. As she introduced Bishop to Brazilian language and culture, Helena Morley at the same time revived the memories and longings of her childhood. She wrote to her Aunt Grace, after not receiving the awaited letter of shared reminiscence:

Oh – I was hoping you'd go into detail about "Helena Morley" – don't you think she was funny? And didn't a lot of it remind you of G V? – The false pregnancy – "the town's a regular asylum" – because her dress was white "they may even think I have two"? and so on. (9 Apr. 1958, VC)

Attempting to nudge Aunt Grace into nostalgic play, Bishop asks, in effect, didn't the book remind you of our old world together; didn't you feel it, too? As Bishop was completing her work on the *Diary* she was drafting "Sestina." May Swenson wrote about the poem, "It has that almost surrealistic feeling of some room way down deep in memory, or in a dream, that's been dark, and suddenly the light is turned on and every detail is seen, as on a far away stage, tiny but very clear" (28 Oct. 1955, WU). When Bishop looked away – into a diary distant from her in time and place, but entirely familiar in the pull of emotion – she stumbled upon her grandmother's kitchen and, as Swenson intuited, was able to turn on the light that revealed her relationship with her grandmother.

When Marianne Moore reviewed *The Diary of "Helena Morley,"* she mistook the author's preface for Bishop's own. She quotes Dona Alice, "Happiness does not consist in worldly goods but in a peaceful home, in family affections, – things that fortune cannot bring and often takes away" (*CPr* 526;[23] *Diary* xxxvii), and she attributes these words to "Miss Bishop." In her mistake, Moore fuses the writer who introduces and translates – the woman who had not had that home and those ready affections – and the writer who appreciates them in the preface to her adolescent diary. Moore, who had in 1954 completed her own quite Moore-like "translations" of La Fontaine, was unaware of her review's fusion but pleased with the partnership: "The real excitement, Elizabeth is that it is as much you as it is Diary" (9 Dec. 1957, VC).

An Anthology of Twentieth-Century Brazilian Poetry, the collection of originals and translations Bishop coedited with Emanuel Brasil, steers clear of any suggestion of a relationship between translating and translated poets. Bishop and Brasil wrote brief biographies of the Brazilian authors in their introduction and within the table of contents. Each poet's bibliography follows the collection, and only at the end are the translators' names and profiles listed, the service people, as it were. In her review of the *Anthology,* Helen Vendler praises the translator-poets' "self-effacing work" (18). The tone of the introduction is uncharacteristically formal for Bishop, highly organized, and void of first-person narrative and anecdote. She, or she and Brasil, are not to be present here. But her translations of poems and stories, like her translation of the *Diary,* defy such a barrier.

Whether she wrote her first draft of "For Grandfather"[24] before or after she translated Carlos Drummond de Andrade's "Travelling in the Family," the affinities are haunting:

> I looked in his white eyes.
> I cried to him: Speak! My voice
> shook in the air a moment,
> beat on the stones. The shadow
> proceeded slowly on
> with that pathetic travelling
> across the lost kingdom.
> But he didn't say anything.
>
> I saw grief, misunderstanding
> and more than one old revolt
> dividing us in the dark.
> The hand I wouldn't kiss,
> the crumb that they denied me,
> refusal to ask pardon.
> Pride. Terror at night.
> But he didn't say anything.
>
> Speak speak speak speak.
> I pulled him by his coat
> that was turning into clay.
> By the hands, by the boots
> I caught at his strict shadow
> and the shadow released itself
> with neither haste nor anger.
> But he remained silent.[25]

Drummond de Andrade's father and Bishop's grandfather lead the poets forward into the desert of Itabira and through the snows to the North Pole. The dreamlike details pass before the poet-speakers, who are frightened, eager, and frustrated that they cannot grasp and hold onto the dead patriarchs. The same doubt troubles both speakers, about where he or she is in relation to them. Like Bishop's poem, Drummond de Andrade's is ambivalent about whether his speaker confronts his father directly, whether he looks into his father's eyes or faces only his shadow. The "waters cover his moustache" at the end; the hoar frost hangs on Bishop's grandfather's. Father and son close in a "ghostly embrace"; Bishop's kiss remains a projection. The affinity is not a coincidence. Bishop and Drummond de Andrade knew each other only through a stiffly formal correspondence, but, steeped in the terms of Drummond de Andrade's painful return to an unfinished relationship, Bishop discovered or revised her own.

Bishop's first published translations of Brazilian poems were from João Cabral de Melo Neto's *The Death and Life of a Severino: A Pernambuco*

Christmas Play, 1954–1955; she did not know Cabral de Melo at all. She translated three of the eighteen sections in 1963,[26] shortly before the Portuguese was set to music by Chico Buarque de Holanda. Bishop's "note on the poet" in *Poetry* describes the poem as resembling traditional "Brazilian folk-plays," with its theme of the wanderer "fleeing from drought and starvation. He overhears conversations, sees green grass and a river, talks to a woman, meets a funeral, etc." (18) as he migrates east from the interior to the coast. During the years of Castelo Branco's military regime, Buarque de Holanda's musical drama, staged by students at São Paulo's Catholic University, became popular as a leftist appeal against social injustice (E. Burns 513). The poem had not yet achieved this political stature when Bishop wrote her *Poetry* note, though it had by the time of the *Anthology*'s publication. There too, however, Bishop avoided political reference: Cabral de Melo's "first book *Stone of Sleep* (1942) showed the characteristics of his mature style: striking visual imagery and an insistent use of concrete, tactile nouns" (xxi).

Bishop's representation of poet and poem hardly prepares us for the translation that follows. The first section of the poem concludes:

> We are many Severinos
> and our destiny's the same:
> to soften up these stones
> by sweating over them,
> to try to bring to life
> a dead and deader land,
> to try to wrest a farm
> out of burnt-over land.
> But, so that Your Excellencies
> can recognize me better
> and be able to follow better
> the story of my life,
> I'll be the Severino
> you'll now see emigrate.

Calculatedly an emigration with political consequences, the whole of the first section uses verbal and rhythmic repetition to exhibit this Severino as an everyman; this is not one man's death and life but the death and life of a people starving and without political power. His anger and self-pride are nowhere evident in Bishop's introductions nor in her own prose about the interior. For the duration of the translation, however, the precise English terms of these emotions are necessarily her own. Although Severino's life ["*a história de minha vida*" (*Anthology* 128)] was even farther removed from Bishop than that of the *Menina*, "Helena Morley," the poignant inflections of Bishop's translation demanded from her more than a knowledge of poetics and Portuguese.

The second section moves by haunting repetitions. Our Severino meets the "brothers of souls," caretakers of the pauper dead, Bishop's note explains, who are carrying the corpse of a "Severino farmer." The speaker's many questions receive unsatisfactory answers. There are no satisfactory answers:

> – But did he have fields
>   brothers of souls,
>   how could he plant
>   on the barren rock?
> – In the thin lips of sand,
>   brother of souls,
>   in the stones' intervals,
>   he planted straw.
> – And was his farm big,
>   brothers of souls,
>   was his farm so big
>   that they coveted it?
> – He had only two acres,
>   brother of souls,
>   on the mountain's shoulder,
>   and neither one level.
> – Then why did they kill him,
>   brothers of souls,
>   why did they kill him
>   with a shotgun?
> – It wanted to spread itself,
>   brother of souls,
>   this bullet bird wanted
>   to fly more freely.

We could look backward to the fourth of the "Songs for a Colored Singer" to hear these rhythms in Bishop's own poetry or forward to her last poem, "Sonnet," to hear the words' echo:

> Freed – the broken
> thermometer's mercury
> running away;
> and the rainbow-bird
> from the narrow bevel
> of the empty mirror,
> flying wherever
> it feels like, gay!

Sixteen years later, the words were still in place in Bishop's mind. Except in the resonances of words and rhythms, however, Bishop would not have written this poem. She did not, on her own, have access to the voices of a village of poor farmers. Nor would she have been able, or have chosen, in her own poetry, to utter their anger at social and economic oppression and their awareness of their disempowerment in the face of "Your Excellencies" or their bullet birds. In choosing to translate these sections of the work, however, she extended her own reach into the political and social concerns of a speaker otherwise wholly removed from her.

In the winter of 1962–3, Bishop translated, as she wrote Lowell (8 Jan. 1963, HL), five of Clarice Lispector's stories;[27] the following summer she wrote him that

> I suppose we are getting to be "friends" – but she's the most non-literary writer I've ever known, and "never cracks a book" as we used to say – She's never read anything, that I can discover – I think she's a "self-taught" writer, like a primitive painter. (12 July 1963, HL)

The terms of their friendship sound familiar. Drawn to what she considers Lispector's "primitive" un-self-consciousness, once again, Bishop discovers her own double point of view.

In the longest of the three translations she published, "The Smallest Woman, in the World," a French explorer discovers a pregnant African woman, seventeen and three-quarters inches tall. His necessity for ethnographic order overcoming him, he quickly names her – Little Flower – and sets about to "classify her among the recognizable realities" by "collect[ing] facts about her" (501). Once the explorer has identified his subaltern object, it is up to the readers of the Sunday newspaper that features his article to reject or appropriate her. One woman looks away: "It gives me the creeps." Another falls in love with her, decidedly mourning her lack. Where one child feels empathy with what she interprets as the small woman's great sorrow, another wants her to "be our toy!" (503). One mother controls her own conflicted emotions by rationalizing, "It isn't human sadness," another, by scrubbing her son all the harder in his bath and, in the bathroom mirror, forming a "deliberately refined and social smile, placing a distance of insuperable millenniums between the abstract lines of her features and the crude face of Little Flower" (504).

Lispector most likely had not read "Brazil, January 1, 1502" by the time she wrote the story, since the poem and the story were published in the same year and since it is unlikely the poem reached a Brazilian audience, at least until it appeared in *Questions of Travel*. Translating this story about the latter-day conquistador, his people back home, and the "maddening little wom[a]n," Bishop meets an unwitting sequel to her own poem. When the imperial powers have spoken, Lispector turns, in a move Bishop reaches toward but only rarely achieves in her own poetry, to the voice of the subaltern subject herself. The small, pregnant woman in Africa is heartily laughing, "experiencing the ineffable sensation of not having been eaten yet. [. . .] It was a laugh such as only one who does not speak laughs. It was a laugh that the explorer, constrained, couldn't classify" (505). It was a self-acknowledging laugh that befuddles appropriation, of which Hélène Cixous's Medusa would be proud.

Explaining Little Flower's profound love for the explorer – "having no other resources, she was reduced to profundity" (506) – as determined not by logic but by the unconditional generosity of her spirit, Lispector romanticizes the difference between these subjects, only to undercut difference altogether in her close: "Little Flower answered 'Yes.' That it was very nice to have a tree of her own to live in," her eyes deepening as if to say, "it is good to own, good to own, good to own" (506), and thus seizing as her own a prime tenet of the imperialist's ethos. Lispector's story offers Bishop voices for the women (and the latter-day conquistadors), whom she herself had worked to hear. Daring to listen to history's silences, Lispector explored the "maddening" and found in it a laugh of self-appreciation, love, and a not so alien pleasure in her daily possessions.

Within the dialogue of her translations Bishop discovers intimate guides to Brazil. Likewise, her own writing about Brazil, where cultural and political differences meet, asserts in its tones, structures, and thematic insights that representation is in part a collaborative effort. Her relationships extrinsic to the writing, with a Brazilian poet, friend, or guide, make vitally complex her enactment of subject–subject relationships within the piece. Just as Ruy led Bishop repeatedly to revise her impressions during their trip to Vigia, and the community watch for the burglar on the loose as well as her research on the socioeconomics of Rio framed her ballad, so her outsider's distance from the voices along the Rio São Francisco or in the Brazilian mines colored her representations of these experiences. Within the ballad, then, Bishop's double point of view allows her to set the observing burglar beside the observing rich, for a moment erasing the difference that seems so inevitably to divide them. Within the story, Bishop-as-tourist converses with Ruy-as-guide, each investing the desires and interpretations of the other with the shades of his and her difference. Alert to the situatedness of speakers and subjects throughout her writing on Brazil, Bishop may not hear the words being called by the "maddening little women" or the squatter's children at play, but her poems inevitably concern themselves with the dynamics that bind and distance her speakers and her subjects in relationships of power, possession, and love.

6

Closing Together

Robert von Hallberg opens his book about contemporary American culture poetry saying he will discuss the variety of excellent poems written in recent decades about what poets "have taken to be the range of thought and experience most central to American life" (1). He defines the "center" as synonymous with "public life," "social institutions," "cultural authority," and "national spirit," and he lists examples of poems his study excludes because they do not address this center. Elizabeth Bishop's "One Art," her 1976 villanelle about the loss of love, is one such poem; it does "not relate directly to my subject" (2).

Bishop would have been the first to agree with his definition of the center. She wrote to Robert Lowell, after reading *Life Studies,* that

> I am green with envy of your kind of assurance. I feel that I could write in as much detail about my Uncle Artie, say – but what would be the significance? Nothing at all. He became a drunkard, fought with his wife, and spent most of his time fishing . . . and was ignorant as sin. It is sad; slightly more interesting than having an uncle practising law in Schenectady maybe, but that's all. Whereas all you have to do is put down the names! And tha fact that it seems significant, illustrative, American, etc., gives you, I think, the confidence you display about tackling any idea or theme, <u>seriously</u>, in both writing and conversation. In some ways you are the luckiest poet I know![1]

Lowell's poetry had access to America's cultural veins simply because he had familial roots in American poetic and political history. Bishop, on the other hand, was an orphan of unimportant stock, off in Brazil at the time of this letter; hers was the "eye of the outsider," as Adrienne Rich put it,[2] or so Bishop projects it here.

In this closing chapter I will argue that Bishop's poetry, particularly her late poetry, defies such distinctions of inside and outside; or rather, it enacts a slippage, locating the "significant, illustrative, American, etc." center precisely in the voices of the traditionally marginalized – children, tourists, an island recluse, a stray dog, the clutter of a poet's desk. Her poetry challenges a notion of "centralized culture" (von Hallberg 4), through a perspective both subtle and daily, fully attentive to culture as it is constituted not necessarily in institutional actions but always in human interactions. In a departure from the concerns of her 1960s Brazil writing, Bishop's late, reflective poetry locates history and politics in the daily relationships of power, alienation, curiosity, identification, and love that bring into focus the less seen shades and less heard intonations of culture, which might lead us to quite different conclusions about it. While several of her new poems would reenvision the memories of her 1950s and 1960s Nova Scotia writing, she punctuated the break by publishing *The Complete Poems* in 1969, before returning to the poems, several of which she had begun decades earlier, that would make up *Geography III* (1976).

In the summer of 1970 she wrote Lowell about her solitary life in her Ouro Prêto house:

> I also have a "cannon-ball" stove, I brought two – the other's a Franklin, for the sala, – burning away, and I just realized last night as the lights failed in the kitchen and I fried myself an egg by the light of the oil lamp, that probably what I am really up to is re-creating a sort of de luxe Nova Scotia all over again, in Brazil. And now I'm my own grandmother. (15 June 1970, UT)

Her solution – to make her own Nova Scotia in Brazil by embodying her grandmother and assembling a turn-of-the-century kitchen – is a return to an earlier theme. In a series of nostalgic letters in 1963, amid the Brazilian political upheaval, but before Macedo Soares's suicide and Bishop's years of personal unease, Bishop wrote her Aunt Grace about Nova Scotia land. She asked her to send clippings of houses for sale in Great Village. She mused over an advertisement for a lighthouse house that Aunt Grace had sent her, responding with longing:

> How much land goes with that lighthouse? I want some land and some woods and a brook – and a pasture for a cow! And some old apple trees – When does it begin to get spring-like? May? (I have no heavy coat!) Shad and salmon – and clams! – and I love to go fishing, you know – any kind of fishing – (28 Oct. 1963, VC)

In 1963 she dreamed of buying the fields of the childhood she had represented in "In the Village"; in 1970 she re-created the kitchen she had drawn in "Sestina." In Boston, when she purchased her final home, the apartment at Lewis Wharf, she determined that she was settled when she had her Franklin stove (letter to Barkers, 30 July 1973, PU). While her life was coming round, so was her poetry. In *Geography III* and in the poems that followed, she worked to bring her worlds together and to closure. By 1978 she had received the $21,000 Guggenheim Fellowship for work on her books of memory and loss, *Grandmother's Glass Eye,* and the book-length poem "Elegy," which in draft form she called "Aubade and Elegy," to Lota de Macedo Soares.

Bishop may have likened herself to her sandpiper in her 1976 *Books Abroad* Prize acceptance speech, but she would not have written "Sandpiper" in the 1970s. As if in conversation with her earlier poetry's pragmatic skepticism about resting places, Bishop explores the parameters of closure here. The moments when "the world is / minute and vast and clear" are not more prolific in these poems, but they are sustaining: there is an acceptance in her acts of bringing things together that they will not clash, as there was not in "Roosters" or "Arrival at Santos," that they can be claimed slowly and gradually, as there was not in "Invitation to Miss Marianne Moore," that no one will sneak up behind and destroy the vision, as there was not in "The Riverman." Structurally and thematically, these poems endeavor to make the moments hold, even when loss threatens around the edges or at the core.

Never giving up the other element of her pragmatism – her fascination with each subject's movement in relation to others – her late poetry is a culmination of a lifelong exploration of subject–subject relationships. Excepting "Pink Dog" (1979), which satirizes class degradation in Rio and "12 O'Clock News" (1973), which views the horrors of war from the vantage point of the writer's nighttime desk,[3] this poetry looks most consistently through memory to the moments where individual subjects discover or reveal their relation to one another. Bishop plunges the child Elizabeth into the world with which she had never before had to identify, in "In the Waiting Room"; "The Moose" dissolves the time and distance between Nova Scotia and Boston, as the people traveling together discover a common voice. In "Crusoe in England," first titled, ironically, "Crusoe at Home," Bishop continues her exploration of the concept of home, working here to accommodate the death of an intimate at home's center. "One Art" brings together a life's worth of losses in an attempt to reconcile lost love. Writing of sexuality and mourning in unpublished poems of these years, Bishop exposes most poignantly an "I," "an *Elizabeth,*" as she says in "In the Waiting Room," who is our guide into the interior. She began several of the major poems of *Geography III* – "In the Waiting Room," "The Moose," "Crusoe in England," "12 O'Clock News" – in Brazil and completed them in Boston, beginning amid a domestic life becoming increasingly crowded by Macedo Soares's service to an always volatile Rio government and completing them while teaching and traveling to speaking engagements and prize committee meetings and while battling the anemia of the last few years of her life. In different ways, each of these poems confronts the space between worlds, where, whether or not oppositions have in fact, as she says in "Santarém," "resolved, dissolved, straight off," inner and outer realities, north and south, island and mainland "homes," war and not-war inevitably meet. Perhaps "Santarém" best represents memory's reconfiguration of both the political and her personal upheavals of the 1960s: while the events lurk at the poem's edges, the speaker turns to the compelling intimacy of daily relationships between rivers, riverboats, and the people who live in and visit this place:

> Of course I may be remembering it all wrong
> after, after – how many years?
>
> That golden evening I really wanted to go no farther;
> more than anything else I wanted to stay awhile
> in that conflux of two great rivers, Tapajós, Amazon,
> grandly, silently flowing, flowing east.
> Suddenly there'd been houses, people, and lots of mongrel
> riverboats skittering back and forth
> under a sky of gorgeous, under-lit clouds,
> with everything gilded, burnished along one side,
> and everything bright, cheerful, casual – or so it looked.
> I liked the place; I liked the idea of the place.
> Two rivers. Hadn't two rivers sprung
> from the Garden of Eden? No, that was four
> and they'd diverged. Here only two
> and coming together. Even if one were tempted
> to literary interpretations
> such as: life/death, right/wrong, male/female
> – such notions would have resolved, dissolved, straight off
> in that watery, dazzling dialectic.[4]

In its elegiac tone the poem conflates nostalgia for the Amazon with a more prosaic, harried life in Boston. The "literary interpretations" that one might apply to the scene come from Bishop's 1970s teacher's vocabulary, not her tourist's. The 1962 draft refers only to "whatever grand interpretation you like best." Our academic means of defining opposition, she shows in revision, become meaningless in the face of the vital chaos of this moment. Any black-and-white reading of the racial, religious, class, and political divisions of Brazil, as Bishop repeatedly stressed in letters and as the poem's anecdotes illustrate, is rendered absurd by the underlit tones of burnished clouds that color the poem. Definition is necessarily left to the quite daily terms of anecdotes, which record a specific circumstance as they speak to a larger philosophical or cultural reality.

Bishop closes "Santarém" with a confrontation of cultures by three ordinary people:

In the blue pharmacy the pharmacist
had hung an empty wasps' nest from a shelf:
small, exquisite, clean matte white,
and hard as stucco. I admired it
so much he gave it to me.
Then – my ship's whistle blew. I couldn't stay.
Back on board, a fellow-passenger, Mr. Swan,
Dutch, the retiring head of Philips Electric,
really a very nice old man,
who wanted to see the Amazon before he died,
asked, "What's that ugly thing?"

A gift is given; the wasps' nest bond between this Brazilian and this American bridges a cultural gap for a moment, until she must (is free to) leave. The tourist reboards the ship, where alienation reigns. The gift, the appreciation, the leave taking, and the shipboard condescension depend in part on a set of cultural assumptions given to and accepted by each of the members. Yet at the same time the poem recognizes the blurring of any cultural conclusion: the speaker is complicitous with the pharmacist in the face of Mr. Swan's disdain; at the same time she allies herself with Mr. Swan, "fellow-passenger," aboard their mutual tourist ship. These inconclusive relationships hardly answer to the spliced oppositions she posed earlier – "life/death, right/wrong, male/female"; rather, they reveal that ordinary individuals quietly crossing the slash marks that define cultural difference can shift the boundaries or change the definitions so as to make room for the work of daily relationships.

"In the Waiting Room," *Geography III*'s first poem after the passages Bishop excerpted from an 1884 geography textbook, approaches geography not as a location of places but as the means for reading the identity and the differences among people. The textbook asks generic questions: *"What is Geography?" "What is the Earth?" "What is a Map?" "What is in the East? In the West?"* "In the Waiting Room" takes up the challenge, as poems throughout Bishop's career have done, but it does so most daringly. As if sweeping away the net before walking the tightrope, she removes the shields of map and tourist's persona that protected the speakers in the poems opening geographies I and II: facing the void, the child Elizabeth plunges into the world, with which she had never before had to identify:

Without thinking at all
I was my foolish aunt,
I – we – were falling, falling,
our eyes glued to the cover
of the *National Geographic*,
February, 1918.

> I said to myself: three days
> and you'll be seven years old.
> I was saying it to stop
> the sensation of falling off
> the round, turning world
> into cold, blue-black space.
> But I felt: you are an *I*,
> you are an *Elizabeth*,
> you are one of them.[5]

"*What is Geography?*": it is the connection of the almost-seven-year-old girl to the African women whose breasts hang and whose necks are ringed with wire and to the "dead man slung on a pole" that she faces in the *National Geographic*. "*What is a Map?*": it is the way we endeavor to represent our divisions and our connections. What is "the interior," besides the destination at the end of a poem of self-mockery?: it is the place where she must shed the convenient terms of geography and where, if she does not become overwhelmed, as in her 1960s travel prose, she must explore the "awful" fit between herself and that which she is not:

> Why should I be my aunt,
> or me, or anyone?
> What similarities –
> boots, hands, the family voice
> I felt in my throat, or even
> the *National Geographic*
> and those awful hanging breasts –
> held us all together
> or made us all just one?

"The family voice" expands in waves for the child, from her aunt, who screams of pain, to the gray strangeness of the other waiting patients, to the women, the babies, and the dead man represented in the *National Geographic*. Any recognition of her own identity would seem to depend on some recuperable sense of boundaries that might mark what she includes and what in all this world includes her. But these, she discovers, have to do with neither her own nature nor others' so much as with the "unlikely" moment of their coming together here in the waiting room, where there is a scream of pain that could come, as David Kalstone in part points out, from "inside" any of them.[6]

Closing the poem without any pretense of being able to solve the perplexity of boundary, Bishop nonetheless offers the child an increased clarity about, at least, the geography of her place and time:

> Then I was back in it.
> The War was on. Outside,

in Worcester, Massachusetts,
were night and slush and cold,
and it was still the fifth
of February, 1918.

She has not fallen off the turning world; she has survived this encounter,
and she rejoins what is again simply the dentist office waiting room
with a new assurance about what she is rejoining. Spondaically stressing
her sense of place in the first line of this closing stanza, she only
gradually releases her clutching hold. The capitalized war gives the day
its most precise definition; the day's actuality depends on this main
historical event. Naming the town, the child gains further grounding.
It is not "home"; its mention provides no warmth. It simply offers a
helpful fact, as the war does, in confirming where she is. Reminding
herself of weather and date, her beat becomes regular and iambic, so
that by the time she has all the facts firmly in place she can lengthen
her line from trimeter to a slower tetrameter and release her grip, in
a feminine ending whose sounds blend into the silence that follows.
She is in this waiting room, of it, yet not bound to it or strangled by
it. Being one of its members, whatever that entails, seems by the end
a clarified possibility.

Bishop enclosed a draft of the poem in her letter to Lowell about the
cannon-ball stove and the frying eggs. In the same letter she responded
to the closing lines of his final poem in *Notebook*, "Obit," which read as
follows:

> I'm for and with myself in my otherness,
> in the eternal return of earth's fairer children,
> the lily, the rose, the sun on dusk and brick,
> the loved, the lover, and their fear of life,
> their unconquered flux, insensate oneness, their painful 'it was . . .'
> After loving you so much, can I forget
> you for eternity, and have no other choice? (261)

Bishop was disturbed by his assertion of love, presumably for his es-
tranged wife, Elizabeth Hardwick, and addressed her own deepest intimacy:

> Those lines of yours, Cal darling – "After loving you so much" – etc
> – I sometimes wish you had't written them or I hadn't read them. They
> say everything, and they say everything I wish I could somehow say
> about Lota, but probably never shall. I am trying to do a small book
> of poems for her, or about her – but it is still too painful. (15 June 1970,
> UT)

All the feelings are mixed. Her pained response to Lowell's expression
of love, her renewed thoughts of her childhood home, and the vast and

seemingly bottomless blurring of disparate worlds in her poem were
stuffed into a single envelope and sent to Lowell. The rebuke in the letter
of both Lowell's disturbingly easy expression of love and her own inability to express it at all, and the child's recognition in the poem of her
boundaryless connection to the world's pain, speak to a similar question
about the responsibility of poetry: how can one, Bishop seems to assert,
begin to articulate one's cultural or historical connections if one cannot
even find adequate words for one's greatest intimacies? Bishop's late
poetry, especially, makes central the difficulty, the pain, and the rewards
of those relationships, in all their dailiness.

As David Kalstone points out in *Five Temperaments,* several of Bishop's
Geography III poems are reenvisionings of earlier writing, "In the Waiting
Room," for instance, internalizing the pain only watched in "In the
Village" (34–5). Bishop did not revise her published writing, as Lowell
did repeatedly during these years, although she read every version of
every poem he wrote. When she returned in the 1970s to the territory
of her former writing, she did so because there was a particularly vital
depth unexplored. Here there is a new intensity: there is no looking
away, no cow to take to pasture or candy to buy, but only a steady
facing of the blurring lines between her childhood self and this incomprehensible world. Even still, the constant gaze is not enough: she could
not yet articulate her love for Lota, and its inarticulability, she told
Lowell, was wrenching.

Bishop's next published poem, "Crusoe in England,'"[7] bears witness
to that pain, discovering through it a story not quite told by Daniel
Defoe. She began the poem amid the upheavals in 1963 (letter to Lowell,
27 Aug. 1963, HL); her rereading of Darwin in June 1971 and a trip to
the Galápagos in August with her friend Alice Methfessel, whom she
had met her first year at Harvard (1971), gave her the natural setting
with which to finish.[8] More precisely, one could say that she conceived
the poem, whether she remembered doing so or not, when she was
vacationing with Margaret Miller on the island of Cuttyhunk in July
1934. She recorded in her notebook:

> Mr. Van Wuthenaur wanted to "simplify life" all the time – that's the
> fascination of an island. That is also why it is fun to be in a difficult
> situation for a few hours, in which you have to make clothes out of
> { }, tie machinery together with strings, eat berries, etc. On an island
> you live all the time in this Robinson Crusoe atmosphere, making this
> do for that, and contriving and inventing. [. . .] A poem should be
> made about making things in a pinch – & how it looks sad when the
> emergency is over. Margaret is good at this.

Complaining and bragging, her poem's Crusoe relishes having an
audience for whom he may provide such details of his solitary life now

past. For four pages he details his island, its animals and plants, his ingenious inventions, and the endless time he found ways of filling. But when he begins to recount Friday's appearance, he is jogged from his memory into his present loss:

> Just when I thought I couldn't stand it
> another minute longer, Friday came.
> (Accounts of that have everything all wrong.)
> Friday was nice.
> Friday was nice, and we were friends.
> If only he had been a woman!
> I wanted to propagate my kind,
> and so did he, I think, poor boy.
> He'd pet the baby goats sometimes,
> and race with them, or carry one around.
> – Pretty to watch; he had a pretty body.
>
> And then one day they came and took us off.

Bishop's poem downplays the hierarchy Defoe establishes between the two men. Although Crusoe speaks for Friday, he does so less as colonizer than as surviving, mourning friend. Shifting from primer-style prose to a tone of indrawn desire, from playful attraction and affection to the white space that holds inarticulable memory, Bishop reflects the difficulty of finding an accurate language with which to describe someone one knows so intimately. Never relocating the joy in his story, Crusoe breaks it off abruptly and in a single line narrates their removal from the island, by what is here an intrusive "they." This is the last we see of Friday until the closing lines, and as much as we will know of their life together, besides what we surmise from the understatement and the silence.

An exchange of letters with James Merrill, interestingly parallel to that with Swenson regarding "The Shampoo," followed an April 1974 reading of the poem at the Guggenheim Museum in New York. Merrill asked, tentatively and apologetically, for elaboration of the relationship of Crusoe and Friday:

> Something strikes me as not quite right about Friday when he appears; about what you do with him. The poem's last line, it's true, gives the full resonance of feeling earlier withheld or deflected into the landscape + fauna. Yet I wondered: why that faintly dismissive tone – "poor boy" and his "prettiness"? Why that, I mean, without some expression of the relation that makes him "dear" as well. A lot will go without saying, and does. But I found I was yearning for, say, some lines about how they communicated, Crusoe + Friday: did they make a language? of sounds? of signs? [. . .] The poem is so magnificent, and so touching, and so strong (for me) except at this one turning where something seems to wobble unintentionally. (19 Apr. 1974, VC)

Though the drafts that might have more explicitly defined their relationship have been lost, Bishop had apparently written and then cut the lines he sought. Three years after the poem's publication, she explained its gaps as practical decisions:

> Actually, there was quite a lot more in the last 2 or 3 parts of that poem – then I decided that it was growing boring [. . .] and that the poem shd. be speeded up toward the end and not give too many more details – so I cut it quite a lot. – the rescue to one line, etc. If I can find the original mms. here (under the ping-pong table, no doubt) I might be able to put back a few lines about Friday. I still like "poor boy" – because he was a lot younger; and because they couldn't "communicate" (ghastly word) much, Crusoe guesses at Friday's feelings – but I think you are right and I'll try to restore or add a few lines there before the piece gets to a book. In fact, now that I think of it, I can almost remember 2 or 3 lines after "we were friends" – that's where something is needed, probably. (20 Apr. 1974, VC)

Crusoe and Friday are distant, fictional figures whose lives Bishop represents by adding and cutting, or so her letter asserts; she has stored the details of their relationship under the ping-pong table. Her response suggests that, if she chose, she could reconstitute this relationship simply by restoring lines "where something is needed." But when the poem "gets to a book" two years later, only one word has changed from her *New Yorker* version, in a description of the billy goat's pupils. That which "wobble[s] unintentionally," the loss, remains intact, just as the "mysteriousness" of the love did in "The Shampoo."

Throughout the poem, Crusoe cherishes the memory of his island, keeping the story current in the retelling. But after the break in his narration – the white space of his and Friday's removal from the island – his possessions and his memories become diminished things, looking "sad," as Bishop wrote in 1934, "when the emergency is over." His knife that had "reeked of meaning" now "won't look at me at all. / The living soul has dribbled away." Enacting Crusoe's alienation as the tea-kettle's tears do the child's pain in "Sestina," the knife becomes simply an artifact, fit for the museum's efforts toward historical preservation. The loss of Friday, however, cannot fit:

> The local museum's asked me to
> leave everything to them:
> the flute, the knife, the shrivelled shoes,
> my shedding goatskin trousers
> (moths have got in the fur),
> the parasol that took me such a time
> remembering the way the ribs should go.
> It still will work but, folded up,

looks like a plucked and skinny fowl.
How can anyone want such things?
– And Friday, my dear Friday, died of measles
seventeen years ago come March.

Bishop began receiving requests from libraries for her papers in 1963. The hundreds of ragged slips of paper, holding scratches of used and unused poetic phrases, must have seemed to her just as uninteresting as the "shrivelled shoes" or the moth-eaten trousers to Crusoe, for whom these museum curiosities had been his daily necessities. Requests from Boston University in 1968, from the Library of Congress in 1969, and from Smith College in 1970 must have held for her the bitter irony of the closing lines of this poem: that which really matters cannot be preserved. Macedo Soares and Friday cannot be restored, no matter how many lines one retrieves or how much one offers for the collection.[9] In the understatement of Crusoe's loss of Friday, the abruptness and incompleteness of this closing sigh, we feel the greatest loss. Bishop reveals only the corner of Crusoe's pain, not by any means the "everything"; her close is the inbreath to Lowell's exhale. While Lowell's love finds consolation in "eternity," Bishop confronts the ordinary pain before which museum archives and narrative recountings must stop short. If those means of preserving culture are to do so with accuracy, they must find a way to account for such vitally central but necessarily quiet elements of it.

Five years later in her villanelle "One Art,"[10] which von Hallberg made a point of excluding, Bishop focuses on the pain of loss. To convey the cultural centrality of these intimate emotions, the poem avails itself not of the rhetoric of "public life" or "national spirit" but of the daily losses that fringe the loss of a dear friend. Within the bounds of this tight form[11] the poem keeps its gaze steady:

The art of losing isn't hard to master;
so many things seem filled with the intent
to be lost that their loss is no disaster.

Lose something every day. Accept the fluster
of lost door keys, the hour badly spent.
The art of losing isn't hard to master.

Then practice losing farther, losing faster:
places, and names, and where it was you meant
to travel. None of these will bring disaster.

I lost my mother's watch. And look! my last, or
next-to-last, of three loved houses went.
The art of losing isn't hard to master.

I lost two cities, lovely ones. And, vaster,
some realms I owned, two rivers, a continent.
I miss them, but it wasn't a disaster.

– Even losing you (the joking voice, a gesture
I love) I shan't have lied. It's evident
the art of losing's not too hard to master
though it may look like (Write it!) like disaster.

Confronting a series of daily frustrations, "One Art" takes on the challenge of mastering disaster by balancing taut structure and casual tone, defiance and pain, the daily and the extraordinary. Perhaps most clearly drawn here, the balance is hardly new to Bishop's poetry. From "The Man-Moth" to "The Prodigal" and beyond, Bishop had worked similar ground, knowing her subjects' pain intimately enough that she could in single poetic utterances voice it and the empathy or love that might begin to compensate. She most explicitly articulated the connection of rawness and salve in an unfinished late–1940s piece about Sable Island, called "The Deadly Sandpile":

> Anyone familiar with the accent of Nova Scotia will know what I mean when I refer to the Indrawn yes [. . .], – saying "yes", or a word half-way between "yes" & "yeah", while drawing in the breath at the same moment. It expressed both commiseration & an acceptance of the Worst, and it occurred to me as I walked over those fine, fatalistic sands, that Sable Island with its mysterious engulfing powers was a sort of large-scale expression of the Indrawn Yes.

Both the island and the Nova Scotian articulate pain – the perpetually returning sea-washed sand holds within it the tales of the mariners' drowning offshore; the Yes's inbreath re-utters the pain's initial shock – and the compensatory tones of a community's call and response. When Bishop takes on something like this paradox in her own poetic project, her Indrawn Yes depends, as I argued in the preceding chapter, on the relationality of her subject positions wherein no single subjectivity can engulf the poem's emotion.

Bishop discovered such a balance for "One Art" gradually, as we see in studying the fifteen extant drafts.[12] The first draft is actually a set of instructions, entitled "How to Lose Things," "The Gift of Losing Things," and finally "The Art of Losing Things." She writes that she is so "fantastic lly good at losing things / I think everyone shd. profit from my experiences." In an amusing letter two years earlier, Bishop consoled her aging Aunt Grace for her forgetfulness: "This, I feel, is no disgrace . . . at the moment I can't find 1. my checkbook. 2. my extra reading glasses. 3. 1 pr. of earrings 4. my WILL. . . . . so you see, maybe it's a family failing . . . " (21 Feb. 1973, VC). She considered in the first and sixth drafts including these reading glasses, but opted instead for door keys, whose metrical count is smoother.

She is also more explicit in this first draft than she would be again about the loss motivating the poem – her estrangement from Alice Methfessel, her closest companion:

> One might think this would have prepared me
> for losing one average-sized not ~~especially~~ ———— exceptionally
> beautiful or dazzlingly intelligent person
> (except for blue eyes)   (only the eyes <u>were</u> exceptionally beautiful and
> But it doesn't seem to have at all . . .   the hands <u>looked</u> intelligent)
>   the fine hands

In later drafts, Bishop incorporated Methfessel's blue eyes into the rhyme: "(eyes of the Azure Aster)" in draft 10 and "(eyes of the small wild aster)" in draft 11. By draft 12, she removed the telling color altogether, realizing that while the specificity of a "you" was vital, the identifying details were not (perhaps she was remembering the "indecen[cy]" of her specificity in "The Shampoo"). Choosing instead to identify the "you" through the humor of her body language, Bishop tested in draft 13

>   joking one
>   (that ~~funny~~ voice; ~~that~~ gesture)
> ~~And losing~~ you ~~now (a special voice, a gesture)~~ (funny voice; one gesture)

Most discussions of the poems suggest that Bishop is working once again to articulate her loss of Macedo Soares.[13] That most painful and still unapproachable death, as well as the more recent death of Marianne Moore in 1972, hovers about the poem as part of a composite of intimates loved and lost. But Macedo Soares is not specifically addressed here. The loss of her constant friend, Methfessel, was in actuality more feared than final. Bishop wrote the poem amid the several-month estrangement; by the time it was published, they were back together in Boston (letters to Baumann, 29 Nov. 1975 through 13 Mar. 1976, VC). Regardless of the relative magnitude of losses, the poem suggests precisely as it is stating the opposite, one loss is no preparation for another; the original pain affords one nothing in the confrontation of the new pain.

Already in the first draft she conceived the poem as a villanelle and seemed more sure about her secondary, -ent, rhyme than she was about her primary one, for which she tested "geography," "scenery," "key," and "ever," "never," "forever," "~~never again~~." By the second draft she had settled on the "master"–"disaster" base and had a working list of rhymes to draw from. The poem's drafts reveal a fascinating process of emerging detail. Beginning with a skeletal plan of daily losses, geographic ones, and the irresolvable human absence, the poem unfolds in an exquisite slow motion, when we watch it from draft to draft. Her loss of houses, for example, brought on the following set of revisions:

> my last, or
> next-to-last of ~~three~~ loved houses went
> into nowhere away ~~somewhere~~, but they weren't a disaster. (draft 9)

> My last, or
> next-to-last of three loved   houses. ~~They~~ went.
> ~~off into nowhere, but they weren't disaster~~. (draft 10)

> My last, or
> next-to-last of three loved houses went.
> ~~But nothing quite so serious as disaster.~~ (draft 11)

The force of the poem, from the first line's defiance forward, propels us toward the painful showdown of the last stanza. Not surprisingly, this stanza underwent the most revision. Several things had to happen here: the "you" had to emerge by startling yet seem as inevitable as the "I love you" that closes "Insomnia." If the poem were to achieve its balance – if the casual tone of humor and defiance were to recognize the pain at its edges and the ordinary were to hold a tenuous place for the extraordinary – then this stanza had to offer most firmly its Indrawn Yes of empathy and acceptance and at the same time its refusal to relinquish its hearty defiance. The stanza accomplishes this, metrically, in a challenge to the forces of the villanelle. "Even," an extra foot in a deliberately regular poem, is a test of strength, vital to the poem's progression and a defiance of its form. The loss expressed in this stanza is the most extreme, but *this, too,* I can overcome, the "Even" asserts, breaking out of pentameter to do so.

But the drafts reveal in their repeated, dissatisfied return to the same question the poem's most poignant lack of resolve about whether it will recognize this loss among the others, whether in fact this loss, too, is no disaster:

> No – I am lying – (draft 4)

> All that I write is false, it's evident
> The art of losing isn't hard to master.
> oh no.
> anything at all anything but one's love. (Say it: disaster.) (draft 9)

> above's all lies and it
> ~~I've written lies above~~. It's evident (draft 10)

Draft 11 continued in this vein, revising the command to herself from

"Say it" to "Write it." In draft 12, alone, she revised the stanza half a
dozen times, and finally, with a few small changes,

> above's all lies now. It is evident

became

> above's not lies, but it is evident.

Likewise in the same draft the last line underwent a difficult revision,
Bishop clearly struggling with the pain as she wrote and crossed out her
efforts:

> with this exception. (~~Stupid! Write!~~)
> (<u>Write it!</u>)   this disaster.
> ~~except this less (Oh, write it!) this~~ disaster.

>   seems
> but this ~~loss is~~ (Go on! write it!) ~~is~~ disaster.

The stanza wavered as well about whether it would mention love specifically, whether "~~losing love~~" (draft 7) or the "you" who entered in
draft 10 was responsible for the seemingly unrelenting disaster. Draft 13
set forth the ambivalence:

>   joking one
> (that ~~funny~~ voice; ~~that~~ gesture)
> ~~And losing~~ you ~~now (a special voice, a gesture)~~ (funny voice; one gesture)
> doesn't mean I've lied. It's evident
> the loss of love is possible to master,
> even if this looks like (Write it!) like disaster.

Draft 14 was a breakthrough: here she discovered a way to integrate the
"love" and the "you" metonymically, in the way that life might. Finding
raw love within a loved effect, she enjambed the line so that love would
look back to its specific source and outward toward the generalized loss:

> In losing you (a joking voice, a gesture
> I love), ~~I haven't lied.~~ It's evident

Having it both ways she could finally make the strong statement "I love,"
which in itself defied the lie, by quieting her insistence on opposition.
The compromise of love and loss was the nuance of truth she sought.
"It may look like (*Write* it!) like" a terrible lie, but in the poem's formal
control and defiance and in its articulation of the place of love in loss,
she has mastered something. The long process of writing this poem has
taken her from a disaster so inarticulable that it called the lie on her entire
poem to a disaster masterable, because she has recognized it, contained
it, and discovered how to balance her defiance and her acceptance.

    Bishop gives the Indrawn Yes its most explicit voice in "The Moose,"[14]
the poem she would perhaps have never finished if not for an upcoming

Phi Beta Kappa ceremony at which she was invited to speak.[15] Here she focuses on the relationship of strangers on a night bus from Nova Scotia to Boston, providing a new setting for her old question, posed a year before in "In the Waiting Room": what "made us all just one?" The tightly rhymed stanzas of "The Moose" orchestrate the scene, bringing people together quietly, gradually, so gradually it seems nothing has changed, when at the end the impressive mundanity of the moose helps them discover their common voice. The "irreducible center of public life" – I refer again to von Hallberg's distinction (4) – is precisely here, among people living daily life together.

Bishop made the bus trip herself, following a visit in 1946 to her childhood home in Great Village, Nova Scotia:

> – we hailed it with a flashlight and a lantern as it went by the farm late at night. Early the next morning, just as it was getting light, the driver had to stop suddenly for a big cow moose who was wandering down the road. She walked away very slowly into the woods, looking at us over her shoulder. The driver said that one foggy night he had to stop while a huge bull moose came right up and smelled the engine. "Very curious beasts," he said. (Letter to Moore, 29 Aug. 1946, V:05:03, RM)

The moose would play a crucial role in her poem. For years, she told Elizabeth Spires in her 1979 interview, she had her ending, the first few stanzas, and a "stack of notes" for the four pages of poetry in the middle (62).

Bishop opens "The Moose" with a series of prepositional phrases and adverbial clauses, developing the setting in expanding waves and delaying the verb until the scene is drawn:

From narrow provinces
of fish and bread and tea,
home of the long tides
where the bay leaves the sea
twice a day and takes
the herrings long rides,

where if the river
enters or retreats
in a wall of brown foam
depends on if it meets
the bay coming in,
the bay not at home;

where, silted red,
sometimes the sun sets
facing a red sea,
and others, veins the flats'
lavender, rich mud
in burning rivulets;

on red, gravelly roads,
down rows of sugar maples,
past clapboard farmhouses
and neat, clapboard churches,
bleached, ridged as clamshells,
past twin silver birches,

through late afternoon
a bus journeys west.

The bus meets the well-prepared scene, teeming with the life of nature's cycles and with human beings' civilizing structures. But as the bus gathers the people, who, we assume, fill the houses, cook the fish, and serve the bread and tea, it resets them, including them in its own small, traveling world, removed just enough from home that they can reflect on it. Their conversations speak to the present moment of the homes just left and to a larger time and space, less attached to any distinct moment. Among them there is,

in the creakings and noises,
an old conversation
– not concerning us,
but recognizable, somewhere,
back in the bus:
Grandparents' voices

uninterruptedly
talking, in Eternity.

The physical closeness invites the quiet, hypnotic talk into the night, and in that talk lies an ahistorical intimacy: these are not a specific somebody's grandparents; these voices come from capitalized grandparenthood itself. The rhyme mirrors the quiet repetition of a pattern we know so intimately we have forgotten it. Almost every stanza repeats at least two sounds, sometimes three, but rarely perfectly, usually in off-rhyme, so that we hear a repetition buried within the line, as within memory.[16]

In its span of writing, "The Moose" rivals "Santarém." Bishop encountered the moose in 1946; she began writing the poem in the mid-1950s, as she informed her Aunt Grace on two occasions, when she repeated that she wanted to dedicate it to her (2 Dec. 1956, 20 May 1958, VC); she finished, published, and read it at Harvard's Phi Beta Kappa awards ceremony in 1972. The poem encompasses twenty-six years of Bishop's life, including her two decades in Brazil. If it does not concern itself with the "dominant" in American, Canadian, or Brazilian culture, it does allow its grandparently passengers to articulate the culture where

they are, at the very center of their daily lives, where what is important
are the

> deaths, deaths and sicknesses;
> the year he remarried;
> the year (something) happened.
> She died in childbirth.
> That was the son lost
> when the schooner foundered.
>
> He took to drink. Yes.

While the passengers rehearse life in its cycles and aberrations, the poem's
speaker listens, hears snatches only, but fills in the rest of the common
story, since she knows it all already.

Midway through a stanza that settles the voices into sleep, the poem
jolts with the unexpected, the moose that disrupted Bishop's bus journey
and held a place for itself in the poem:

> Towering, antlerless,
> high as a church,
> homely as a house
> (or, safe as houses).
> A man's voice assures us
> "Perfectly harmless. . . . "
>
> Some of the passengers
> exclaim in whispers,
> childishly, softly,
> "Sure are big creatures."
> "It's awful plain."
> "Look! It's a she!"
>
> Taking her time,
> she looks the bus over,
> grand, otherworldly.
> Why, why do we feel
> (we all feel) this sweet
> sensation of joy?
>
> "Curious creatures,"
> says our quiet driver,
> rolling his r's.
> "Look at that, would you."
> Then he shifts gears.
> For a moment longer,
>
> by craning backward,
> the moose can be seen
> on the moonlit macadam;

then there's a dim
smell of moose, an acrid
smell of gasoline.

These people have accommodated deaths and alcoholism; they have built
tiny villages that assert only the briefest of pauses in a bus's journey
between stretches of Nova Scotian bay, marsh, and forest. They are
sturdy, and with "that peculiar / affirmative. 'Yes . . . ' / A sharp, indrawn
breath," they acknowledge their commiserating acceptance of life and
death. But they are not jaded, and they know when life becomes surprising. All eyes on the houselike, churchlike moose, the passengers are
transfixed together by the epitome of the daily and the plain in the figure
of something at the same time "otherworldly." They know this creature,
who in her appearance and slow, casual, self-assured demeanor is strik-
ingly already a part of the world they know, and they know nothing
about her. They feel the joy in the mutuality of that paradox, she watching them, they watching her, all strangers and all familiars brought
together on this "moonlit macadam," because of the coincidence of this
bus ride.

Willing these people to "stay awhile," as she put it in "Santarém,"
she simply does not write the moment at which they begin to return
from moose and gasoline to their separate worlds. For more than twenty
years, Bishop knew the literary, epiphanic moment that would discover
their bond and inevitably end the poem. Intervening life – and perhaps
the postmodern turn in poetry toward the ordinary, the irrelevant, and
the unsortably chaotic, which she never explicitly acknowledged, except
as she watched the changes in Lowell's poetry – gave her a way of writing
about sleeping, snoring, and ageless conversation. The moose simply
allows these very average lives to come together, in what Bishop apologetically called an "old-fashioned umpty-umpty nostalgic poem" (to
Howard Moss, 21 Mar. 1972, NYP). In the midst of revising this poem
she told Lowell, "I'm sick of being simple" (2 July 1972, UT). The poem
captures life so simply that one could overlook the fact that it is precisely
here, as easily as one could pass the road sign "Five Houses" without
noticing it, on one's journey through the hinterlands of Nova Scotia.[17]

Bishop claimed more than once that she hated "being simple." She
closed her interview with George Starbuck lamenting that she hadn't
"said anything profound," unlike Moore, who "always said something
to make one think very hard about writing, about technique – and Lowell
always says something I find mysterious . . . " (330). But whether or not
she could articulate it, Bishop's simplicity gave her access to the surprising; in her scrupulous focus on the surface, she peeled the human
layers that made it up. "12 O'Clock News,"[18] which James Merrill called

"the saddest poem you've ever written" (letter to Bishop, 30 Nov. 1972, VC) and which Adrienne Rich called "the poem-about-an-artifact which becomes the poem-as-artifact" ("Outsider" 16), oversimplifies by splicing the quite different settings of her writing desk and the Vietnam War, as a means for exploring how we create, label, write, and destroy another culture.

The poem did not address a specific war when she first conceived it more than twenty years earlier; then, her desk objects were the buried tenor for an elaborately metaphoric battle scene.[19] When she returned to the poem in the midst of the Vietnam War and the barrage of narrated footage that brought it home to America, she understood better the import of her conjunction of desk and war. Juxtaposing a prose report of the "situation" in a primitive, shelled village with a marginal list of things on her desk, Bishop reveals in layers the ways we silence and speak for the other:

<blockquote>
As you all know, tonight is the night of the full moon, half the world over. But here the moon seems to hang

gooseneck motionless in the sky. It gives very little light; it could
lamp be dead. Visibility is poor. Nevertheless, we shall try to give you some idea of the lay of the land and the present situation.
</blockquote>

Reversing the order by which we disguise our own voice in seeming objectivity, Bishop foregrounds the moment of writing so as to make most obvious the ways it colors what is written. The poem inspires both Rich's and Merrill's reactions, because it is all objects, irony, and cold wit about the war and because, by refusing to pose as the righteous poet deploring the horrors of war, Bishop reveals the sadder fact that any partial understanding potentially reproduces the degradations it means to describe. Condescending in its assessments and opinions, her newscaster gives us distorted soldiers that are really desk objects, who, because they appear so backward and foolish, seem to have caused their own disarray and death:

<blockquote>
At last! One of the elusive natives has been spotted! He

typewriter appears to be – rather, to have been – a unicyclist-courier
eraser [. . . .] Alive, he would have been small, but undoubtedly proud and erect, with the thick, bristling black hair typical of the indigenes.

From our superior vantage point, we can clearly see into a sort of dugout, possibly a shell crater, a "nest" of soldiers.
ashtray They lie heaped together, wearing the camouflage "battle dress" intended for "winter warfare." They are in hideously contorted positions, all dead. We can make out at least eight
</blockquote>

bodies. These uniforms were designed to be used in guerrilla
warfare on the country's one snow-covered mountain peak.
The fact that these poor soldiers are wearing them *here,* on
the plain, gives further proof, if proof were necessary, either
of the childishness and hopeless impracticality of this inscrutable people, our opponents, or of the sad corruption
of their leaders.

In each draft she revised toward further condescension, carating in "superior" before "vantage point," "sad" before "corruption," "elusive"
before "natives," who are "inscrutable" rather than "mysterious." She
mocks the superiority of her speaker, who can condemn the "childishness" of and identify as "our opponents" people about whom he admits
to knowing little; she mocks these dead soldiers, who are so absurd,
once dead; she mocks herself for having created the twisted butts in the
first place.

In the simplicity of her juxtapositions and the hyperreduction of the
issues, Bishop reveals war as not only the activity of killing but also the
degrading reportage of that killing. The ease with which news reporters
name and define the other implicates them in the experience of the war
at home. Even the most mundane of writer's tools plays a part, the poem
asserts to the point of absurdity. In its refusal to slip from this ironic
public voice to a voice of more private perplexity, which might serve
to dissociate the realms of the public and the personal, this poem calls
attention to the implication of the daily in the events of the world.

A departure from most of the poems of *Geography III,* the desk objects
in "12 O'Clock News" represent a quite different sort of agency than
do those in most of Bishop's poems. In such poems as "In the Waiting
Room" or "Santarém" the details of daily life, pressured by the offstage
world, are themselves laden with the poem's emotions. The aunt's
scream, for instance, forces the child to question her place in an incomprehensible world; the pharmacist's wasps' nest binds tourist and native
for a moment together. Enacting the poem's emotions, then, scream and
wasps' nest bridge the distance between subjects. In "12 O'Clock News,"
however, the desk objects' agency – they are the tools that serve our
writing and mislabeling of the other – must be read through a primary
metaphoric function: the typewriter is the escarpment; the cigarette butts
are the dead soldiers, etc., engulfing and rather insidiously replacing the
recreated other. Because of that rhetorical slippage, these objects are
uncharacteristically removed both from the emotions of the poem's subjects and from the public concerns they evoke. Tightly ironic, they enact
distance rather than bridge it.

If "12 O'Clock News" is Bishop's most insistently public and distanced poem of these years, a poem she drafted perhaps a few months later is her most intimate. "Vague Poem (Vaguely love poem)" remained unfinished and unpublished.[20] Closing in a stunning, lyrical sexual play between lovers, the poem progresses by means of layered stories about the Oklahoma setting, the crystalline formation – rose rock – and the shrub that shares its name – rock rose:

> The trip west –
> – I think I dreamed that trip.
> They talked a lot of "Rose Rocks"
> or maybe "Rock Roses"
> – I'm not sure now, but someone tried to get me some.
> (And two or three students had.)
>
> She said she had some at her house.
> They were by the back door, she said.
> – A ramshackle house.
> An Army house? – No. "a Navy house." Yes,
>   that far inland.
> There was nothing by the back door but dirt
> or that same dry, monochrome sepia straw, I'd seen everywhere.
> Oh she said the dog has carried them off.
> (A big black dog, female, was dancing around us.)
>
> Later, as we drank tea from mugs, she found one,
> "a sort of one". "This one is just beginning. See –
> you can see here, it's beginning to look like a rose.
> It's – well, a crystal, crystals form –
> I don't know any geology myself..."
> (Neither did I.)
> Faintly, I could make out – perhaps – in the dull,
> rose-red lump of apparently soil?
> a rose-like shape; faint glitters... Yes, perhaps
> there was a secret, powerful crystal at work inside.
>
> I almost saw it:turning into a rose
> without any of the intervening
> roots, stem, buds, and so on; just
> earth to rose and back again.
> Crystalography and its laws:
> something I once wanted badly to study,
> until I learned   that it would involve a lot of arithmetic, that is, mathematics.
>
> Just now, when I saw you naked again,
> I thought the same words: rose-rock; rock-rose...
> Rose, trying, working, to show itself,
> forming, folding over,
> unimaginable connections, unseen, shining edges.
> Rose-rock, unformed, flesh beginning, crystal by crystal,

clear pink breasts and darker, crystalline nipples,
rose-rock, rose-quartz, roses, roses, roses,
exacting roses from the body,
and the even darker, accurate, rose of sex –

Behind these images of intimacy – the paired rocks and roses – lies a cohesive history of relationships in Bishop's writing. Rock roses from Gregorio Valdes's garden are, in Bishop's 1939 essay, placed without seeming significance atop Gregorio's coffin by the large cluster of mourners, before the Cuban men will depart from their families to witness the funeral (*Prose* 56). Just as quietly, roses and rock roses proliferate at the gathering of Faustina, her dying mistress, and the visitor. The word slips and reverses, becoming rose rocks, a crystal common in Oklahoma, where Bishop gave a reading (letter to Aunt Grace, 21 Feb. 1973, VC); as such they are the excuse for a visit to the home of an eager student and an entry into conversation. By the time the double image of rocks and roses has become an impression in the naked body of her lover, beckoning her with its inchoate form to further exploration, it is already part of a history of personal connections in Bishop's writing. "They were by the back door, she said." Like the "map-makers' colors," we could say, after Robert Mazzocco, that the "back door" is "emblematic of everything about" Bishop. Offering not its centrality or authority but its dailiness, its relative privacy, even its false lead as the location of rose rocks, this back door opens onto companionship, mutual confusion, discovery of the crystals' "secret" and the roses' sexuality, unexpectedly and at the same time inevitably, as ordinary life would, without conscious preparation and announcement. The "Just now" echoes the "Just so" that introduced the conquistadors' invasion in "Brazil, January 1, 1502." Similarly, the pattern that includes it develops gradually and suggestively; similarly, its arrival is surprising, and it reopens the pores of the entire poem that must accommodate it. It is vital in both poems, as in "The Moose," that there really is nothing new in the closing element; its inherency in the preceding scene and in Bishop's writing over several decades is precisely what makes it surprising. The sexuality of these roses is a back-door surprise, where something we have known as intimately as a lover's breast visits us with colors and textures that make it seem suddenly new.

The secondary surprise for a reader of Bishop's work is that this stanza exists at all: Bishop simply did not write explicitly about sex. She wrote the last extant poems that approached the body in the late 1940s – "O Breath," her dream poem about holding an unconscious lover, and her poem about awaking together with a lover. Publishing only the first, she intended to jolt no reader with her bursts of sexuality. But here these other poems are. Her softened, tender attention to the pleasure of breasts is so rare because it keeps nothing at bay; there is no "myster[y]" and no "host of guests" in the garden waiting to condemn this love. The rose rock not only is a metaphor, like the land and sea of "The Map" or the "still explosions" of lichen in "The Shampoo," but is, finally, the lover's body itself. The poem approaches this nakedness not with the self-protective defiance of "One Art," but through the back door that quietly grounds the interior. Yet this more self-revealing interior could not be published.

Bishop left "Aubade and Elegy," her poem of mourning for Lota de Macedo Soares, much farther from publication. She completed her Guggenheim year with only rough and painful notes, probably typed years earlier.[21] She defined the project atop a page of memories of Macedo Soares: "Make it in sections, some anecdotal, somelyrical different legth – never more than two short pages –" Quickly and without proofreading, she typed things to consider including:

> small hans, small feet   the Beardsley sillhoute –
> the Pierrot cotume – the English underdarwers and littlesokc –
> the 1st communion –
> the chip-on-the h shoulder – the of God, the books – the books –
> athesit, pride, pride pride –
>
> [...]
>> the sdoor slamming, plaster-falling – the cok and I laughing helplessly
>> ont the other side of the door
>> An d oh the dream – te house, tehe desire – Bonniers – Museums –
>> and oh the contry's ingtatirud e- misnuderstanding – WASTE

The repeated "oh" and "of [oh] God" tell as much as the images and the glimpses at stories: the pain in her exclamations is the sticking point, holding her to these memories as if the words themselves would yield up the woman. Repetition is a vital element in elegy – as in the "Indrawn Yes" – creating pattern, providing continuity, controlling while expressing grief within the comforts of its rhythm.[22] But repetition is not a movement toward consolation here; this is a broken-record repetition, from which the poem needs to be jarred to a new idea:

> the poor cats come for our breakfast
> They hesitate at your door the Siamese gives a faint howl
> they run and jump onto my bed
>
> the smell of the earth, the smell of the black-roasted coffee
> as fine as fine humus as black

no coffee can wake you no coffee can wake you no coffee can wake you

No coffee

they hesitate at your door; they look back at me, big-eyed

Bishop found the perfect waking image, potent Brazilian *cafezinho,* but the line spins round ineffectively. The final, trailing "No coffee" suggests a repetition ended only because the cats came back to mind, not because anything has been resolved in the appeal to the coffee that has failed the lover. In the first draft Bishop reused her old analogy for this relationship – "your life slowed to that of the rock first the lichen then the rocks" – but she did not rediscover the concert of overlapping images of love that included these rocks and lichens in "The Shampoo," nor did she find anything like the closure of Wordsworth's "rocks, and stones, and trees" ("A Slumber Did My Spirit Seal") in her images, which in the first draft precede the coffee lament. Macedo Soares is not an abstract, Words-worthian spirit who can join the ground in its perpetual motion. If she is not a fighting subject, she is simply dead.

In "North Haven," Bishop's published elegy about Robert Lowell, there is consolation in the lists of flowers and birds and in the explicit attention to Lowell's completed cycle:

Nature repeats herself, or almost does:
repeat, repeat, repeat; revise, revise, revise.

[...]

You left North Haven, anchored in its rock,
afloat in mystic blue... And now – you've left
for good. You can't derange, or re-arrange,
your poems again. (But the Sparrows can their song.)
The words won't change again. Sad friend, you cannot change.

Locating death in its place within and apart from renewal, Bishop could write this elegy, publish it in 1978, arrange with Herb Yellin to have Kit Barker do a pen and ink drawing, and republish it as a broadside in 1979.[23] In its repeated calls to nature, the poem compensates for grief, as it acknowledges that Lowell can now no longer follow nature's patterns. But the patterns, she insists, continue. Nature in "Aubade and Elegy" is represented instead as the unapproachable Samambaia view:

~~and~~ the seven lines of mountains gently shouldering each other

away from the sun gently away from the sun, one by one

white like a bowl of milk

The scene is beautiful but distant, surrounded on this draft page by empty space. The milklike fog she characterized more than twenty years earlier in a letter to Moore (8 July 1952, RM) leads her not to homey comfort but to the stillness of lichen and rocks, whose description in draft 2 follows the bowl of milk. Not traversible or habitable, nature here offers a panorama but not a means toward closure as does "A Slumber Did My Spirit Seal," nor a force of continuity as does "North Haven."

Hovering over all is "the black wave ~~of your death~~," which recalls the "big black wave" that overwhelms the child in the waiting room. If these drafts are those to which Bishop referred in her July 1970 letter to Lowell, the coincidence is not surprising: this great loss put her in mind of the child's first awful knowledge of the world's pain and her place in it. Here, instead, any external world is closed off:

> No revolution can catch your attention.
> You are bored with us all. It is true we are boring.

There can be no viable, "natural" context for this suicide, no encompassing anecdotes, and no closure of the life, the relationship, or the poem. The extant fragments acknowledge this fact in a way that completion and publication never could. Perhaps Bishop sensed this when she returned to these drafts in 1977 in order to apply for the Guggenheim but then took the set of projected poems no farther. She wrote the elegy for Lowell in this year instead, returned in 1978 and 1979 to the Brazilian setting to write "Santarém" and "Pink Dog," and enacted a defiant closure in "Sonnet."

Bishop had no idea that she would die when she did. Everyone has a story about what she was doing in the last months and days of her life to suggest that she was as engaged in it as ever. She had an assortment of ailments – a hernia, rheumatism, anemia – and she was drinking, but none of this was new.[24] She and Methfessel returned from a trip to Greece and England in May; they went to North Haven in July and August. She was hospitalized for her anemia for five days in late September (letter to Barkers, 30 Sept. 1979, PU), then promptly returned to work. She signed "North Haven" broadsides on September 26 (MacMahon 118) and met the next day with William Goodman of Godine's, regarding the Jewett anthology (Goodman to Bishop, 27 Sept. 1979, VC). Brett Millier records a letter Bishop was writing on the morning of her death to chastise John Nims: she did not want his *Harper Anthology* to footnote unfamiliar words in her poems (Millier, "Bishop" 63). She had scheduled a reading the following evening at Harvard. No signs point to efforts at closure. She wrote no eleventh-hour letters to her friends; there are few extant letters from these last months. Life was progressing daily, until a brain aneurysm on October 6 stopped it.

"Sonnet," published three weeks after Bishop's unexpected death, pares life to the barest images of desired freedom, in what seems almost prescient access to the precarious line between life and death:[25]

Caught – the bubble
in the spirit-level,
a creature divided;
and the compass needle
wobbling and wavering,
undecided.
Freed – the broken
thermometer's mercury
running away;
and the rainbow-bird
from the narrow bevel
of the empty mirror,
flying wherever
it feels like, gay!

Nominally a sonnet because it consists of fourteen lines, as well as a clearly demarcated – though reversed – sestet and octave, the poem breaks all the form's traditions of rhyme and meter. Sounds and emotions disregard the boundaries of the staged polemic, and the range of emotions is packed into four disconnected images – the bubble, compass needle, ball of mercury, and mirror's edge. These apersonal and ahistorical objects call forth the emotions of entrapment and liberation, but do so neither in the terms of a "significant, illustrative, American, etc." struggle for freedom, nor in those of the daily efforts of an ordinary individual toward that end. Rather, the poem is in important ways self-canceling; its images escape the clutch of the emotions they call forth. The poem's end teases with its own seeming access to a freedom removed from the ordinary world of emotions Bishop has engaged throughout her poetry, emotions in which we are still caught.

The drafts of the poem suggest how conflated and conflicted the images were, as she was discovering the important relation of caught and freed. The first draft[26] is clearly discomfited: being "caught" does not provide certainty; yet uncertainty offers not freedom but "drifting."

Caught – the bubble   (SONNET!)
in the spirit-level
—and the uncertain, too.   (MM's "enchanting thing")
        and, equally uncertain
        the compass needle –
        A—What was that thought? ?
    – something like { } bubble
                in a spirit-level.   (blindly)

Oh   Brain,   bubble the   compass needle
~~bubble bubble~~   the false north –
in the spirit-level,
slipping, ~~slithering~~   (?)   shifting;
~~uncertainly~~ the compass-needle
uncertain in the   ~~wilderness~~
                                            drifting

"MM's 'enchanting thing'" is Marianne Moore's kaleidoscopic poem
"The Mind Is an Enchanting Thing" (*CP* 134–5). The mind there ma-
neuvers independently, "feeling its way as though blind." It is powered
by memory and the strength it gathers from the poem's diverse figures,
"the apteryx-awl/as a beak" and "the dove-/neck animated by/sun,"
for instance. "Conscientious inconsistency" notwithstanding, it is in sync
with its other body parts and with the surrounding world; it is certainly
never "caught." Bishop's "Brain, bubble"[27] acts "(blindly)" in this draft,
like Moore's, but the uncertainty is of a different order. It is unsettling,
not "enchanting."

The discomfort does not yet have a paired opposite. The octave's
mirror appears in this draft simply as one more image to work with; the
rainbow has not found its wings:

                the bevel
        at the mirror's edge, bit of
flicking   a rainbow

the caught–freed dichotomy enters in the second draft. The bubble becomes "trapped," as does the needle; conversely, the rainbow-bird "flies
free, flies free   gay," and the thermometer's "silver," following the
rainbow-bird, is "running away." But alongside a stanza testing these
movements, Bishop introduced the ambivalence: she challenged her images with the paradox "broken, free" splicing the one state with the
other. The dash of the published version simply solidifies that working
paradox: "Freed – the broken."

Over the next few drafts, she discovered how important the opposition
of entrapment and liberty was to her poem's frame, but she never gave
up the ambivalence that made both positions problematic. The compass
needle is indecisive; the spirit-level's bubble is a "creature divided": she
discovered the latter image in draft 3 and the former in draft 4. In drafts
4 and 5 the compass needle is "seeking, seeking," while the thermometer's silver "runs, runs away." In seemingly opposed motions, both
react with parallel nervousness: they are not where they want to be, but
they do not know where that is. Nor does the poem provide them any
context that might support their search. Each image must discover its
true north in this highly asocial poem, void of companionship and resting

spots. In drafts 5 and 6 the mirror is "indifferent" and alternately "obliv-
ious" to its edge's flying; in the published poem, it is "empty." Any
flight risks loneliness, or loss.

But that is where Bishop's last published poem ends. The closing
stresses –

> flying wherever
> it feels like, gay!

– assert neither "go to hell" nor "I love you" specifically, but they echo
them. At the same time they are insistently located nowhere in particular.
Defiantly disengaged from cultural and personal history, "Sonnet" seems
to take everything back, the *"Elizabeth"* of "In the Waiting Room," the
"sweet/sensation of [mutual] joy" of "The Moose," the resting spot of
"Santarém," where two rivers come together. Yet closure here is the
obverse that validates closure elsewhere in Bishop's poetry. The closing
word, "gay," is an utterance of sexual liberation – hers, ours, her time's
– and it is at the same time a simply social pleasure. The spirit-level,
compass, thermometer, and mirror embody our ambivalent desire for
freedom, and they are at the same time too abstract to be claimed by
any belief system. The rainbow-bird can fly "wherever/it feels like"
flying but in doing so is already beyond our reach. Bishop puts us in the
position of the curious but fearful child in "First Death in Nova Scotia,"
who can only follow with her mind her dead cousin Arthur's journey
down "the roads deep in snow": as a poem "Sonnet" is so neat, so
complete; it ought to satisfy, but, because it flies free of the daily spread
of emotions Bishop's poetry has taught us to trust, it leaves us hungry.
The rainbow-bird is released from the "empty mirror," the mercury
from the thermometer, and the poem closes without looking back at the
ambivalence and tension that produced this release. The poem's closing
stresses defiantly do not look back, but we must. We mourn the absence
of "an *Elizabeth*" here, because we are still in that world, discovering
how to make our battlefields, political upheavals, and painful intimacies
livable. We know that the caught and the freed and the freed and the
broken are inextricably intertwined. If the poem gives us access to nothing more personal, it insists we be aware of this. But then it flies off,
leaving us, the child in the parlor straining to see where cousin Arthur
has gone. Elizabeth Bishop has escaped from her posthumously published
poem. Intrigued but afraid to follow, because this freedom eludes our
divisions and connections, our emotional and daily centers, we want her,
instead, "back in it," where she has shown us we are.

Notes

Introduction

1 Bishop told George Starbuck about her literary inheritance in her 1977 interview (Schwartz and Estess 319).

2 After writing two stanzas of the long poem *Homage to Mistress Bradstreet*, Berryman became stuck for five years, during which time he rethought the entire project in order to discover how to write the seeming disjunction between what he considered to be the abstraction of her rhyme and her quite real passion and suffering, a dualism that, he felt, was also his own. His process is discussed in these concise terms in the anonymous introduction to Berryman's work in *The Norton Anthology of American Literature*, Vol. 2.

3 I am making use of Charles Altieri's opening definition of the divergence of postmodernist poetry from modernism (605).

4 *Partisan Review* 28 (1961): 594–611.

5 Rorty 148–50. Giles Gunn's reading of Rorty's pragmatism has been helpful to me here (69–71).

6 Jeredith Merrin points me to a passage in William Carlos Williams's 1925 essay on Moore, with which Bishop would have been familiar: "With Miss Moore a word is a word most when it is separated out by science, treated with acid to remove the smudges, washed, dried, and placed right side up on a clean surface" (Merrin, *Humility,* 58; Williams 128). Puzzling over the phrase, Bishop returned with her own terms: her acid does not "treat"; it eats.

7 Remy de Gourmont 115, quoted in Sanford Schwartz 57–8.

8 See Christopher Reid's London *Sunday Times* blurb on the cover of *Elizabeth Bishop: The Complete Poems: 1927–1979,* as well as such critics as Jerome Mazzaro, Jan Gordon, Thomas Travisano, and Jeredith Merrin.

9 Arthur Schlesinger, Jr.'s phrase (133), quoted in Cornel West 150.

10 Dewey here cites James's essay "Does Consciousness Exist?" 172.

11 "Being There" and "Being Here" are the opening and closing chapter titles of *Works and Lives.* See Clifford and Marcus for examples of this greater anthropological "nervousness" (Geertz 130).

12 Spivak, "Can the Subaltern Speak?" 308.

13 While I approach this term through a reading of pragmatism and postmodern gender and cultural theory, its more direct origins are in the object-relations theories delineated in the 1950s by D. W. Winnicott and more recently by theorists of infant development such as Daniel Stern and feminist theorists such as Nancy Chodorow. Taken together, these theorists are concerned with, in Winnicott's terms, "the intermediate area of experience" (2), wherein an infant both interacts with and creates the other – the blanket or teddy bear – and with intersubjectivity, or the daily, intimate relations among people. This focus on, as Nancy Chodorow puts it, a subjectivity that is in its "very structure fundamentally implicated in relations with others" (156) is set in opposition to Freud's drive theory and to Margaret Mahler's theory of separation-individuation, for their mutual premise that the subject is motivated by needs or anxieties that launch him or her from an unbounded merging toward greater ego differentiation from the mother. Disputing such an original undifferentiation, Stern studies a range of collaborative activities engaged in by parent and child from the earliest days of their relationship ("Early Development" 72–6). He posits a primary "we self," which is never wholly "I" nor "we" but is located in a third position, in which "something [can] happen that could not happen without the commingling of behaviors from each" (*Interpersonal World* 101). He and most object-relations theorists do not consider, as de Lauretis, Spivak, and Geertz do, the unbalanced power and gender relations inherent in any such "commingling." Nancy Chodorow picks up the argument at this point, asserting that neither relationality nor gender can be defined adequately in the absence of the other; in combination, we can begin to understand the "variability and fluidity in gender salience" in any relationship, as we are recognizing the "gender hierarchy and relations of inequality" at stake (197).

14 *Trial Balances* collected well-established poets' introductions of new ones. Moore selected for publication three of Bishop's poems, "The Reprimand," "Three Valentines," and "The Map," and elaborated on what she expected of poetry and found in Bishop's work.

15 Recent critics have picked up Lowell's suggestion of polarities in Bishop's art to understand particular thematic or emotional shiftings in her poetry. In her 1977 essay Helen Vendler discusses "the domestic and the strange" (Schwartz and Estess 32), an opposition that leads in her essay to an analysis of the more frightening polarity for Bishop between domesticity and absence or loss. Vendler looks both at some of the most personal and at some of the more exotic poems to explore the range of meanings held for Bishop in the highly charged idea of "home." David Lehman addresses the issue of enclosed space for Bishop, looking closely at "In Prison" and related poems to explore the paradox of freedom in enclosure, of poetic freedom within knowledge of belatedness. Lehman's argument falters because it is too little an understanding of Bishop's own position within this paradox and too much an imposition on her of given insights about the workings of the imagination. Bonnie Costello looks at the way tone and language construction in Bishop's poetry create their own paradox: questions and poses of impersonality make for disorientation, which is in turn her means toward discovery. Travel is the sustained metaphor here. Costello's attention to syntax allows her to address the complex relationship with the reader, which Bishop establishes in her movement between distancing disorientation and "total immersion" ("Impersonal and Interrogative").

16 In her 1971 essay Rich discusses her emergence as a woman writer as a breaking away from the kind of female poet who preceded and surrounded her – for example, the poet who, "like Marianne Moore and Elizabeth Bishop, [. . .] kept sexuality at a measured and chiseled distance in her poems" (*Lies* 36). Other woman poets have struggled with their inability to embrace Bishop; see also Kathleen Fraser 157. Jane Cooper writes that Bishop was to admire, not to use, and then puts the fact into "a poem with capital letters," which begins:

> john berryman asked me to write a poem about roosters.
> elizabeth bishop, he said, once wrote a poem about roosters.
> *do your poems use capital letters?* he asked. *like god?*
> i said. *god no,* he said, *like princeton!* (43–4)

Diane Wakoski writes about Bishop's rejection of her actually, in a letter – a response to Wakoski's request for a grant recommendation – and again, but worse, in Wakoski's dream: "As I reached the door, I saw on the other side Elizabeth Bishop just as she appeared in Victor's photo in *Preferences.* She was signaling me to go away, even though I had a guest apartment in the building. I said I wanted to come in, and she told me I shouldn't come in because I stood for the kind of poetry she had spent her life fighting against. I said she was wrong. She didn't understand what she was saying. The light glared on the flat glass sheet of the door, and as the light got stronger, I could no longer see her reflection, only my own" (115).

17 David Kalstone, "Trial Balances"; Lynn Keller, "Words Worth a Thousand Postcards"; Bonnie Costello, "Friendship and Influence." More recent discussions of the Bishop–Moore relationship include Kalstone, *Becoming a Poet,* Keller, *Re-making It New,* and Merrin, *An Enabling Humility.*

18 Brett Millier's critical biography, which will assuredly become central to Bishop studies, is forthcoming from University of California Press. Robert Giroux is currently editing a volume of Bishop's letters.

19 "Sandpiper." All poems quoted, unless otherwise noted, are from *The Complete Poems: 1927–1979.*

20 Millier's dissertation reads Bishop's work in the context of her personal history, the first chapter detailing the chronology of Bishop's life. Rather than repeat what Millier has already done and will do comprehensively in her forthcoming critical biography, I highlight here only those biographical facts that have a direct bearing on my argument and discussion.

1. Articulating a Personal Poetics

1 She made similar statements in other interviews with Elizabeth Spires 80 and with Sheila Hale and A. S. Byatt 61. See also an excerpt from a letter to Joan Keefe 1739.

2 Bogan goes on to do precisely this, because, as she sees it, "beneath surface likenesses, women's poetry continues to be unlike men's, all feminist statements to the contrary notwithstanding." "Verse" 173. Bishop wrote May Swenson that she was highly annoyed with Bogan's article, because she made a special plea for women's "tenderness and affection" (Bogan's phrase) (17 June 1963, WU). Decades earlier, in a letter to John Hall Wheelock, Bogan mentioned a *New Republic* offer to edit a women's poetry anthology: "They [*New Republic*] have, as you know, already published groups of Middle-Western verse, and whatnot. They are now about to divide mankind horizontally rather than vertically, sexually rather than geographically. [. . .] The thought of corresponding with a lot of female songbirds made me acutely ill" (1 July 1935). *Letters* 86.

3   She told Ashley Brown in her 1966 interview that socialism was "the popular thing" at Vassar, but, she said, "I felt that most of the college girls didn't know much about social conditions." She closed the comment with "I'm much more interested in social problems and politics now than I was in the '30's" (293–4). This interview took place at her home in Brazil in 1966; in Brazil, politics became a personal issue for Bishop, vitally impinging on her life. Reading and learning from her Latin American contemporaries, living in view of poverty and violence, Bishop's political sensibilities formed and made their quiet way into her published and especially into her unpublished writing.

4   Bishop wrote long, autobiographical letters to Anne Stevenson when Stevenson was preparing her book. Gary Fountain is currently working on a collection of oral histories begun by Peter Brazeau, and Brett Millier has likewise conducted dozens of interviews toward her critical biography. My own work has led me to Alice Methfessel, intimate friend of Bishop and executor of her estate, who has been invaluable in questioning my biographical hypotheses and confirming factual detail, to Ilse and Kit Barker, longtime friends of Bishop, who have provided me with rich anecdotes and helpful corrections, and to Miss Elsee Layton, a Great Village friend of Bishop's mother, with whom I have talked and corresponded.

5   The date, 29 May 1934, was confirmed in a letter by Craig Brown, executive director of the Nova Scotia Hospital, to me (29 Aug. 1988). The date of Gertrude Bishop's death will become particularly important in Chapters 2 and 4, where I discuss Bishop's relation to her mother.

6   In her review essay, Bishop compares Wallace Fowlie's idealized early impressions of Boston with her own. She recalls a swan-boat ride with her mother when she was three, and a swan's biting and drawing blood from her mother's finger (Schwartz and Estess 282). The early memory was a profound one for Bishop; it is a recurrent image in her unpublished memoirs about her mother.

7   "The Country Mouse" was written in 1961 and published for the first time in *Collected Prose* 13–33.

8   "The U.S.A. School of Writing" was written in 1966 and first published in *New Yorker*, 18 July 1983: 32–8.

9   Written between 1969 and 1979, "Efforts of Affection: A Memoir of Marianne Moore" was first published in *Vanity Fair* (May 1983): 44–60.

10   Bishop was an alcoholic. Her letters to her New York doctor, Anny Baumann, describe her breakdowns and hospitalizations during her toughest periods in the late 1940s and early 1950s. She began an Antabuse program in 1954 and

with only occasional lapses was faithful to it until her last few years. She details this program and each of the Brazilian doctors' procedures in letters to Baumann (VC).

11   In her correspondence throughout the stages of preparation and publication of *North & South,* mostly with Ferris Greenslet at Houghton Mifflin, Bishop exhibited the polite aggression that came to characterize her business prose. In the following letter, for instance, she made very clear how she wanted her book to look: "I dislike the modern unglazed linen bindings so very much that I wondered if I could have a glazed one? And could it be dark grey? I think that quite a dark gray with a gilt "NORTH & SOUTH" down the back would look nice, don't you? – and if gilt is not possible may be a dark blue lettering? Looking over the mms. as a whole it seems to me a slightly squarer than usual book would suit it – [. . .] Is there any possibility that I can have something to say about the type?"

When Greenslet asked her if she had a particular type in mind, she was prepared with an answer, "Baskerville monotype, 169E, 11 point" (Bishop letters to Ferris Greenslet, 11 Jan., 22 Jan. 1946, HL)

12   See especially Henri Cole. Bishop reiterates these influences in slightly varied form in interviews with Sheila Hale and A. S. Byatt 61 and with Ashley Brown 292. In 1934 she published in her college journal an essay she wrote on Hopkins, "Gerard Manley Hopkins: Notes on Timing in His Poetry." She admired and felt challenged by Auden but claims not to have been influenced by him (Brown 294–5; Starbuck 319–20). Her 1930s combination of sophistication, form, and politics in her sestina "A Miracle for Breakfast" and in "Sleeping Standing Up," for instance, seems reminiscent nonetheless of Auden. Likewise, her 1964 "Burglar of Babylon" recalls Auden's 1930s ballads, "Victor" in particular.

13   Several recent feminist dissertations discuss Bishop among her contemporaries, though most are as yet unpublished. For discussion of the Barker–Bishop relationship, see my "Recording a Life."

14   Houghton Mifflin rejected the manuscript. The short stories were not published until 1984 in *Collected Prose.*

15   See letters to Robert Lowell, 11 Oct. 1963, HL, and to Ilse and Kit Barker, 14 Oct. 1963, PU.

16   To respect her friend's privacy, I follow what has become a tradition in Bishop scholarship to omit her name here and throughout.

17   "Sonnet" was first published in *New Yorker,* 29 Oct. 1979: 38. Bishop died of a brain aneurysm on 6 Oct. 1979.

18   For a photograph of *Fear,* see Nello Ponente 99.

19   Bishop was invited to become a poetry reviewer for the *New Yorker* in March 1970, but she never completed or submitted a review (see letter to Howard Moss, 20 Mar. 1970, NYP).

20   There is a gap in Bishop's letters to Lowell from 5 Dec. 1953 to 20 Nov. 1954. If there is a missing letter during this year, it would be the logical place for her to have mentioned to Lowell Jewett's influence on her, were there to be such mention at all. Bishop refers on 20 May 1955 to a long, missing letter, but it is unclear whether she means a letter during that 1954 gap or another entirely.

21 David R. Godine, Inc. had been negotiating this edition with her.

22 Despite her reservations, she met with William Goodman of Godine's for further discussion on 27 Sept. 1979, nine days before her death.

23 In their article about Dickinson and Bishop, Lynn Keller and Cristanne Miller show the parallel manipulations of language of these two writers. They do not, however, examine Bishop's letters discussing Dickinson, and they mention only in passing her two reviews about her – "Love from Emily" and "Unseemly Deductions." Joanne Feit Diehl discusses neither letters nor reviews in her essay on Bishop, Dickinson, and the American sublime.

24 She typed the later draft on her IBM Selectric, which she acquired in October 1972 in Boston (EB to RL, 26 Oct. 1972) and which she used most consistently the rest of her life.

25 The books quoted here are from a collection of Bishop's reading library held by the Houghton Library, Harvard University.

26 O'Connor makes reference to this suggestion, although Bishop never did the review. O'Connor to Bishop, 9 Apr. 1959; *The Habit of Being* 326.

27 This letter (11 May 1963) is in Bishop's archives at the Vassar College Library.

28 She published reviews of poetry, fiction, and a collection of letters in Walnut Hill School's *Blue Pencil* and in the *Vassar Review*. See MacMahon 139–41 for references. "Gregorio Valdes" was first published in *Partisan Review* 6.4 (1939): 91–7.

29 "Sandpiper" was first published in *New Yorker*, 21 July 1962: 30.

30 For years she wrote this phrase, or alternately "tact and embarassment," in her notebooks alongside fragments of poems and notes about difficult emotions, particularly love. Writing the phrase as often as she did, she must have had something larger in mind to do with these individual pieces. Though she tried to define the terms, she never assembled the whole or drew the explicit connections.

2. Writing Intimacy

1 "The Map" was first published in October 1935 in *Trial Balances*. Bishop then included it in *North & South*. She wrote Anne Stevenson on 20 Mar. 1963 that "the first 5 in the book [...] were written in N. Y, in 1934–35" (WU).

2 Bishop recommended the article to a Mrs. Koncel, who sent her a paper she wrote on "Over 2,000 Illustrations and a Complete Concordance" (26 Apr. 1972, VC). See also Jan Gordon 12–13, John Hollander 244, and Lee Edelman 180.

3 The writing of the poems in *North & South* and *Poems: North & South – A Cold Spring* spans the years 1934 to 1953, from Bishop's college graduation to her life with Lota de Macedo Soares in the mountains of Brazil (though all but the last two – "Arrival at Santos" and "The Shampoo" – were written in the 1940s, before she left for Brazil). The poems range widely in setting – New York, Maine, Paris, Key West, Brazil, and places that exist only in the imagination – including both postmodern travel poems and surrealist blurrings of time and place. Bishop wrote in a variety of styles and forms, from persona poems to bluesy black dialogue, from the sestina and double sonnet to the parody of all form and rhyme in the overworked triplets of "Roosters," from intimate expressions of emotion to exercises in objectivity, and from the antiwar to the quasi-socialist to the consciously aesthetic.

4 Most recent discussions of Bishop's personal "I" examine it toward some other end. Robert Dale Parker, for instance, attempts to address Bishop's anxieties, but his New Critical training translates emotional states into literary ones; hence, he discusses her "unbelief in the self, a fear that, once having felt the vocation of *poet,* a poet still anxiously awaits the calling of any particular poem" (ix). In her essay "Bishop's Radical 'I,'" Lois Cucullu discusses the "I" in its connection with the "eye," which together are radically pluralistic, questioning, and challenging. Politically incisive, Cucullu's argument nonetheless disregards human relationships in its study of relationships as they are constructed in ideology and in language: "The eye/I and, more obviously, the map are subjects of this poem; their interaction calls attention to the hierarchical relationships and rhetoric operating in the poem that more discursive forms of discourse usually suppress" (251). Lorrie Goldensohn's 1988 essay focusing on an unpublished 1940s love poem is one important exception. Tracing the poem biographically and through the imagery of other poems about love, Goldensohn treats poetic intimacy quite literally as the various articulations of love between two people. I attempt here to strike a middle ground between Cucullu's ideological-rhetorical and Goldensohn's literal analyses.

5 As she wrote in her notebook, "If one had such a place to throw things into, like a sort of extra brain, and a chair in the middle of it to go and sit on once in a while, it might be a great help – particularly as it all decayed and fell together and took on a general odor" (late Aug. 1935).

6 While I find problematic Marilyn Farwell's embrace of the duality of "sameness" and "difference," I find quite helpful her designation of "lesbian narrative space" as a space "defined by fluid instead of rigid boundaries" (97), in which women are each other's "primary presence" (quoted from Adrienne Rich, "Power and Danger" 250) in a relational sameness that realigns standard associations of self and other. In "Zero Degree Deviancy" Catharine Stimpson encompassed in her definition of lesbian fiction the writer and reader, as well as the character, thus making it possible to include in Bishop's "lesbian narrative space" such a poem as "The Gentleman of Shalott," which addresses most specifically a homoeroticism that is male.

7 The entry itself is undated; the first succeeding date, a page later, is 18 Aug. 1934. Bishop was most likely on vacation with Margaret Miller and her mother on the Massachusetts island of Cuttyhunk at the time of this entry, since she was there for much of this summer and entries surrounding this one make reference to the sea. Bishop kept journals irregularly from the 1930s through the early 1950s.

8 Bishop's notebook entries during the summer of 1935 suggest what in conversation Alice Methfessel called a "crush" on Margaret Miller, a Vassar friend and artist who later became one of the founding members of the Museum of Modern Art in New York. Bishop's mid-1930s letters to Moore speak with

equal frequency of Miller and Louise Crane, another intimate from Vassar, an extremely wealthy woman, also involved with the foundation of MOMA and with the republican cause in the Spanish civil war. Bishop traveled in Europe with Crane from the summer of 1935 until the following spring, and again in 1937. Miller was with them during some of each trip. All three women were in New York in 1934–5, when, Bishop told Stevenson, she wrote the poem.

9 Critics have generally overlooked the sensuality of "The Map." Anne Stevenson states that the poem is about the "relationship between art and life" (*Bishop* 72). Bonnie Costello more recently argues that the map, for Bishop, is a vehicle of "imaginative engagement, a way of seeing in and through time" (*Questions* 235). Alfred Corn discusses the land and water as allegorical representations of the conscious and unconscious mind and then connects them with divisions of land and water in Genesis (149–50). Concerned with Bishop's reenvisioning of the literal, Lee Edelman opposes "the truth of history or fact *per se*" to "the more 'delicate' matter of representation . . . , the functioning of poetic coloration, or trope" (180). Thomas Travisano is interested in the poem's emotional ambivalence – its choice of an imaginative geography and its need for the lingering material facts (41–2). Lynn Keller discusses the freedom of the map's coloration, which has nothing to do with, say, "the imposition of colonial rule" (*Re-making* 108). Lois Cucullu takes such an argument back one step to assert that in their defining, boundary-erecting nature, "maps are artifacts of a patriarchal and imperial culture" (249). But Bishop, Cucullu continues, questions and revises this sovereign position by revealing the map as illusion; she thus "challeng[es] the hierarchy of discourses and those who engage in objective discourse" (252).

10 "The Gentleman of Shalott" was first published in *New Democracy* (Apr. 1936): 36.

11 "The Weed" was first published in *Forum and Century* (Feb. 1937): 114. Bishop told Stevenson (20 Mar. 1963, WU) that she wrote the poem on Cape Cod. She spent the summer of 1936 there with Margaret Miller and her mother. Several poems from these years reflect Bishop's interest, while in Europe in 1936, in surreal art and literature. She especially admired Klee and Schwitters. In his essay on Bishop's "surrealist inheritance," Richard Mullen analyzes her verbal connections with this art form. He quotes a letter from Bishop to himself, saying that she did not know the surrealists personally but was "much interested" in them. Mullen points out what aspects of surrealist art Bishop did and did not re-create in her writing, but he neglects to historicize her relation to the movement. Surrealism was baggy, long-lasting, and constantly in flux. While its main effort throughout was to enact a "crisis in consciousness" (André Breton, Second Manifesto of Surrealism, 1929), the interpretations of this varied widely over the years and across the range of artists and writers connected with the movement. Bishop was in Paris in the mid-1930s, but she had little to do with the surrealism of those years, which had become increasingly politicized under Breton's lead, antifascist and antipacifist. The poems she wrote after her Paris stays had much more to do with the early 1920s artistic experimentations by Klee, Chirico, and others into dream and the unconscious, into childhood as a source for adult

imaginings and primitivism as a manifestation of this (see also Maurice Nadeau and Uwe Schneede on surrealism).

12 Readings of the poem that argue Bishop into a single position, such as Robert Dale Parker's chapter-long discussion of "The Weed" as Bishop's anxiety over creativity and over procreation (3–21) – the latter is wholly unfounded – necessarily fall short.

13 Luce Irigaray figures the love and terror of such a struggle with the double metaphor of *"la glace"* – the mirror and ice that bind and pain mother and daughter – in "And the One Doesn't Stir without the Other." Melanie Klein asserts that "the most profound anxiety experienced by girls" is "the daughter's wish to destroy her mother, to see her old, worn out, marred," a wish absolutely intrinsic to her need to repair and restore her ("Infantile Anxiety-Situations" 234–5). "The Weed," however, closes by refusing to recognize this latter need.

14 The process of their writing relationship during these years is documented by David Kalstone, *Becoming a Poet,* chap. 2.

15 I am suggesting here a division of the mother and a displacement onto Moore of the introjected "good breast" that, in Melanie Klein's terms, the infant splits off from the "bad" one. Such splitting, however, never satisfies: "Through its identification with a good object [at the expense of the bad one] and through the other mental advances which this implies, the ego [. . . is exposed] to fierce conflicts. Some of its objects (an indefinite number) are persecutors to it, ready to devour it and do violence to it. [. . .] Every internal or external stimulus (*e.g.* every real frustration) is fraught with the utmost danger: not only bad objects but also the good ones are thus menaced by the id, for every access of hate or anxiety may temporarily abolish the differentiation and thus result in a "loss of the loved object." [. . .] For at this stage of his development loving an object and devouring it are very closely connected" ("Psychogenesis" 285–6).

As my intent is not to read the psychoanalytic functioning of "The Weed" or its author, I do not engage the complexity of Klein's argument in this essay about the potential formation of a depressive personality. I am intrigued nonetheless by the connections in time and theme between this poem and Bishop's oddly doubled engagement with her two "mothers."

16 Sandra Gilbert and Susan Gubar stress Bishop's ambivalence about her mentor in this poem, but they have to stretch the poem and Moore's August 1948 letter of thanks to do so here, as one does not have to in the case of Bishop and Moore's 1930s and early 1940s relationship. Their purposes in poetry had diverged by 1948; Bishop does not pretend otherwise in her poem or essays about Moore. Their love and mutual respect, however, remained constant. (Gilbert and Gubar must cut their quotation of Moore's letter short, for instance, to suggest sarcasm, where the letter in its entirety is much more one of pleasure and appreciation.) *No Man's Land* 211–14.

17 Bishop modeled the rhythm on Pablo Neruda's somber poem about a friend who has died, "Alberto Rojas Jiminez Comes Flying" (36–43).

18 "The Man-Moth" was first published in *Life and Letters To-day* 14.3 (1936): 92–3.

19 The notebook entry is undated but immediately follows a newspaper clipping of 17 July 1935.

20   "Love Lies Sleeping" was first published in *Partisan Review* (Jan. 1938): 14–15.

21   "The Prodigal" was first published in *New Yorker*, 17 Mar. 1951: 30.

22   Kalstone, "Prodigal Years," 188. In 1946 and 1947, Bishop made trips home to Nova Scotia, staying in Great Village. It was perhaps during one of these trips that, as she wrote May Swenson, the inspiring incident took place, "being offered a drink of rum in a pig-pen in Nova Scotia at 9 o'clock one morning" (6 Sept. 1955, WU). In the same letter she credits her "stretch with psychoanalysis" as sourcework for this poem. In 1951, after her Yaddo stay and after writing this poem, she returned home once again, shortly before sailing for Brazil, to begin a never-completed study of Sable Island, off the coast of Nova Scotia, famous for a nearby sailing accident that killed her great-grandfather and all of his crew.

23   Ian Hamilton records an anonymous letter stating that they "never made love" (135). See also an unpublished poem of Lowell's about their time together in Stonington – "The Two Weeks' Vacation" – quoted in Hamilton 134–5, 238 and "Water 1948," the first of Lowell's "Four Poems for Elizabeth Bishop" in *Notebook* 234.

24   Bishop recorded no trip in which she crossed the equator with Hemingway. Either the imagery of horizons and the equator central to the poem is metaphoric or Hemingway is transposed onto her trip to South America, in which she met the Miss Breen of "Arrival at Santos." The latter relationship is recorded in a notebook from these years.

25   The first three poems were originally published as one, entitled "Rain Towards Morning" in *Partisan Review* (Jan. 1951): 41–2; the last, "O Breath," was published in *Partisan Review* (Sept. 1949): 894.

26   "Insomnia" was first published in *New Yorker*, 23 June 1951: 34. Bishop wrote "Insomnia" at Yaddo, where, she admitted in letters, she was dissatisfied and drinking.

27   This poem immediately precedes drafts of a poem called "Faustina II," suggesting a 1947 dating at the earliest, since "Faustina, or Rock Roses" was published in February 1947.

28   Again, precise dating is impossible. In her essay on this poem, Lorrie Goldensohn writes that handwritten drafts are preceded and followed by "notes and scraps that echo the images and descriptive language of 'The Bight,' published in 1948" (40). Goldensohn published the poem for the first time, after having been shown these notebooks and some letters during a research trip to Brazil and making arrangements that facilitated the Vassar College Library's purchase of them from Linda Nemer. The first two chapters of Goldensohn's *Biography of a Poetry* are devoted to the poem and its rediscovery.

29   Bishop wrote "The Shampoo," as letters quoted in the text suggest, in the summer of 1953. It was first published in *New Republic*, 11 July 1955: 19.

3. Turning History Under

1   "In Prison" was first published in *Partisan Review* 4.4 (1938): 3–10. All stories, unless otherwise noted, are quoted from *Collected Prose*.

2 In this 5 May 1938 letter she criticizes Louis MacNeice for his *Poems,* which she calls a "spotted, helter-skelter thing," and Edmund Wilson, whose "applications" in particular she labels "short sighted and, I think, ignorant." *Poems* does have several poems that take a polemic stance on anticommunism, individualism, and war. Wilson was working through the 1930s on his history of Marxism and historical interpretation of literature; in 1940 he published the culmination of this work, *To the Finland Station.*

3 Between 1935 and 1952, roughly the years of her first two books of poetry, she published nineteen pieces of poetry and prose in *Partisan Review.* During the same period, she published twelve pieces in the *New Yorker,* the journal that was to become her major source of publication in the 1950s through the 1970s.

4 Margaret Homans characterizes the division between North American and French feminism (she qualifies her division so as not to essentialize them geographically) in terms that shed insight on the split between Bishop's and Moore's aesthetics. North American feminism, she argues, trusts that "language itself is impartial," even though cultural and ideological expectations have historically silenced women. Consequently, women can and do write their experience: they can be known in language. French feminism believes that language is a constructed order that itself limits expression, particularly the expression of the feminine, which is in Lacanian terms outside that order. The feminine is necessarily the "silent object," the "fictive or absent referent" (xi–xii). Bishop's trust in the power of her poetry to reveal people can be seen in the former light, while Moore's animals and plants, which shield the poem from the dangerous and finally inarticulable force of human emotions, can be located in the latter. Though any such assessment is necessarily reductionist, it nevertheless spotlights a fundamental difference between these two poets.

5 "A Miracle for Breakfast" was first published, along with "Paris, 7 A. M.," "From the Country to the City," and "Song," as "Two Mornings and Two Evenings" in *Poetry* (July 1937): 182–4.

6 Much of the genre was supported by the Federal Writers' Project. The poetry was direct, unembellished, and its subject was the historical moment of its production. See, for example, Jack Salzman and *American Stuff.* Bishop read and enjoyed the latter: "We've both [she and Louise Crane] been enjoying it – I thought that almost every one of the stories had something very interesting about it, didn't you?" (letter to Moore, 27 Mar. 1938, V:05:01, RM).

7 In a letter to Moore from Sevilla on 6 Apr. 1936, for instance, she responded defensively and with guilt to a comment of Moore's: "Oh dear – I am worried by your speaking of my "leisurely" life – my conscience is troubling me so badly these days that it takes it for a confirmation of the very worst. And it is particularly bad since so many people I know are having such a difficult time. We are coming home at the end of June and I am going to try to work and study much more seriously and thoroughly than I ever have before. Not that that in any way has anything to do with other people's difficulties," (V:04:30, RM).

8 In a 20 Mar. 1963 letter to Anne Stevenson, Bishop dated the writing of some of her poems, including "Paris, 7 A. M." and "A Miracle for Breakfast": these were written in the fall and winter of 1936–7 in Paris and New York. "The

Hanging of the Mouse" was also published in 1937 (*Life and Letters To-day* 17.9: 111–12), and its overlapping details suggest a similar period of writing.

9 Whether or not Richard Wilbur read Bishop's "Paris, 7 A. M." in *Poetry*, he uses very similar images in his explicit war poem, "First Snow in Alsace," where snow, once again, connects this war with childhood nostalgia.

10 Bishop to Lynn Keller, postmarked 19 July 1979 (VC).

11 For examples, see Oscar Williams.

12 "Sleeping Standing Up" was first published in *Life and Letters To-day* (Nov. 1938): 55.

13 "Roosters" was first published in *New Republic*, 21 Apr. 1941: 547–8.

14 In the original *New Republic* version of this poem, three bullets marked section breaks here and before the line "In the morning." In *North & South* the second break is clearly marked with blank space, but the first disappears. "St Peter's sin" falls at the top of the page and no extra space has been left to signify a break. I have seen no evidence that Bishop directed this alteration or later ones restoring the blank space, so it was most likely an uncaught printer's error. In subsequent published versions, the size of the break varies, depending on where the stanza falls on the page.

15 "Now now" is hardly Moore's usual syntax; I am assuming that this is a typo, and that she meant "not now."

16 See Susan Schweik, "Writing War Poetry" 536–40, regarding Moore's public and private writings on war. Moore's emphasis is the immorality of militarism and the universality of its guilt.

17 Bishop began mentioning Cootchie, the woman, in her 5 May 1938 letter to Moore and sent her the poem in February 1940 (RM). She published both "Cootchie" and "Jeronymo's House" (changed in *North & South* to "Jerónimo's House") in *Partisan Review* 8 (Sept./Oct. 1941): 382–4.

18 "Songs for a Colored Singer" was first published in *Partisan Review* 11 (Fall 1944): 429–32.

19 Years later, she wrote to May Swenson about her love of the blues: "I hadn't had a chance to play the Johnson record – any record – until I got up here. Didn't you like it? – or maybe you don't like pure blues the way I do. I think it's superb – heavens! – Flavio, who shares my tastes, & I sent Lota to another part of the house and listened to all of it. – Then some Bessie Smith, who sounds ultra-professional after him. – [. . .] The trouble is that after the record I keep putting everything every thought, into blues form – and very little of my thinking makes good blues, alas. "Brazil Blues" all right – but they have their own forms –" (3 Oct. 1963, WU).

20 Bishop read Brooks and wrote one of her small handful of book reviews on *Annie Allen* in 1950.

21 Marshall Stearns discusses background and features of blues (104–5). Loretta Burns analyzes forms of closure in blues lyrics (229). Houston Baker discusses blues theoretically by way of introduction to his study, which sees the "blues matrix" as central to an Afro-American literary history.

22 In 1944 Bishop began seeing an allergist and a psychiatrist, Dr. Ruth Foster, both in New York (Stevens to Bishop, 26 Nov. 1944; Moore to Bishop, 18 Oct. 1944; Bishop to Baumann, Aug. 1948, VC).

23   "Faustina, or Rock Roses" was first published in *Nation,* 22 Feb. 1947: 214.
24   Faustina's unabashed requests for cognac as payment for work or for nothing
at all become anecdotal in Stevens's letters to Bishop in New York (VC).

4. Gathering in a Childhood

1   Neither entry is dated; this rough dating is made possible by dates of surrounding entries.

2   She used the paper for reading notes from the New York Public Library
and for two courses – "Family of Curves," at the New School for Social Research,
and "Early Keyboard Music," given by Ralph Kirkpatrick.

3   The alternating blank and grid pages are numbered consecutively from 1
through 14, each number repeated. She wrote phrases or notes on the back of a
few pages as well. She typed ten additional pages of notes, which I have not
been able to date but which are lighter in tone and subject matter than the very
private manuscript stories; only a couple of stories here are direct revisions of
the extant manuscript material.

4   Though she had returned to these notes to print the date "1934" below the
typed heading

BAROQUE ART
Prof. Panofsky   N.Y.U.
I   Sept. 30th

it is unlikely that she took the course that fall. While it is always a possibility
that she took the course twice, she reported to Marianne Moore on 15 Sept. 1936
that "I am coming back the 20th, I think – because I have decided to take Mr.
Panofsky's course in the Baroque, at the Metropolitan, beginning around then"
(RM, V:04:30). Although the locations do not match, the dating does seem
accurate: on the back of the last page of notes for this course there is draft material
for "The Hanging of the Mouse," which she was working on in the fall and
winter of 1936–7.

5   Both stories were first published posthumously in *Collected Prose.*

6   In the late 1970s it seems she planned to revise and expand the unfinished
work in a volume of poems she proposed to the Guggenheim Foundation,
"Grandmother's Glass Eye." They granted her $21,000 for the year 1978–9 for
the project, as well as for continued work on her prose book and on a book-
length poem, "Elegy."

7   She was introduced to psychology and psychoanalysis during her second
trip to Europe. That summer she met Bryher, who tried to convince her to
undergo psychoanalysis, but with Moore's encouragement (MM to EB, late Aug.
1937, V:04:31, RM), she refused (EB to MM, 2 Sept. 1937, V:04:31, RM). Bishop
discussed with Moore her reading of Karen Horney, *The Neurotic Personality of
Our Time,* and her plans to read Ernest M. Ligon, *The Psychology of Christian
Personality* (14 May 1942, V:05:03, RM). In late 1955 she began reading Ernest
Jones's three-volume study of Freud, which she mentioned in three letters to the
Barkers (26 Jan., 23 Mar. 1956, 28 Nov. 1957, PU). In the March letter she
wrote, "He's a beautiful writer, along with everything else, even in translation,
compared to all the other psychological writing I've ever read." In this letter

also, she mentioned rereading Melanie Klein's *Psychology of Children,* which she found "superb." In the November letter she referred to her 1940s analysis in reference to this new reading: "Sometimes I wish I could go back to the analyst I went to and do the whole thing over again . . . I'd do it much better; however, when one can do it well one doesn't need to, I suppose." Her reading of Jones's Freud was coincident with her writing of "Sestina" and her translation of *The Diary of "Helena Morley,"* and before she began the typed version of the unpublished swan-boat poem about her mother.

8 Since Bishop drops the male persona here, I do so as well. She uses "I"; I refer to the child in this dream with the self-identifying female pronoun.

9 "In the Village" was first published in *New Yorker,* 19 Dec. 1953: 26–34.

10 "Gwendolyn" was first published in *New Yorker,* 27 June 1953: 26–31.

11 Bishop wrote these poems on paper used for about a year, from late 1955 until late 1956. Wherever possible, I match paper with that of notebooks, drafts of published poems, or letters whose dates are intact. Usually, however, she used personalized stationery for letters, so this last, most accurate method of dating is only occasionally useful. In the case of typescripts, it is possible to suggest rough dates on the basis of the typewriter used. Bishop typed the blueberry-picking poem and the elegy, for instance, on her Royal, which she acquired while at Yaddo ("a GIFT," EB to RL, 7 Nov. 1950, HL) and which she used most often in Samambaia, until 1957. (She also had a "Baby Hermes," which she had had for years; she used it less frequently.) When she was in New York for several months working in 1957, she bought a Royal Portable and brought it back with her to Brazil (EB to RL, 26 Apr. 1957, HL). When she and Macedo Soares began living much of the time in the Rio apartment in 1959, she took the Royal Portable with her. In December 1962, she got an Olympia Portable, "with accents," for Samambaia and traveling (EB to MS, 2 Jan. 1963, WU). She acquired a Smith Corona with accents in San Francisco, and brought it as well as the Royal back with her to Ouro Prêto in the early 1970s. There is less consistency obviously than these known dates suggest, for instance, when she left her "Royal in Rio because it was so awkward to manage on the bus and we're going back the first of next week" (EB to MS, 26 Mar. 1959, WU).

12 For her single typed version, she used the Royal Portable she acquired in 1957. An earlier draft is in a notebook a few pages after drafts of "Sestina."

13 Bishop published "Memories of Uncle Neddy" almost two decades later in *Southern Review* 13 (1977): 786–803.

14 Lacan defined metonymy as the "eternally stretching forth towards *the desire for something else*" (167), which it can never reach. We might liken this to Chase Twichell's discussion of the emotion that is *"written around* as though it were each poem's center of gravity," or "hollow spot" (131). I am arguing, however, that while this might be the child's vision here, the poet in the same breath embraces objects, gestures, and repeated phrases not as metonyms standing in for an absent center but as agents with a vital subjectivity of their own that allows for a decentering and so an accommodating of the emotion.

15 "Sestina" was first published in *New Yorker,* 15 Sept. 1956: 46.

16   My dating here is based on the notebook paper Bishop used for these drafts, which matches that used for drafts of "Argument," "At the Fishhouses," "Over 2,000 Illustrations and a Complete Concordance," and "A Cold Spring," poems published between 1947 and 1952. She mentions "the story about Nova Scotia [. . .] the one with the dog" in a letter of 18 Oct. 1950 to Loren McIver, suggesting that McIver might illustrate it for her (VC). The 1970s revision is on notebook paper she used for years in Boston.

17   There was an Una Layton in town, a friend of Grace, a year older (Elsee Layton to myself, 21 Jan., 6 Mar. 1988).

18   Bishop scripted "Swan-Boat Ride" on paper she used for a fourth extant draft of "A Cold Spring" (1952). There is a brief draft entitled "A Ride on the Swan-Boats" in a Brazil notebook between drafts of "Sestina" and "The Grand-mothers." The untitled draft, beginning "My mother made of dress-goods" was typed on the Royal Portable; thus, it was written after 1957.

19   As in my Chapter 2 discussion of "The Weed," it is not difficult to read through this injured mother to Melanie Klein's discussion of the infant's frightful effort to restore the injury she has in her unconscious fantasy inflicted on the bad breast, which in turn endangers the introjected good breast and, consequently, the child's own ego ("Psychogenesis" 286): "The attempts to save the loved object, to repair and restore it, attempts which in the state of depression are coupled with despair, since the ego doubts its capacity to achieve this restoration, are determining factors for all sublimations and the whole of the ego-development [. . .] It is a 'perfect' object which is in pieces; thus the effort to undo the state of disintegration to which it has been reduced presupposes the necessity to make it beautiful and 'perfect.' [. . .] The real object was felt to be unattractive — really an injured, incurable and therefore dreaded person" (290).

I find Klein's terms provocative, but because I am not pursuing her discussion of the depressive position either of this poem or of Bishop, I offer this passage as an overlay rather than as an avenue of interpretation.

20   "First Death in Nova Scotia" was first published in *New Yorker,* 10 Mar. 1962: 36.

21   There are four extant drafts; all are typed. Bishop typed the first draft on her Olympia Portable, the second and most of the third on the IBM Selectric she acquired in Boston in October 1972 (EB to RL, 26 Oct. 1972, UT), and the beginning of the third and the fourth draft on her Smith Corona, which she brought with her (as well as the Olympia) when she began teaching at Harvard in 1970. Once she got the IBM, she rarely used another typewriter, except, occasionally, the portable Olympia. Her handwritten revisions on each draft of this poem, however, make any other ordering of these drafts impossible.

22   For the sake of continuity, I have incorporated her handwritten revisions into my transcription. All revisions of this last draft are matters of punctuation or a movement of words, except the last line, in which she crossed out "Please, Grandpa! Stop!" — phrasing she used as well in the second and third drafts.

23   "Phyllis" is Phyllis Sutherland, Aunt Grace's daughter, with whom Bishop corresponded in the 1950s through the 1970s.

5. Confronting Brazil

1 Gayatri Spivak, *In Other Worlds*, 204. See my Introduction for a fuller quotation.

2 For background on Brazilian history and politics see Peter Flynn, Riordan Roett, and Thomas Skidmore.

3 "Arrival at Santos" was first published in *New Yorker*, 21 June 1952: 24, and "Questions of Travel" in *New Yorker*, 21 Jan. 1956: 40.

4 "Squatter's Children" was first published in *Anhembi* (São Paulo), Apr. 1956: 288–9. In a footnote, the editor roughly translates the title into Portuguese as "Filhos de favelado," or "Children of the Slum Dweller." The poem was then printed in *New Yorker*, 23 Mar. 1957: 36.

5 "Manuelzinho" was first published in *New Yorker*, 26 May 1956: 32.

6 Robert von Hallberg's political analysis of contemporary poetry includes a discussion of "Manuelzinho," which, he argues, responds with a mild liberalism to the issues of class exploitation that it raises, offering "both servants and a clear conscience" (126–9).

7 In his reading of the juncture between Wagley's and Bishop's representations, Thomas Travisano discusses Bishop's tonal shift, transforming Wagley's historical distance into the riverman's present awe, humility, and respect for the *sacaca* (158–62). "The Riverman" was first published in *New Yorker*, 2 Apr. 1960: 40.

8 Wagley is actually quoting President Truman's Inaugural Address of 20 Jan. 1949: "More than half of the people of the world are living in conditions approaching misery. Their food is inadequate. They are victims of disease. Their economic life is primitive and stagnant. Their poverty is a handicap and a threat both to them and to prosperous areas." Two pages later Wagley endorses Truman's claim, regarding the "primitive and stagnant" economy of the Amazon Valley (4).

9 Bishop found particularly compelling a dog's access to language. In her 1966 interview with Ashley Brown, she similarly described herself, when asked about her command of Portuguese: "After all these years, I'm like a dog: I understand everything that's said to me, but I don't speak it very well" (291).

10 It is unclear whether the other Amazon poem she refers to is an early draft of "Santarém," which she published in 1978, or another very rough poem that she called "On the Amazon." The first extant draft of "Santarém," which begins, "after two years, / I may remember it all wrong" (VC), suggests a 1962 dating, since Bishop went to the Amazon in the spring of 1960. A missing draft is always possible, however.

11 "Brazil, January 1, 1502" was first published in *New Yorker*, 2 Jan. 1960: 26.

12 Lynn Keller and Cristanne Miller are concerned with the female lineage of the poem, exploring the poet-as-tapestry-maker as a figure parallel to the enduring Indian women, who retreat by means of their repetitive calls into the wilderness. Primary concern for Bishop's identification with the poem's female figures, however, delimits interpretations of the poet's own appropriations (539–42).

13   Bonnie Costello considers the reader/participant's eye toward different ends: she is concerned with the tensions in Bishop's writing that move her images (and the represented issues) from foreground to background, so that the reader is alternately pulled into conspiracy with and pushed away from speakers and poetic subjects ("Vision" 353–6).

14   Bishop recorded her own annoyance with Brazilian male chauvinism and overt sexism in letters to May Swenson, 10 Aug. 1953 and 9 Feb. 1961 (WU), and to the Barkers, 4 Mar. 1961 (PU). Collected with her notes toward *Brazil* is a list of truck bumper stickers she saw, including the following:

> WOMEN – HERE I COME!
> NO PASSENGERS – Without tight skirts
> WOMAN * STILL THE BEST BRAZILIAN PRODUCT
> IT DOESN'T PAY BUT IT'S AMUSING
> (on a beaten up old truck) LOVE WAS MY RUIN (VC)

15   Robert von Hallberg's is the best political reading of "Brazil, January 1, 1502." He discusses Bishop's projection throughout the poem of the "Christian imperialists'" vision onto the landscape and her consequent implication in "the appropriation of that territory" (80–1).

16   The poem was first published as "The Burglar of Babylon" in *New Yorker*, 21 Nov. 1964: 56–7. Bishop then issued the poem as a book with woodcuts by Ann Grifalcani.

17   See Introduction, note 11.

18   The essay commemorating Rio's quatricentennial engages topics from history, politics, and Brazilian social structures to Carnival and its sambas. *New York Times Magazine*, 7 Mar. 1965, 30, 84–6.

19   Mary Morse, Bishop and Macedo Soares's friend and neighbor, had, by 1965, adopted two Brazilian children.

20   Bishop wrote May Swenson, for instance, about her trip with Aldous Huxley to Brasília and to a post of the Indian Protection Service on a branch of the Xingú, adding, "I have written a long long piece about it which I am now re-writing, and I hope I can sell it somewhere –" (25 Aug. 1958, WU). She mentioned the article to Anny Baumann as well (4 Dec. 1958, VC). It is not, however, among her papers at Vassar or any other reporting library.

21   *Collected Prose* 111. "A Trip to Vigia" was first published in *New Yorker*, 6 June 1983: 34–8.

22   See, for instance, letters to Robert Lowell, 26 May 1963, HL; to May Swenson, 11 Nov. 1963, WU; to Anne Stevenson, 8 Jan. 1964, WU; and her interview with George Starbuck, 315–16.

23   Moore begins the quotation, "That happiness" (there is no "That" in the text), and she leaves off the *s* in "affections."

24   The first draft is on the Olympia Portable she acquired in 1962. See Chapter 4, note 21, for details about this poem's dating. It is likely that she had at least read Drummond de Andrade's poem in Portuguese before beginning "For Grandfathers." Clearly, however, the subsequent drafts of her poem postdate her translation.

25   Bishop's translation of "Travelling in the Family" was first published in

Poetry (June 1965): 181–4, and was reprinted alongside the Portuguese in *Anthology* 56–61.

26 Bishop's translation of *The Death and Life of a Severino* was first published in *Poetry* (Oct.–Nov. 1963): 10–18, and was reprinted alongside the Portuguese in *Anthology* 126–39.

27 Three, "The Smallest Woman in the World," "A Hen," and "Marmosets," were published in *Kenyon Review* 26 (1964): 500–11. As with the Xingú and Brasília piece, the two stories not published are not among Bishop's extant papers.

6. Closing Together

1 Letter to Lowell, 14 Dec. 1957. She was, as she told Lowell in a "March ??
[1959]" letter, "half-way through" her story about Uncle Arthur, "Memories of Uncle Neddy" (HL).

2 Rich 16. Eavan Boland has also written movingly about Bishop's poetry "from the edges, from the margins" (90).

3 "Desk at Night" was her original title for a precursor to "12 O'Clock News," much more conventional in style, which she wrote at Yaddo in 1950. Below her manuscript is a draft of a letter to Katherine White at the *New Yorker*, to whom she had planned to send the poem. At the second draft stage, she decided to emphasize the riddling nature of the poem by titling it, simply, "Little Exercise." The battlefield was first attached to a historical war when she returned to the poem in the 1970s, calling the first of these drafts "News Report."

4 "Santarém" was first published in *New Yorker*, 20 Feb. 1978: 40. The first extant draft begins:

> I may remember it all wrong,
> after two years

Bishop traveled on the Amazon in February 1960, so, if we can trust her accuracy, the draft is datable to 1962.

5 "In the Waiting Room" was first published in *New Yorker*, 17 July 1971: 34.

6 Kalstone draws the connection between the inside of child and aunt, but the poem's text allows for an even wider reading:

> And then I looked at the cover:
> the yellow margins, the date.
> Suddenly, from inside,
> came an *oh!* of pain

Inside the yellowed cover there lies just as much potential for a scream of anguish. *Becoming a Poet*, 245–56.

7 "Crusoe in England" was first published in *New Yorker*, 6 Nov. 1971: 48.

8 See letters to James Merrill, 6 June, 27 Sept. 1971, VC, and to Dr. Anny Baumann, 9 Sept. 1971, VC.

9 Emotional content aside, Bishop was always practical. Aware of the monetary worth of her papers, she wrote to her Aunt Grace the year after the poem was published, "I have to get a good many – pounds and pounds – of valuable papers into this country because I must sell them as soon as possible, to support me in my rapidly approaching old age" (17 June 1972, VC).

10   "One Art" was first published in *New Yorker*, 26 Apr. 1976: 40.

11   Bishop varies the villanelle form somewhat. Whereas the last line of the first stanza should be identical with the last line of the third and fifth stanzas and the poem's closing line, Bishop retains the closing term "disaster" but makes each of these lines a thematic variation on the others. The opening line of the poem is, as the form dictates, identical with the last line of the second and fourth stanzas, but it goes through a slight but important variation in the poem's penultimate line.

12   Brett Millier's analysis of these drafts in her dissertation is finely detailed (150–9). She uses the Vassar College Library's numbering, while I have renumbered the drafts according to apparent revisions, so our discussions of particular numbered drafts vary (we agree from draft 9 on). There is a possibility of error in either case, of course, since Bishop did not number them.

13   The most recent of these is Lorrie Goldensohn's *The Biography of a Poetry* 261.

14   "The Moose" was first published in *New Yorker*, 15 July 1972: 27.

15   Or so she put it to Elizabeth Spires 62–3.

16   As Stephen Yenser has pointed out in correspondence with me, "In this poem Bishop always 'rhymes' the last line in a stanza with one preceding" line in the stanza.

17   This dirt road, on which there are still five farmhouses, runs toward the water from Route 2, the highway along the northern shore of the Minas Basin, where are found the highest tides in the world. Five Houses is west of Great Village, before the road turns north and into the New Brunswick woods.

18   "12 O'Clock News" was first published in *New Yorker*, 24 Mar. 1973: 37.

19   George Starbuck 320. The early drafts are alternatively titled "Desk at Night" and "Little Exercise" and dated 1950 (see note 3 above). Bishop discusses with Starbuck the effects of "the times" on her early and published poems, in both the writing and the interpreting.

20   I transcribe here the second of two extant typescript drafts, using her handwritten wording in the case of revisions. Although Bonnie Costello suggests a late-1940s chronology for the poem (*Questions* 74), the earliest it could have been written is October 1972, as she used the IBM. She went "west" to Oklahoma on two occasions, in February 1973 and again in April 1976 with John Ashbery, to receive her *Books Abroad* award.

21   The four extant pages of notes and drafts are typed on the Smith Corona, which she used less frequently in the middle to late 1970s than she did her IBM. These are most likely the poems to which she referred in her 15 June 1970 letter to Lowell.

22   Sacks 23–5. Peter Sacks's first chapter, "Interpreting the Genre: The Elegy and the Work of Mourning," discusses the psychological and ritualistic movements through loss to consolation in the elegiac form.

23   Barker's drawing is of the view from the house at which they stayed together in North Haven, looking toward Penobscot Bay and Mount Megunticuk (Kit Barker to myself, 4 Mar. 1987). Bishop signed 150 copies.

24   See letters to Barkers, 30 Aug. to 9 Sept., 27 to 30 Sept. 1979, PU; see also letters to Baumann, 7 Jan., 30 June 1978, VC.

25   Bishop died on 6 Oct. 1979. "Sonnet" was first published in *New Yorker*, 29 Oct. 1979: 38. While it was her last published poem, it was not her last written; "Pink Dog" was. As Lloyd Schwartz tells me, "Sonnet" was accepted by Howard Moss and held at the *New Yorker* for much of the year 1979. The version published in the *New Yorker* replaces the line "a creature divided" with "contrarily guided," although none of the extant drafts suggest that revision and although, in dictating the poem to Lloyd Schwartz, who was to read it at Bishop's memorial service, Howard Moss quoted the line "a creature divided." There is some suggestion that Bishop telephoned in the revision, but definitive records do not exist.

26   The six drafts that I discuss here are all in manuscript form; the numbering is my own, based on a word-by-word study of Bishop's revisions. Elizabeth Spires reprints this first draft preceding her *Paris Review* interview (56).

27   In her December 1991 paper Jeredith Merrin draws the fascinating but of course uncanny connection between this "Brain, bubble" and the brain aneurysm that caused Bishop's death.

Bibliography

Altieri, Charles. "From Symbolist Thought to Immanence: The Ground of Postmodern American Poetics." *Boundary 2* 1.3 (1973): 605–41.

American Stuff: An Anthology of Prose & Verse by Members of the Federal Writers' Project. New York: Viking, 1937.

Auden, W. H. *Another Time*. New York: Random House, 1940.

Baker, Houston A., Jr. *Blues, Ideology, and Afro-American Literature: A Vernacular Theory*. Chicago: U of Chicago P, 1984.

Bishop, Elizabeth. "As We Like It." Spec. Marianne Moore issue of *Quarterly Review of Literature* (Ed. José Garcia Villa) 4.2 (1948): 129–35.

   The Ballad of the Burglar of Babylon. With woodcuts by Ann Grifalcani. New York: Farrar, Straus & Giroux, 1968.

   Brazil (with the editors of *Life*). Life World Library. New York: Time, 1962.

   The Collected Prose. Ed. Robert Giroux. New York: Farrar, Straus & Giroux, 1984 (*Prose*).

   The Complete Poems. New York: Farrar, Straus & Giroux, 1969.

   The Complete Poems: 1927–1979. New York: Farrar, Straus & Giroux, 1983 (*Poems*).

   Correspondence with the Houghton Mifflin Company. Houghton Library, Harvard University, Cambridge, Mass. (HL).

   Correspondence with James Merrill. Elizabeth Bishop Collection. Vassar College Library, Poughkeepsie, N.Y. (VC).

   Correspondence with Anne Stevenson. Elizabeth Bishop Collection. Olin Library, Washington University, St. Louis, Mo. (WU).

   Correspondence with May Swenson. May Swenson Papers. Olin Library, Washington University, St. Louis, Mo. (WU).

   "Flannery O'Connor, 1925–1964." *New York Review of Books,* 8 Oct. 1964: 21.

   Geography III. New York: Farrar, Straus & Giroux, 1976.

   "Gerard Manley Hopkins: Notes on Timing in His Poetry." *Vassar Review* (Feb. 1934): 5–7.

   "Laureate's Words of Acceptance." In Ivask 12.

Letters to Ilse Barker and Kit Barker. Elizabeth Bishop Collection. Princeton University Library, Princeton, N.J. (PU).

Letters to Anny Baumann. Elizabeth Bishop Collection. Vassar College Library, Poughkeepsie, N.Y. (VC).

Letters to Grace Bowers (Aunt Grace). Elizabeth Bishop Collection. Vassar College Library, Poughkeepsie, N.Y. (VC).

Letter to Dorothee Bowie. Elizabeth Bishop Collection. Vassar College Library, Poughkeepsie, N.Y. (VC).

Letter to Joan Keefe. 8 June 1977. Rpt. in *The Norton Anthology of Literature by Women*. Ed. Sandra M. Gilbert and Susan Gubar. New York: Norton, 1985. 1739.

Letter to Lynn Keller. Elizabeth Bishop Collection. Vassar College Library, Poughkeepsie, N.Y. (VC).

Letters to Robert Lowell. 1947–70. Robert Lowell Collection. Houghton Library, Harvard University, Cambridge, Mass. (HL).

Letters to Robert Lowell. 1970–7. Robert Lowell Collection. Harry Ransom Humanities Research Center. University of Texas, Austin (UT).

Letter to Loren McIver. Elizabeth Bishop Collection. Vassar College Library, Poughkeepsie, N.Y. (VC).

Letters to Marianne Moore. Papers of Marianne Moore. Series V: Correspondence. Rosenbach Museum and Library, Philadelphia (RM).

Letters to Howard Moss. Elizabeth Bishop Papers. Henry W. and Albert A. Berg Collection. New York Public Library. Astor, Lenox and Tilden Foundations (NYP).

"Love from Emily." Rev. of *Emily Dickinson's Letters to Doctor and Mrs. Josiah Gilbert Holland*, by Theodora Van Wagenen Ward. *New Republic*, 27 Aug. 1951: 20–1.

"The Man-Moth" Discussion. In *Poet's Choice*. Ed. Paul Engle and Joseph Langland. New York: Dial, 1962. 103–5. Rpt. in Schwartz and Estess 286.

North & South. Boston: Houghton Mifflin, 1946.

North Haven. Broadside. Northridge, Calif.: Lord John, 1979.

"A Note on the Poet." Introduction to her translation of João Cabral de Melo Neto's *The Death and Life of a Severino*. *Poetry* (Oct.–Nov. 1963): 10–18.

"On the Railroad Named Delight." *New York Times Magazine*, 7 Mar. 1965: 30–1, 84–6.

Poems: North & South – A Cold Spring. Boston: Houghton Mifflin 1955.

Questions of Travel. New York: Farrar, Straus & Giroux, 1965.

Rev. of *Annie Allen*, by Gwendolyn Brooks. Unsigned. *United States Quarterly Book List* (Mar. 1950): 21.

"Unseemly Deductions." Rev. of *The Riddle of Emily Dickinson*, by Rebecca Patterson. *New Republic*, 18 Aug. 1952: 20.

"What the Young Man Said to the Psalmist." Rev. of *Pantomime, A Journal of Rehearsals*, by Wallace Fowlie. *Poetry* (Jan. 1952): 212–14. Rpt. in Schwartz and Estess 282.

Bishop, Elizabeth, and Emanuel Brasil, eds. With an introduction by Bishop and Brasil. *An Anthology of Twentieth-Century Brazilian Poetry*. Middletown, Conn.: Wesleyan UP, 1972.

Blake, William. *William Blake's Writings*. Vol. 1: *Engraved and Etched Writings*. Ed. G. E. Bentley, Jr. Oxford: Clarendon P, 1978. 185–6, 194–5.

Bloom, Harold, ed. *Elizabeth Bishop*. Modern Critical Views. New York: Chelsea, 1985.

Bogan, Louise. Rev. of *North & South*, by Elizabeth Bishop. *New Yorker*, 5 Oct. 1946: 113. Rpt. in Schwartz and Estess 182–3.

What the Woman Lived: Selected Letters of Louise Bogan, 1920–1970. Ed. Ruth Limmer. New York: Harcourt Brace Jovanovich, 1973.

"Verse." *New Yorker*, 27 Apr. 1963: 173–5.

Boland, Eavan. "An Un-Romantic American." *Parnassus: Poetry in Review* 14.2 (1988): 73–92.

[Brant, Alice (Dayrell)]. *The Diary of "Helena Morley."* Trans. and ed., with an introduction by Elizabeth Bishop. 1957. New York: Ecco, 1977. Trans. of *Minha Vida de Menina: Cadernos de Uma Menina Provinciana nos Fins do Século XIX*. 2.ª ed. Rio de Janeiro: J. Olympio, 1944.

Breton, André. *Manifestoes of Surrealism*. Trans. Richard Seaver and Helen Lane. Ann Arbor: U of Michigan P, 1969.

Brooks, Gwendolyn. *A Street in Bronzeville*. New York: Harper, 1945.

Brown, Ashley. "An Interview with Elizabeth Bishop." *Shenandoah* 17.2 (1966): 3–19. Rpt. in Schwartz and Estess 289–302.

Browne, Thomas, Sir. "The Garden of Cyrus." 1658. In *The Works of Sir Thomas Browne*, Vol. 1. Ed. Geoffrey Keynes. Chicago: U of Chicago P, 1964. 173–226.

Burns, E. Bradford. *A History of Brazil*. 2d. ed. New York: Columbia UP, 1980.

Burns, Loretta S. "The Structure of Blues Lyrics." In *More Than Dancing: Essays on Afro-American Music and Musicians*. Ed. Irene V. Jackson. Contributions in Afro-American and African Studies 83. Westport, Conn.: Greenwood, 1985. 221–37.

Cabral de Melo Neto, João. *Morte e Vida Severina: Auto de Natal Pernambucano (1954–1955). Duas Aguas (Poemas Reunidos)*. Rio de Janeiro: J. Olympio, 1956. 169–254.

Chodorow, Nancy J. *Feminism and Psychoanalytic Theory*. New Haven, Conn.: Yale UP, 1989.

Cixous, Hélène. "The Laugh of the Medusa." Trans. Keith Cohen and Paula Cohen. *Signs* 1.4 (1976): 875–93.

Clifford, James, and George Marcus, eds. *Writing Culture: The Poetics and Politics of Ethnography*. School of American Research Advanced Seminar. Berkeley and Los Angeles: U of California P, 1986.

Cole, Henri, ed. "Elizabeth Bishop: Influences." A version of a 13 Dec. 1977 talk by Elizabeth Bishop. The Acadamy of American Poets "Conversations." *American Poetry Review* (Jan./ Feb. 1985): 11–16.

Coleridge, Samuel Taylor. *Collected Letters*, Vol 1. Ed. Earl Leslie Griggs. Oxford: Clarendon, 1956.

Cooper, Jane. "Nothing Has Been Used in the Manufacture of This Poetry That Could Have Been Used in the Manufacture of Bread." *Maps and Windows*. New York: Macmillan, 1974. 29–58.

Corn, Alfred. "Elizabeth Bishop's Nativities." *Shenandoah* 36.3 (1986): 21–46.

Rpt. in Corn, *The Metamorphoses of Metaphor: Essays in Poetry and Fiction* (New York: Sifton-Viking, 1987), 144–72.

Costello, Bonnie. *Elizabeth Bishop: Questions of Mastery*. Cambridge, Mass.: Harvard UP, 1991.

"The Impersonal and the Interrogative in the Poetry of Elizabeth Bishop." 1977. In Schwartz and Estess 109–32.

"Marianne Moore and Elizabeth Bishop: Friendship and Influence." *Twentieth Century Literature* 30 (Summer–Fall 1984): 130–49.

"Vision and Mastery in Elizabeth Bishop." *Twentieth Century Literature* 28 (Winter 1982): 351–70.

Croll, M. W. "The Baroque Style in Prose." In *Studies in English Philology*. Ed. Kemp Malone and Martin B. Ruud. Minneapolis: U of Minnesota P, 1929. 437–43.

Cucullu, Lois. "Trompe l'Oeil: Elizabeth Bishop's Radical 'I.'" *TSLL: Texas Studies in Literature and Language* 30.2 (1988): 246–71.

Darwin, Charles. *The Autobiography of Charles Darwin and Selected Letters*. Ed. Francis Darwin. 1892. New York: Dover, 1958.

Defoe, Daniel. *Robinson Crusoe*. 1719. New York: Norton, 1975.

de Lauretis, Teresa. *Technologies of Gender: Essays on Theory, Film, and Fiction*. Theories of Representation and Difference. Bloomington: Indiana UP, 1987.

Des Brisay, Ella. Letter to Joseph Summers. Elizabeth Bishop Collection. Vassar College Library, Poughkeepsie, N.Y. (VC).

Dewey, John. *Democracy and Education: An Introduction to the Philosophy of Education*. 1916. New York: Macmillan, 1922.

Experience and Nature. 1925. La Salle, Ill.: Open Court P, 1958.

The Influence of Darwin on Philosophy and Other Essays in Contemporary Thought. 1910. New York: Smith, 1951.

Donoghue, Denis. *Connoisseurs of Chaos: Ideas of Order in Modern American Poetry*. 1965. New York: Columbia UP, 1984. 246–81.

Drummond de Andrade, Carlos. "Viagem Na Família." *José. Poesias*. Rio de Janeiro: J. Olympio, 1942. 213–16.

Eberhart, Richard. "A Note on War Poetry." In Oscar Williams 18–20.

Edelman, Lee. "The Geography of Gender: Elizabeth Bishop's 'In the Waiting Room.'" *Contemporary Literature* 26.2 (1985): 179–96.

Farwell, Marilyn R. "Heterosexual Plots and Lesbian Subtexts: Toward a Theory of Lesbian Narrative Space." In *Lesbian Texts and Contexts: Radical Revisions*. Ed. Karla Jay and Joanne Glasgow. New York: New York UP, 1990. 91–103.

Faulkner, William. *As I Lay Dying*. 1930. New York: Random House, 1964 ed.

Feit Diehl, Joanne. "At Home with Loss: Elizabeth Bishop and the American Sublime." In *Coming to Light: American Women Poets in the Twentieth Century*. Ed. Diane Wood Middlebrook and Marilyn Yalom. Women and Culture. Ann Arbor: U of Michigan P, 1985. 123–37.

Flynn, Peter. *Brazil: A Political Analysis*. A Benn Study: History; Nations of the Modern World. London: Benn; Boulder, Colo.: Westview, 1978.

Frankenburg, Lloyd. *Pleasure Dome: On Reading Modern Poetry*. Boston: Houghton Mifflin, 1949.

Fraser, Kathleen. "On Being a West Coast Woman Poet." *Women's Studies* 5 (1977): 153–60.

Freyre, Gilberto. *The Masters and the Slaves [Casa-Grande & Senzala]: A Study in the Development of Brazilian Civilization.* Trans. Samuel Putnam. New York: Knopf, 1946.

New World in the Tropics: The Culture of Modern Brazil. New York: Knopf, 1959.

Geertz, Clifford. *Works and Lives: The Anthropologist as Author.* Stanford, Calif.: Stanford UP, 1988.

Gilbert, Sandra M., and Susan Gubar. *No Man's Land: The Place of the Woman Writer in the Twentieth Century.* Vol. 1: *The War of the Words.* New Haven, Conn.: Yale UP, 1988.

Gioia, Dana. "Studying with Miss Bishop." *New Yorker,* 15 Sept. 1986: 90–101.

Goldensohn, Lorrie. *Elizabeth Bishop: The Biography of a Poetry.* New York: Columbia UP, 1992.

"Elizabeth Bishop: An Unpublished, Untitled Poem." *American Poetry Review* (Jan./ Feb. 1988): 35–46.

Gordon, Jan B. "Days and Distances: The Cartographic Imagination of Elizabeth Bishop." *Salmagundi* 22–3 (1973): 294–305. Rpt. in Bloom 9–19.

Gourmont, Remy de. *Selected Writings.* Trans. Glenn S. Burne. Ann Arbor: U of Michigan P, 1966.

Gunn, Giles. *The Culture of Criticism and the Criticism of Culture.* New York: Oxford UP, 1987.

Hale, Sheila, and A. S. Byatt. "Women Writers in America." *Harpers & Queens* (July 1978): 58–71.

Hamilton, Ian. *Robert Lowell: A Biography.* New York: Random House, 1982.

Hardwick, Elizabeth. "Flannery O'Connor, 1925–1964." *New York Review of Books,* 8 Oct. 1964: 21.

Harrison, Victoria. "Recording a Life: Elizabeth Bishop's Letters to Ilse and Kit Barker." *Contemporary Literature* 29.4 (1988): 498–517.

Hollander, John. "Questions of Geography." Rev. of *Geography III,* by Elizabeth Bishop. *Parnassus: Poetry in Review* 5 (1977): 359–66. Rpt. as "Elizabeth Bishop's Mappings of Life" in Schwartz and Estess 244–51.

Homans, Margaret. *Bearing the Word: Language and Female Experience in Nineteenth-Century Women's Writing.* Chicago: U of Chicago P, 1986.

Hopkins, Gerard Manley. *Journals and Papers of Gerard Manley Hopkins.* Ed. Humphry House and Graham Storey. New York: Oxford UP, 1959.

Hughes, Langston. *Selected Poems of Langston Hughes.* New York: Random House, 1990.

Irigaray, Luce. "And the One Doesn't Stir without the Other." *Signs* 7.1 (1981): 60–7.

This Sex Which Is Not One. 1977. Trans. Catherine Porter and Carolyn Burke. Ithaca, N.Y.: Cornell UP, 1985.

Ivask, Ivar, ed. "Homage to Elizabeth Bishop, Our 1976 Laureate." Spec. issue of *World Literature Today* 51.1 (1977): 4–52.

James, William. *The Writings of William James: A Comprehensive Edition*. Ed. John. J. McDermott. Chicago: U of Chicago P, 1977.

Jarrell, Randall. "The Poet and His Public." *Partisan Review* 13 (1946): 488–500. Rpt. in Schwartz and Estess 180–1.

Jewett, Sarah Orne. *The Country of the Pointed Firs*. 1896. Preface by Willa Cather. The Traveller's Library. London: J. Cape, 1951.

"John Berryman." Unsigned. Introduction to his poems. *The Norton Anthology of American Literature*, Vol. 2. New York: Norton, 1989.

Johnson, Alexandra. "Geography of the Imagination." Interview with Elizabeth Bishop. *Christian Science Monitor*, 23 Mar. 1978: 20–1.

Jones, Ernest. *The Life and Work of Sigmund Freud*. 3 vols. New York: Basic Books, 1953–7.

Kalstone, David. *Becoming a Poet: Elizabeth Bishop with Marianne Moore and Robert Lowell*. Ed. Robert Hemenway. New York: Farrar, Straus & Giroux, 1989.

"Elizabeth Bishop: Questions of Memory, Questions of Travel." In *Five Temperaments: Elizabeth Bishop, Robert Lowell, James Merrill, Adrienne Rich, John Ashbery*. New York: Oxford UP, 1977. 12–40.

"Prodigal Years: Elizabeth Bishop and Robert Lowell, 1947–9." *Grand Street* 4.4 (1985): 170–93.

"Trial Balances: Elizabeth Bishop and Marianne Moore." *Grand Street* 3.1 (1983): 115–35.

Keats, John. *The Poems of John Keats*. Ed. Jack Stillinger. Cambridge, Mass.: Belknap Press of Harvard UP, 1978. 282–3.

Keller, Lynn. *Re-making It New: Contemporary American Poetry and the Modernist Tradition*. Cambridge Studies in American Literature and Culture. Cambridge UP, 1987.

"Words Worth a Thousand Postcards: The Bishop/Moore Correspondence." *American Literature* 55 (1983): 405–29.

Keller, Lynn, and Cristanne Miller. "Emily Dickinson, Elizabeth Bishop, and the Rewards of Indirection." *New England Quarterly* 57.4 (1984): 533–53.

Klein, Melanie. "A Contribution to the Psychogenesis of Manic-Depressive States." 1935. In *Contributions to Psycho-Analysis, 1921–1945*. The International Psycho-Analytic Library No. 34. Ed. Ernest Jones. London: Hogarth, 1948. 282–310.

"Infantile Anxiety-Situations Reflected in a Work of Art and in the Creative Impulse." 1929. In *Contributions to Psycho-Analysis, 1921–1945*. The International Psycho-Analytic Library No. 34. Ed. Ernest Jones. London: Hogarth, 1948. 227–35.

Lacan, Jacques. "The Agency of the Letter in the Unconscious or Reason Since Freud." In *Ecrits: A Selection*. Trans. Alan Sheridan. New York: Norton, 1977. 146–78.

Lear, Edward. *Indian Journal: Watercolours and Extracts from the Diary of Edward Lear (1873–1875)*. Ed. Ray Murphy. London: Jarrolds; New York: Coward-McCann, 1953.

Lehman, David. "'In Prison': A Paradox Regained." 1981. In Schwartz and Estess 61–74.

Levertov, Denise. *Relearning the Alphabet*. New York: New Directions, 1970.
Lispector, Clarice. "The Smallest Woman in the World," "A Hen," and "Marmosets." Trans. Elizabeth Bishop. *Kenyon Review* 26 (Summer 1964): 500–11. "The Smallest Woman," trans. of *"A menor mulher do mundo." Laços de Família: Contos*. Rio de Janeiro: J. Olympio, 1960. 77–86.
Lowell, Robert. *Imitations*. New York: Farrar, Straus & Cudahy, 1961.
Interview. *Writers at Work: The* Paris Review *Interviews: Second Series*. Introduction by Van Wyck Brooks. New York: Viking, 1963. 335–68.
Letters to Elizabeth Bishop. Elizabeth Bishop Collection. Vassar College Library, Poughkeepsie, N.Y. (VC).
Life Studies. New York: Farrar, Straus & Cudahy, 1959.
Notebook. Rev. ed. London: Faber & Faber, 1970.
"Thomas, Bishop, and Williams." *Sewanee Review* 55 (Summer 1947): 497–98. Rpt. in Schwartz and Estess 186–7.
MacMahon, Candace W. *Elizabeth Bishop: A Bibliography, 1927–1979*. Charlottesville: UP of Virginia, 1980.
MacNeice, Louis. *Poems*. New York: Random House, 1937.
Mazzaro, Jerome. "Elizabeth Bishop and the Poetics of Impediment." *Salmagundi* 27 (Summer–Fall 1974): 118–44. Rpt. in Mazzaro, *Postmodern American Poetry* (Urbana: U of Illinois P, 1980), 166–98).
Mazzocco, Robert. "A Poet of Landscape." Rev. of *Questions of Travel*, by Elizabeth Bishop. *New York Review of Books*, 12 Oct. 1967: 4–6.
Merrin, Jeredith. *An Enabling Humility: Marianne Moore, Elizabeth Bishop, and the Uses of Tradition*. New Brunswick, N.J.: Rutgers UP, 1990.
"'Pleasure Seas,' 'Sonnet,' and the Gaity of Elizabeth Bishop." Paper presented at the Modern Language Association Conference, San Francisco. 27 Dec. 1991.
Millier, Brett. *Elizabeth Bishop: Life and the Memory of It*. Berkeley and Los Angeles: U of California P, forthcoming.
"Elizabeth Bishop: Life and the Memory of It." Ph.D. dissertation. Stanford University, 1986.
Monroe, Harriet, and Alice Corbin Henderson, eds. *The New Poetry: An Anthology of Twentieth-Century Verse in English*. 2d ed. New York: Macmillan, 1923.
Moore, Marianne. "Archaically New." In *Trial Balances: An Anthology of New Poetry*. Ed. Ann Winslow [Verna Elizabeth Grubbs, pseud.]. New York: Macmillan, 1935. 82–3. Rpt. in *Complete Prose* 327–9.
The Complete Poems of Marianne Moore. New York: Macmillan, 1981 (*CP*).
The Complete Prose of Marianne Moore. Ed. Patricia C. Willis. New York: Sifton-Penguin, 1987 (*CPr*).
Letters to Elizabeth Bishop. Elizabeth Bishop Collection. Vassar College Library, Poughkeepsie, N.Y., unless otherwise noted (VC).
"A Modest Expert." Rev. of *North & South*, by Elizabeth Bishop. *Nation*, 28 Sept. 1946: 354. Rpt. in *Complete Prose* 406–8.
"Senhora Helena." Rev. of *The Diary of "Helena Morley."* Trans. and ed., with an introduction by Elizabeth Bishop. *Poetry* (July 1959): 247–9. Rpt. in *Complete Prose* 524–6.

Mullen, Richard. "Elizabeth Bishop's Surrealist Inheritance." *American Literature*
54.1 (1982): 63–80.

Nadeau, Maurice. *The History of Surrealism.* Trans. Richard Howard. New York:
Macmillan, 1965.

Neruda, Pablo. *Five Decades: A Selection (Poems: 1925–1970).* Ed. and trans. Ben
Belitt. New York: Grove, 1974.

Newman, Anne R. "Elizabeth Bishop's 'Roosters.'" *Pebble: A Book of Reread-
ings in Recent American Poetry* 18–20 (1980): 171–83. Rpt. in Bloom
111–20.

O'Connor, Flannery. *The Habit of Being: Letters.* Ed. Sally Fitzgerald. New York:
Vintage, 1979.

Letters to Elizabeth Bishop. Elizabeth Bishop Collection. Vassar College Library, Poughkeepsie, N.Y. (VC).

The Violent Bear It Away. New York: Farrar, Straus & Cudahy, 1960.

Wise Blood. New York: Farrar, Straus & Cudahy, 1952.

Ostriker, Alicia Suskin. *Stealing the Language: The Emergence of Women's Poetry
in America.* Boston: Beacon P, 1986.

Parker, Robert Dale. *The Unbeliever: The Poetry of Elizabeth Bishop.* Urbana: U
of Illinois P, 1988.

Poirier, Richard. *The Renewal of Literature: Emersonian Reflections.* New Haven,
Conn.: Yale UP, 1987.

Ponente, Nello. *Klee: Biographical and Critical Study.* Trans. James Emmons.
Lausanne: Skira, 1960.

Rich, Adrienne. "The Eye of the Outsider: The Poetry of Elizabeth Bishop."
Rev. of *The Complete Poems: 1927–1979,* by Elizabeth Bishop. *Boston Review*
(Apr. 1983): 16–18.

"Power and Danger: Works of a Common Woman." 1977. In *On Lies, Secrets
and Silence: Selected Prose, 1966–1978.* New York: Norton, 1979. 247–58.

"When We Dead Awaken: Writing as Re-Vision." 1971. In *On Lies, Secrets,
and Silence: Selected Prose, 1966–1978.* New York: Norton, 1979. 33–49.

Roett, Riordan, ed. *Brazil in the Sixties.* Nashville Tenn.: Vanderbilt UP, 1972.

Rorty, Richard. *Consequences of Pragmatism: Essays, 1972–1980.* Minneapolis: U
of Minn P, 1982.

Sacks, Peter M. *The English Elegy: Studies in the Genre from Spenser to Yeats.*
Baltimore, Md.: Johns Hopkins UP, 1985.

Salzman, Jack, ed. *Years of Protest: A Collection of American Writings of the 1930's.*
New York: Pegasus, 1967.

Schlesinger, Arthur, Jr. "Reinhold Niebuhr's Role in American Political Thought
and Life." In *Reinhold Niebuhr: His Religious, Social, and Political Thought.*
Ed. Charles W. Kegley. 1956. New York: Macmillan, 1956. 125–50.

Schneede, Uwe M. *Surrealism.* Trans. Maria Pelikan. New York: Library of
Great Art Movements; Abrams, 1974.

Schwartz, Lloyd, and Sybil P. Estess, eds. *Elizabeth Bishop and Her Art.* Under
Discussion. Ann Arbor, Mich.: U of Michigan P, 1983.

Schwartz, Sanford. *The Matrix of Modernism: Pound, Eliot, and Early Twentieth-
Century Thought.* Princeton, N.J.: Princeton UP, 1985.

Schweik, Susan. *A Gulf So Deeply Cut: American Women Poets and the Second World War*. Madison: U of Wisconsin P, 1991.

"Writing War Poetry Like a Woman." *Critical Inquiry* 13 (Spring 1987): 532–56.

Sexton, Anne. *To Bedlam and Part Way Back*. Boston: Houghton Mifflin, 1960.

Skidmore, Thomas E. *Politics in Brazil, 1930–1964: An Experiment in Democracy*. New York: Oxford UP, 1967.

Southworth, James G. "The Poetry of Elizabeth Bishop." *College English* (Feb. 1959): 213–17.

Spires, Elizabeth. "An Afternoon with Elizabeth Bishop." *Vassar Quarterly* 75.2 (1979): 4–9. Revised and rpt. as "The Art of Poetry XXVII: Elizabeth Bishop." *Paris Review* 23.80 (1981): 56–83.

Spivak, Gayatri Chakravorty. "Can the Subaltern Speak?" *Marxism and the Interpretation of Culture*. Ed. Cary Nelson and Lawrence Grossberg. Urbana: U of Illinois P, 1988. 271–313.

In Other Worlds: Essays in Cultural Politics. New York: Routledge, Chapman & Hall, 1988.

Starbuck, George. "'The Work!': A Conversation with Elizabeth Bishop." *Ploughshares* 3.3–4 (1977): 11–29. Rpt. in Schwartz and Estess 312–30.

Stearns, Marshall W. *The Story of Jazz*. New York: Oxford, 1956.

Stern, Daniel N. "The Early Development of Schemas of Self, Other, and 'Self with Other.'" In *Reflections on Self Psychology*. Ed. Joseph D. Lichtenberg and Samuel Kaplan. Hillsdale, N.J.: Analytic P, 1983. 49–84.

The Interpersonal World of the Infant: A View from Psychoanalysis and Developmental Psychology. New York: Basic Books, 1985.

Stevens, Marjorie. Letters to Elizabeth Bishop. Elizabeth Bishop Collection. Vassar College Library, Poughkeepsie, N.Y. (VC).

Stevenson, Anne. Correspondence with Elizabeth Bishop. Elizabeth Bishop Papers. Olin Library, Washington University, St. Louis, Mo. (WU).

Elizabeth Bishop. New York: Twayne, 1966.

"Letters from Elizabeth Bishop." *Times Literary Supplement*, 7 Mar. 1980: 261–2.

Stimpson, Catharine. "Zero Degree Deviancy: The Lesbian Novel in English." In *Writing and Sexual Difference*. Ed. Elizabeth Abel. Chicago: U of Chicago P, 1980. 243–59.

Swenson, May. *A Cage of Spines*. New York: Rinehart, 1958.

Correspondence with Elizabeth Bishop. May Swenson Papers. Olin Library, Washington University, St. Louis, Mo. (WU).

Tennyson, Alfred. *The Poems of Tennyson*, Vol 1. Ed. Christopher Ricks. London: Longman, 1969. 387–95.

Travisano, Thomas J. *Elizabeth Bishop: Her Artistic Development*. Charlottesville: UP of Virginia, 1988.

Twichell, Chase. "Everything Only Connected by "And" and "And": The Skewed Narrative of Elizabeth Bishop." *NER/BLQ* 8.1 (1985): 130–7.

Van Duyn, Mona. *To See, To Take*. New York: Atheneum, 1970.

Vendler, Helen. "Domestication, Domesticity, and the Otherworldly." 1977. In Ivask 23–8. Rpt. in Schwartz and Estess 32–48.

Rev. of *An Anthology of Twentieth-Century Brazilian Poetry*, ed. with an introduction by Elizabeth Bishop and Emanuel Brasil. *New York Times Book Review*, 7 Jan. 1973.

von Hallberg, Robert. *American Poetry and Culture, 1945–1980*. Cambridge, Mass.: Harvard UP, 1985.

Wagley, Charles. *Amazon Town: A Study of Man in the Tropics*. New York: Macmillan, 1953.

Wakoski, Diane. "Creating a Personal Mythology: Third Lecture." *Toward a New Poetry*. Poets on Poetry. Ann Arbor: U of Michigan P, 1980. 106–19.

Wehr, Wesley. "Elizabeth Bishop: Conversations and Class Notes." *Antioch Review* 39 (1981): 319–28.

West, Cornel. *The American Evasion of Philosophy: A Genealogy of Pragmatism*. Madison: U of Wisconsin P, 1989.

Wilbur, Richard. *The Beautiful Changes, and Other Poems*. New York: Harcourt, Brace, 1947.

Williams, Oscar, ed. *The War Poets: An Anthology of the War Poetry of the 20th Century*. New York: John Day, 1945.

Williams, William Carlos. "Marianne Moore." 1925. In *Selected Essays of William Carlos Williams*. New York: Random House, 1954. 121–31.

Wilson, Edmund. *To the Finland Station: A Study in the Writing and Acting of History*. Garden City, N.J.: Doubleday, 1940.

Winnicott, D. W. *Playing and Reality*. London: Routledge, Chapman & Hall, 1971.

Woolf, Virginia. *Three Guineas*. London: Hogarth, 1938.

Wordsworth, William. *The Poetical Works of William Wordsworth*, Vol. 2. Ed. Thomas Hutchinson. 1914. Rev. ed. Ernest de Selincourt. London: Clarendon, 1944. 216.

Index

Aesop, 86
Almyda, Hannah, 78, 96
Altieri, Charles, 212n3
Amazon, the, 80, 151, 157, 171, 186, 227n10
animal allegory, 86, 89–90
Anthology of Twentieth-Century Brazilian Poetry, An, 27–8, 177, 179
anthropology, cultural, 7–9, 18, 169
architecture, 22–3
archival material, 15–18
Armstrong, Louis, 99
"Arrival at Santos," 72, 147–8, 185, 187, 188; and Brazil travel prose, 171
art, 22; primitives, 39, 151, 171; "unselfconscious" folk culture, 168–9
"As We Like It," 24, 55–7
"At the Fishhouses," 29; and "The Riverman," 155
Auden, W. H., 78, 163, 216n12

Baker, Houston, 223n21
"Baptism, The," 51
Barkers, Ilse and Kit, 26, 207, 215n4
baroque style, 4
Baumann, Anny, 215–16n10
Beat poetry, 1–2, 20, 30
Beppo (dog), 23
Berryman, John, 1, 13, 212n2
Bible, the, 95, 113
Bidart, Frank, 25
Bishop, Elizabeth: alcoholism, 25, 215–16n10, 221n26; as American, 143–4, 145; awards, 25, 102, 172, 175, 185, 206, 208, 230n20; in Boston, 28, 134, 185, 186; childhood, 17, 21, 23, 44,

Chap. 4 passim, 175, 187–9, 190; at Cuttyhunk, 107, 190, 218n7; dreams, 65–6, 117, 157; emerging as poet, 23–5, 50–5, 57; in Europe, 23, 77, 83, 84, 146, 208, 222n7; in Great Village, 21–3, 108, 221n22; health, 23, 25, 28, 125, 185, 208; and her mother, 44, 66, 72, 107, 108, 110, 113–14, 131, 215n6; income, 21, 23, 229–30n9; in Key West, 4, 25, 39, 63, 68, 103, 130, 151; library requests for her papers, 193; literary critic, 16, 20, 28–41 passim, 216n19; Lowell, relationship with, 1, 13, 24–5, 57; on Lowell's work, 173–4, 175, 201; and Macedo Soares, 21–3, 26–7, 70–2, 155, 157, 189; and Methfessel, 28, 190, 195, 208; Moore, personal relation with, 4, 23–5, 49–58, 72; Moore, poetic relation with, 36–7, 50, 80, 94, 95–7, 220n16, 222n4; on Moore's work, 24, 30, 55–8, 79–80, 201, 212n6; in New York City, 23, 24, 27, 43, 58, 63, 68, 84, 103, 107, 108, 130, 224n4; at North Haven, 208, 231n23; in Ouro Prêto, 27–8; poetry of war, 79, 87–96, 185; and politics, 19, 26, 75, 76–9, 84, 144–5, 166; and psychoanalysis, 117, 175, 224–5n7; in Revere, Mass., 23, 124; in Rio de Janeiro, 21, 130, 144, 185; at Samambaia, 22–3, 26, 146; in San Francisco, 27; in Seattle, 27, 130, 131; on Swenson's work, 39–40; as teacher, 39, 40, 186; at Vassar College, 23, 32, 76, 83, 108; in Worcester, Mass., 23, 189; at Yaddo, 24, 25, 26, 61, 131, 221n26

243

Bishop, Elizabeth, correspondence: with
Barkers, 26; with Lowell, 24, 25; with
Moore, 14, 24, 78; with Stevenson, 26;
with Swenson, 26
Bishop, Elizabeth, interviews: with
Ashley Brown, 52, 76, 78, 82, 98, 147,
157; with Alexandra Johnson, 43, 46;
with Elizabeth Spires, 142, 198, 231n26;
with George Starbuck, 19, 201, 230n19;
with Wesley Wehr, 20
Bishop, Elizabeth, letters: about Darwin,
31, 37, 86, 121; about Dickinson, 34–5;
about her family, 21, 107, 131, 132,
183; about Jewett, 33–4; about Macedo
Soares, 70, 189; about Methfessel, 195;
about Moore, 57; about O'Connor, 38–
9; American cultural significance, 183;
American politics, 143–4; "A Miracle
for Breakfast," 82; Boston, life in, 28,
184; "Brazil, January 1, 1502," 161;
Brazil, life in, 22, 25, 26, 27, 145, 146,
160, 161, 168–9, 208; Brazilian politics,
144–6; Brazil travel book, 171–2;
"Cootchie," 97; "Crusoe in England,"
190, 192; descriptive details, 24; *The
Diary of "Helena Morley,"* 174–5, 177;
emotion and objectivity, 29–30;
feminism, 33; frustrations as poet, 26–7,
50, 53, 79; her health, 21, 223n22; her
reading, 4, 49, 175, 224–5n7; "In
Prison," 74–5, 78; "In the Village," 33–
4, 109; "Jerónimo's House," 79; Key
West locals, 96, 97; "Manuelzinho,"
152; "Memories of Uncle Neddy," 109;
New York City, life in, 25; Nova
Scotia, 22, 177, 184, 198; "O Breath,"
64; politics in poetry, 19–20, 30–1, 75;
"Roosters," 95–6; self-assessment as
poet, 1, 12–13, 31, 50–1, 64, 95–6;
"Songs for a Colored Singer," 78, 103,
168; "The Moose," 201; "The Paper
Nautilus," 79, 80, 96; "The Riverman,"
157; "The Shampoo," 71; "The Weed,"
51; transgressions, 71–2, 95, 96;
translation, 173, 174, 181; women
writers, 31–3; *see also* Barkers, Ilse and
Kit; Lowell, Robert; Moore, Marianne;
Moss, Howard; Stevenson, Anne;
Swenson, May
Bishop, Elizabeth, unpublished poems:
"A Baby," 165–6; "A Trip to the

Mines – Brasil," 165, 182; "Aubade and
Elegy," 185, 206–8, 230n21; Aunt
Maud poems, 123–5, 151, 225n11;
"Brasil, 1959," 165; "Capricorn," 165;
"Crossing the Equator," 63; "Elegy"
(book of poems to Macedo Soares),
185, 189, 224n6; "For Grandfather,"
138–40, 141, 177–8, 226n21, 226n22,
228n24; "Grandmother's Glass Eye"
(book of poems), 185, 224n6; "Hannah
A.," 78; "Homesickness," 133–4, 135,
138, 226n16; Hopkins–Dickinson, 34–7,
217n24; "Key West," 97; 1940s love
poems, 44–5, 58, 63, 67–9, 72, 73, 205–
6, 221n27, 221n28; swan-boat/dress
goods poems, 132, 134–7, 138, 140,
141, 225n7, 226n18; "The
Grandmothers," 125–6, 127, 176,
225n12; "Vague Poem," 204–6, 230n20;
on Vargas's suicide, 166
Bishop, Elizabeth, unpublished prose:
"Black Beans and Diamonds" (book of
Brazil travel pieces), 10, 27, 157, 171–2,
175, 228n20; Brazil travel prose, 147,
151, 169–72, 188; "Homesickness," 113,
131–3, 226n16; 1936 memoirs, 16–7, 21,
44, 49–50, 53, 107–9, 112–17, 125, 126,
134, 137, 140, 224n2, 224n3, 224n4;
"Mrs. Sullivan Downstairs," 124;
notebook entries, 1930s, 3, 5, 44, 59,
65, 83, 107–8, 121, 124, 125, 218n7;
notebook entries, 1940s–1950s, 15, 17,
41, 63, 67, 69, 98, 109, 217n30; poetry
reviews, 30, 31, 40; "The Deadly
Sandpile," 194, 221n22; "The Proud
Villagers" (novel), 107–8, 125; on
Vargas's suicide, 166
Bishop, Florence (aunt), in Bishop's
writing, 188
Bishop, Gertrude Bulmer (mother, Easter,
Una/Georgie): in Bishop's writing, 53,
109, 111, 113–21, 127–30, 131–7, 138;
with daughter, Elizabeth, 107; death,
21, 49, 51, 66, 107, 131, 215n5; mental
illness, 21, 131, 143
Bishop, John W. (grandfather), in
Bishop's writing, 124, 131
Bishop, Sarah Foster (grandmother), in
Bishop's writing, 124, 125
Bishop, William T. (father), 21; in
Bishop's writing, 107, 109, 111, 130–1

Continued from the front of the book